EuroPsy

About the Authors

Ingrid Lunt is Professor of Educational Studies at the University of Oxford, and Vice Principal of Green Templeton College, University of Oxford. She is a Past President of the British Psychological Society (1999), the European Federation of Psychologists Associations (1993–1999), and the United Kingdom Inter-Professional Group (1998–2001). She is currently Chair of the European Awarding Committee for *EuroPsy*. Her main research interests are higher education, in particular doctoral education and higher professional learning, comparative postgraduate education, and work-based learning.

José María Peiró is Professor of Work and Organisational Psychology at the University of Valencia, Director of the Research Institute of Human Resources Psychology (IDOCAL), and Senior Researcher at the Research Institute of Economics (IVIE) Valencia, Spain. He is President of the International Association of Applied Psychology and a Past President of the European Association of Work and Organizational Psychology. His main research interests are occupational stress and well-being, youth labour market entry, and climate and leadership in organisations.

Ype Poortinga is Emeritus Professor of Cross-Cultural Psychology at Tilburg University in the Netherlands, and at the Catholic University of Leuven in Belgium. He has been president of the International Test Commission, the International Association for Cross-Cultural Psychology (IACCP), the Dutch Psychological Association (NIP), and the European Federation of Professional Psychologists Associations (EFPA). His most consistent research interest has been in the conditions under which psychological data obtained in different cultural populations can be meaningfully compared.

Robert A. Roe is Honorary Emeritus Professor of Organizational Theory and Organizational Behavior at Maastricht University (The Netherlands) and former Leibniz Professor at University of Leipzig (Germany). He is President of the European Federation of Psychologists' Associations (EFPA) and was founding president of the European Association of Work & Organizational Psychology. His publications cover a broad range of topics related to work and organization. In his recent work, the emphasis is on temporal facets of behavioral and organizational phenomena, on research methodology, and on the interface between psychology and other disciplines.

EuroPsy

Standards and Quality in Education for Psychologists

Ingrid Lunt, José María Peiró,
Ypé Poortinga, & Robert A. Roe

HOGREFE

Library of Congress Cataloguing-in-Publication Data
is available via the Library of Congress Marc Database under the LC Control Number 2014941569

Library and Archives Canada Cataloguing in Publication
Lunt, Ingrid, author
EuroPsy : standards and quality in education for psychologists / Ingrid Lunt, José María Peiró, Ype Poortinga, & Robert A. Roe.

Includes bibliographical references and index.
Issued in print and electronic formats.

ISBN 978-0-88937-438-6 (pbk.).–ISBN 978-1-61676-438-8 (pdf).–ISBN 978-1-61334-438-5 (html)

1. Psychologists–Certification–Europe. 2. Psychologists–Licenses–Europe. 3. Psychologists–Training of–Europe. 4. Psychologists–Professional ethics–Europe. I. Poortinga, Ype H., 1939-, author II. Roe, R. A. (Robert A.), author III. Peiró, José M. (José María), author IV. Title.

BF80.8.L85 2014	150.23'4	C2014-903655-8 C2014-903656-6

http://www.hogrefe.com

PUBLISHING OFFICES
USA: Hogrefe Publishing, 38 Chauncy Street, Suite 1002, Boston, MA 02111
Phone (866) 823-4726, Fax (617) 354-6875;
E-mail customerservice@hogrefe-publishing.com
EUROPE: Hogrefe Publishing, Merkelstr. 3, 37085 Göttingen, Germany
Phone +49 551 99950-0, Fax +49 551 99950-425; E-mail publishing@hogrefe.com

SALES & DISTRIBUTION
USA: Hogrefe Publishing, Customer Services Department, 30 Amberwood Parkway, Ashland, OH 44805
Phone (800) 228-3749, Fax (419) 281-6883; E-mail customerservice@hogrefe.com
UK: Hogrefe Publishing c/o Marston Book Services Ltd, 160 Eastern Ave., Milton Park, Abingdon, OX14 4SB, UK
Phone +44 1235 465577, Fax +44 1235 465556; E-mail direct.orders@marston.co.uk
EUROPE: Hogrefe Publishing, Merkelstr. 3, 37085 Göttingen, Germany
Phone +49 551 99950-0, Fax +49 551 99950-425; E-mail publishing@hogrefe.com

OTHER OFFICES
CANADA: Hogrefe Publishing, 660 Eglinton Ave. East, Suite 119–514, Toronto, Ontario M4G 2K2
SWITZERLAND: Hogrefe Publishing, Länggass-Strasse 76, CH-3000 Bern 9

Hogrefe Publishing
Incorporated and registered in the Commonwealth of Massachusetts, USA, and in Göttingen, Lower Saxony, Germany

Cover design: Daniel Kleimenhagen, Designer AGD
Printed and bound in the Germany

ISBNs 978-0-88937-438-6 (print), 978-1-61676-438-8 (pdf), 978-1-61334-438-5 (epub)
http://dx.doi.org/10.1027/00438-000

Foreword

Psychology is a global profession. Like many other such professions, there is significant variability in how psychology is defined and regulated throughout the world. The challenge for internationalists is to understand how individual countries construct and implement systems of education, training, credentialing and regulation to conform to the local definitions of the profession, and devise ethical codes that meld universal and local contexts. In addition to languages spoken, the historical and political diversity in countries make comprehensive comparisons difficult. Multiple professional gatherings aimed at understanding psychology's global diversity have attempted to map similarities and differences over the past 20 years, with some success.

The United Kingdom (UK), along with the United States (US), has been one of the primary exporters of global psychology. Many psychologists emigrated to the UK and US for education and training and returned to their home countries to develop similar systems. Initially this educational export then import was seen as helpful, but with time countries also became concerned that UK/US perspectives were not consonant with their own socio-political perspectives, cultural issues or preferences for community service. This is particularly true in Asia, the Middle East, Latin America and other parts of Europe. Now, as universities in these regions have created their own graduate programmes and incorporated their local customs, there is less dependence upon education and training taking place elsewhere.

Psychology in these countries has flourished. Internationalists have great interest in learning how these countries educate, train and credential psychologists, primarily because of a need to promote *mobility*. Stevens and Wedding (2004) in their comprehensive coverage of numerous countries argue that international psychology should also address issues of *global* importance. Hall and Altmaier (2008) in their focus on quality assurance stress the importance of promoting an international culture of *accountability*.

Over 30 years ago in 1981 European psychologists began to systematically and collaboratively develop the structures of European psychology when 12 national psychology organisations signed the enabling statutes and formed the European Federation of Professional Psychologists Associations (EFPPA). Since then, EFPPA General Assemblies have met every 2 years. The four authors of this book have been centrally involved in the development and organization of psychology at European level for most of this period.

At about the same time, the European Union (EU) became interested in fostering mobility of professionals across Europe for economic reasons. This necessitated the development of a European standard of education and training for each of the professions. To support psychology's efforts, the EU funded two projects proposed by Ingrid Lunt (1999–2005) under its Leonardo da Vinci programme to develop a framework for training psychologists and also a recognition system, via the creation of a European Diploma. EFPA, now named the European Federation of Psychologists' Associations, agreed to take over these extensive efforts in 2005 and to support the diploma's implementation. The European Diploma became the *EuroPsy* and the European Register was officially initiated by EFPA in 2010, listing psychologists who were determined by their National Awarding Committee (NAC) to meet the *EuroPsy* standards. Thus in 2010 the European Register joined the efforts by the National Register of Health Service Psychologists (US) and the Canadian Register of Health Service Psychologists to identify qualified psychologists who voluntarily applied for credentialing.

In addition to publishing journal articles and book chapters, these four authors have regularly presented the *EuroPsy* at meetings of EFPA at its European Congress of Psychology, the International Union of Psychological Science (IUPsyS) at the International Congress of Psychology (ICP), the International Association of Applied Psychology (IAAP), at its Congress (ICAP), and numerous other national regional and international meetings. However, this book brings together in one volume all the streams of activity related to creating input and output standards for European education, competency identification, assessment, and revalidation, addressing supervision and training, and developing meta- and ethical codes, all positioned and interpreted within the diverse European sociocultural context. There is much to learn about how the *EuroPsy* was conceptualised, negotiated and implemented, and where it is going. These authors are some of the people who know it best and first hand. The book's significance is that it is not just about *EuroPsy* and EFPA but how psychology organisations and psychologists come together to create systems and standards to reach consensus on national and regional levels and to further mobility. So the Europeans have arrived with their book describing the *EuroPsy* as a benchmark and quality standard for the 36 member countries of EFPA. Perhaps it is more relevant to today to use the more inclusive term of *international*. This is what Europe has done for its region, taking the necessary first steps to becoming truly international.

It has been a personal pleasure for me to witness the efforts made by the Europeans over the past 22 years and to learn from their different perspectives. By reading this book, I am certain you will agree.

Judy E. Hall
Executive Officer
National Register of Health Service Psychologists
1200 New York Avenue, Suite 800
Washington, DC 20005, USA

Table of Contents

Acknowledgements

The *EuroPsy* project is the product of the commitment and efforts of a large number of people whose contributions should be acknowledged. First of all, we are appreciative of the commitment and work of all those who worked in the project teams (listed in Appendices 1 and 2). As is evident from Chapter 2, the *EuroPsy* project has spanned a number of years, involving considerable effort, debate and discussion, negotiation and finally consensus. To benefit from continuity and experience, members from this team agreed to form the first phase membership of the European Awarding Committee (EAC); this has now been extended as further members join this important committee: to all members of EAC our appreciation and acknowledgements. There is now a National Awarding Committee (NAC) in 20 countries; their contribution to the success of the *EuroPsy* endeavour is acknowledged. *EuroPsy* began as a research and development project, and was handed over for implementation to EFPA in 2005 at the European Congress of Psychology in Granada, Spain. We are enormously grateful to the head of the EFPA staff, Sabine Steyaert, and to her colleagues, Ivana Marinovic and Valérie Boni, who have worked so hard to effect the implementation of *EuroPsy* and to enable the *EuroPsy* Certificate to be accompanied by a Register and an effective administrative system which contributes to enhancing the quality of psychology education in Europe. Finally, we would like to mention Dr. Judy Hall, a loyal supporter of the project over all its years, who generously agreed to write the foreword, and Robert Dimbleby at Hogrefe Publishers who patiently allowed repeated delays in the agreed date of submission of the manuscript. Beyond those mentioned we greatly appreciate the support and interest from our colleagues in the wider international community of psychologists and we are grateful to the large number of individuals and organisations that have contributed to making *EuroPsy* a reality.

Preface

There are a number of challenges – and opportunities – facing the profession of psychology as we move through the early years of the 21st century. The implications of a rapidly changing world, with increased globalisation and internationalisation, the expansion of new technologies and concomitant developments, changes in demography, economy, and in the relationship between the professions and the state, create new challenges for the profession of psychology. While psychology both as a science and as a profession has a relatively short history, it has achieved remarkable success and significance over a period of less than 150 years, contributing substantially to understanding and explaining human behaviour, and improving human welfare.

The changing context of the 21st century poses new challenges for the profession of psychology. On the one hand there appears to be a greater need than ever before for psychological interventions in a range of fields: hospitals and clinics, schools and education, companies and organisations, and a growing number of other contexts. There is an increasing demand for psychological services to address mental health problems, disaster and crisis situations, trauma of all kinds, stress in the workplace, the well-being of those incarcerated in prisons, or those migrating as refugees, as well as the challenges created by demographic changes, such as ageing, family breakdown or the adverse effects of poverty, unemployment and other social problems. This demand is fuelled in part by psychology's success and the contribution that psychology has made, as well as the promises made to improve human welfare and well-being in a wide range of contexts. We should note here, too, the importance of psychology's contribution to health and well-being in preventing distress as well as developing successful curative interventions.

These societal changes have been accompanied by changes in the role, status and position of professions, and a proliferation of other groups offering similar services in the different areas of practice that are also covered by our profession. The push for greater accountability and the changed relationship between the state, professionals and the client, demands for greater protection of the recipients of psychological services and increased transparency have all had an impact on the position of psychologists in society and the ways in which they provide services. The recent economic crisis and financial arrangements linked with welfare state reforms in European countries equally are affecting the provision of psychological services in various countries.

Psychology is a science-based profession, committed to a scientific perspective towards professional activity and the scientist practitioner approach to education and practice. In its purest form this means a commitment to hypothesis-testing and data-gathering in search of evidence that disconfirms or validates theories, models and interventions and the use of scientific evidence to inform professional practice. This commitment is frequently held up as a feature that distinguishes psychologists from other allied professions. Evidence-based or evidence-informed practice is increasingly held up as the gold standard. This quality standard demands professional aspirations for rigour, for a robust and reflexive interaction between the science and practice of psychology, and for a striving for continuous evaluation and improvement of interventions and professional practice.

Nevertheless, given the complexity of the demands, the scientific evidence available needs to be complemented by other sources of evidence, such as those arising from professional experience, stakeholders' demands and clients' experience. A wise combination of all these sources of evidence may help to contextualise the theoretical models inspiring professional interventions in specific environments and for specific individuals and groups.

Although education and training routes for professional psychologists showed some common features in the second half of the 20th century, there continued to be notable national differences across European countries. These are understandable and reflect the considerable diversity in history, politics, culture, languages and so on found in this region. Such differences have been a matter of concern to the European Union since the formation of the European Economic Community (EEC) in 1957, when its founders articulated a vision of free movement of professionals across the region. The European Union itself has attempted to address this concern through European Directives promoting mobility, and through funds supporting exchange and collaboration across the Member States. The balance between pressures for greater "Europeanisation" and impulses by nation states towards nationalism creates a tension which is also reflected in a balance between top–down and bottom–up initiatives to foster greater convergence and harmonisation.

This European regionalism is developing within the wider context of internationalisation. Globalisation means that students, researchers, practitioners and clients are becoming more mobile. The differences in education and training routes across European countries are also evident across other parts of the world. The past 20 years have seen a number of initiatives seeking to explore greater convergence or comparability across regions of the world. International organisations of psychology, such as the International Union of Psychological Science (IUPSyS), the International Association of Applied Psychology (IAAP) and the International Association for Cross-Cultural Psychology (IACCP), have held regular congresses and fostered international collaboration, capacity building and exchange. A recent and focussed initiative of this kind has been the IUPSyS initiative of 2012, the so-called Dornburg Conference, which aimed to examine psychology education and training at a global level (Silbereisen, Ritchie, & Pandey, 2014). At about the same time (2013) the 5th International Congress of Certification, Licensing, and Credentialing was organised to consider the possibility of identifying core competences of psychologists at a global level. These initiatives reflect a wide interest in comparing systems of education and training for psychologists, making these transparent and comprehensible, and seeing how far it might be possible to develop over-arching frameworks such as those already achieved for ethical principles through the Universal Declaration of Ethical Principles for Psychologists, which was accepted by the major international organisations in 2008 (Universal Declaration, 2008).

This book is about the development of *EuroPsy*, a European standard and benchmark for psychologist practitioners, which achieved consensus across European countries in 2005. Originally designed as a project to improve transparency and comparability of psychologist qualifications, it quickly became seen as a means for enhancing the quality of psychology education and training across European countries and thus improving services to the public. More recently, and with the modernisation of the EU Qualifications Directive, it has become a potential tool to aid mobility. Europe provides an example of powerful regionalisation and is therefore a fertile context for the development of an international standard. Early on *EuroPsy* adopted the definition of the key role of the professional psychologist originally formulated by the British Psychological Society (1998), which states that their main role is "to develop and apply psychological principles, knowledge, models and methods *in an ethical and scientific way* in order to promote the development, well-being and effectiveness of individuals, groups, organisations and society" (italics added here). This commitment to an "ethical and scientific way" demands a robust form of accountability to individual clients, to organisations, to colleagues and to the profession and the public at large.

Like all professions, psychologists commit to abide by ethical codes (see also Chapter 8). As stated above, psychology is a science-based profession, underpinned by the scientist-practitioner model of training (see Chapter 4). Although there are methodological challenges in evaluating the efficacy and effectiveness of psychological interventions and their adaptation in different contexts, it is essential that we use the methods and tools available to seek to ensure the robustness of the methods used by practitioners and to evaluate the effectiveness and efficiency of interventions. Randomised control trials are difficult to organise and often inappropriate for psychological interventions, yet there is a need for transparency and accountability in relation to the methods used by psychologists. This issue is discussed further in Chapters 7 and 8.

EuroPsy has been developed over the past 15 years or so within the context of the European Union and the European Federation of Psychologists Associations (EFPA; see Chapter 2). *EuroPsy* has been accepted by the 36 member associations of EFPA, which includes all European Union Member States. EFPA is currently working towards acceptance by the EU of *EuroPsy* as the basis for a Common Training Framework facilitating automatic recognition of qualifications across Europe (Chapter 3).

As is often the case, the book cannot address all the topics that could have been included. In the course of writing the book, the authors (who have extensive experience both of *EuroPsy* and of psychology in Europe and its organisation) had a number of productive and informative discussions about the different opinions held within the group. Beyond a description of *EuroPsy* it is possible to take a view on its long-term development, which can be outlined only when there is a perspective on where psychology as a profession should be heading. The team of authors discussed the strengths and weaknesses of the profession and the science behind it; the mutual relations between science and practice; and different mechanisms of quality assurance for the profession across the different countries of Europe, including their current state and aspirations for the future. Our shared vision includes the future development of a common education framework and of standards for practice rooted in the scientist-practitioner model, a common model of competences, and the generalisation of supervised practice and continuing professional development as strategies to build the core competences of all psychologists in Europe. Last but not least, we unanimously and strongly endorse that psychologists have to be guided by ethical principles in their practice as formulated in professional codes.

We held somewhat differing views on the risks and threats that the profession may be facing in a mid-term future and how these might be pre-empted. A focal point in these discussions was the continued use of methods which empirical evidence has suggested are obsolete. Undoubtedly, this and other issues will need to be addressed in the future development of *EuroPsy*. However, they are beyond the horizon of the present book, which aims to describe professional standards and competences, where they come from, and where they are today, for the profession of psychology in Europe.

Outline of the book

We start in Chapter 1 outlining the historical context and background to *EuroPsy*. This is followed by Chapter 2 which provides a description of the process of creating *EuroPsy* within this context. Chapter 3 moves on to describe what *EuroPsy* is and how it works. It is followed by five chapters providing detailed information about the major components of *EuroPsy*. Chapter 4 deals with *EuroPsy* in relation to the psychology curriculum. Chapter 5 addresses the use of competences to ensure that professionals perform well and safely. Chapter 6 gives a view of supervised practice and professional education while Chapter 7 discusses the issue of continuing professional development in relation to the revalidation of *EuroPsy* certificates. Chapter 8 reviews the ethical base of professional practice. The remaining two chapters "zoom out" somewhat, with Chapter 9 discussing *EuroPsy* in the current context of the psychological profession in Europe and Chapter 10 providing a conclusion by presenting a perspective on the future of *EuroPsy*.

1 The Emergence of the Psychological Profession in Europe

Psychology is multifaceted and encompasses a scientific discipline with a broad array of subdisciplines, and a profession that provides services through a number of specialisms in various fields of practice. As a body of knowledge it is embedded in a cultural and social context, and combines scientific evidence with common sense. Psychology as professional practice provides services to individuals, families, organisations, communities and a wide range of other groups and users. These services are legitimised by the scientific and expert knowledge used by professional psychologists. Assuring the quality of these services on behalf of clients and the reputation of the profession is a critical issue, which has become even more important in an open and global society where mobility of professionals and users, and the virtual provision of services through the Internet are growing fast and expanding widely.

Psychology as a science originated in Europe during the 19th century, where it merged with different philosophical and scientific traditions and took a variety of forms. Applications to the multiple facets of human and social life grew rapidly over the 20th century across the different countries, though at a different pace depending on historical and contextual circumstances. During the century significant socio-political developments occurred in Europe, including divisions of the continent according to lines drawn by changing coalitions and outcomes of warfare, followed by moves towards a European Union with a consequent emphasis on a common market and mobility of professionals, as well as progress towards an extended welfare state. These developments had a clear influence on the development of psychology as a profession, raising challenges regarding education and quality assurance beyond the borders of individual countries; a European approach was required. *EuroPsy* is a European response to that challenge. In order to fully understand its origins, development and significance, it is important to consider the context in which it emerged.

In this introductory chapter we will provide an overview of this context looking both at internal developments in psychology as a scientific field, an academic discipline and a profession, and at external developments that have occurred over the past century in Europe. The chapter is divided into two main parts, each comprising three sections. The first part takes an internal perspective and describes how the psychological profession has developed with reference to tendencies and trends inside the community of those who consider themselves psychologists. The second part adopts an external perspective and discusses developments in psychology with reference to the national embedding of psychology and changes in the political, economic, social and cultural dimensions of Europe. We believe that both a proximal and a distal approach to the development of psychology in Europe are needed to understand why *EuroPsy* was conceived and how it was designed and launched. Together, the six sections are meant to provide the reader with a background that is needed to understand the nature and significance of *EuroPsy*.

In the first section we provide a brief overview of the development of psychology as a science and how different traditions stimulated growth and diversity, resulting in different psychological schools. The second section will show how, almost since its beginnings, psychology aimed to promote its application in different areas of individual and social life. These efforts to apply psychology drew on psychology as a science and in turn contributed relevant inputs to the science. A growing recognition in European societies of the value of applied psychology (initially, psychotechnics) enabled psychology to contribute to the well-being of individuals and the welfare of these societies. The progress of psychology as a science, the developments of psychological technologies and the social recognition of the value of its applications played an important role in the emergence and the consolidation of psychology as a profession. This was in part achieved through the organisation of psychologists in associations, societies and networks. In the third section we describe some of the ways in which psychology became organised and institutionalised through national and international organisations. The fourth section puts the psychological profession in context. It describes its emergence, growth and diversification, with reference to the national and international environments and events. In the fifth section we consider the transformation of Europe during the last decades of the previous century and the first decade of the current century, and the profound impact that this has had on the psychological profession in Europe. It focuses on the process of European integration and unification, and the way in which this has altered the developments of professional psychology and its future. In the sixth section we widen our scope and look at psychology as one of many professions, examining some new challenges and opportunities that have emerged in its relationship with some of these professions – at the European as well as the national level – and the renewed need for a demarcation of the psychological profession.

The Emergence of Psychology as a Scientific Discipline

Scientific psychology emerged during the second part of the 19th century. Its origin is often dated to 1879 when Wilhelm Wundt (1832–1920) established the Institute of Experimental Psychology at the University of Leipzig, Germany. However, some decades earlier, the conditions for the emergence of psychology as a new science had been created by a number of scientific developments in physiology and an increasing interest in mental phenomena in philosophy, coinciding with institutional changes in German universities (Ben-David & Collins, 1966; Peiró & Carpintero, 1978). This led to problems which had previously been analysed from a philosophical point of view being studied using the scientific methods of physiology, an approach which Wundt developed in his *Principles of Physiological Psychology* (*Grundzüge der physiologischen Psychologie*) published in 1873–1874, which became the first textbook concerned with the new discipline of psychology. Using the experimental protocols of the natural sciences, Wundt introduced the experimental analysis of what he termed "immediate experience" or "consciousness," in studies of psychophysics, reaction times, perception and attention, or, as he called it, "physiologische Psychologie." However he also acknowledged that not all the phenomena of the mind, especially the more complex processes related to society and collective behaviours, could be studied in the laboratory, and proposed to supplement this form of individual experimental psychology with a Völkerpsychologie (a social, cultural or folk psychology). The focus of the new physiological psychology was on general laws of the human mind and its goal was to develop a theory of mental life, with a central interest in the "whole content of consciousness in its immediate being" (Wundt, 1897, I, 3a). Thus, already at this time Wundt established the precedent that there were two very different kinds of methods to investigate psychological phenomena, one laboratory-based experimentation, the other naturalistic observation, which was more suited to the study of psychological processes influenced by social and cultural factors.

A different approach emerged a little later, focussing on individual differences rather than general laws. James McKeen Cattell (1860–1944), a US psychologist and one of Wundt's students who had gained his PhD from Leipzig in 1886, shifted the focus to individual differences as the most fruitful and productive approach to understanding the human mind, consciousness and behaviour. Returning to the US from Europe in the late 1880s, Cattell developed a series of tests of mental measurement (Cattell, 1890). Around 1891 Hugo Münsterberg (1863–1916), also a student of Wundt, developed tests for verbal associations, arithmetic, reading and memory, before moving to Harvard in 1892. For both, the study of individual differences was no longer to be seen as a secondary issue in the search for general laws of the mind, but rather a valuable field of study in itself. Cattell's work reflected the influence of Darwinism and the work of the British scientist, polymath and psychometrician Francis Galton (1822–1911). Variation and adaptation to the environment as the basis for natural selection made individual differences crucially important for the individual–environment fit. Galton's emphasis on individual measurement and the analysis of human differences fitted well with the new developments of functionalism and social Darwinism in the US, where William James, among others, was emphasising a dynamic and functionalist approach to mental phenomena pointing out their central function for adaptation to the environment. In Europe, William Stern (1871–1938) proposed another approach to the study of individual differences, based on the systematic study of diversity and its origins. This approach was more open and programmatic, and included the use of test methods for practical purposes (Stern, 1900, 1911).

Early scholars in the new discipline of psychology were interested both in gaining theoretical and empirical knowledge about mental phenomena, and in seeing how psychological "findings may also contribute their quota to the sum-total of human happiness" (Hall, Baird & Geissler, 1917, p. 6). Psychologists were interested not only in scientific progress, but also in demonstrating the usefulness of psychology in providing solutions to people's problems and needs in different areas of their lives.

It is important to note that different traditions took root across the countries of Europe. Between 1879 and 1897, following Wundt's example, other experimental psychology laboratories were set up in Germany (Göttingen, Berlin, München, Würzburg), the Netherlands, Italy, Russia, Denmark, France, Belgium, Switzerland, Austria, England and Poland (Misiak & Sexton, 1966). However, psychology in Europe was also strongly influenced by other important developments at that time. Perhaps one of the most significant influences was that of the Viennese physician and neurologist Sigmund Freud (1856–1939) who was using a case study technique to develop psychoanalysis. In 1885 Freud had travelled to France to study with Jean-Martin Charcot, neurologist at the Salpêtrière Hospital in Paris, who was using hypnosis to experiment with the phenomenon of hysteria. Freud later claimed that this visit was instrumental in changing the course of his career and turning him towards clinical psychoanalysis.

Initially, the new scientific psychology was developed almost exclusively at universities, but soon research work began to be undertaken in hospitals, schools and other more "real-life" settings. Concepts and methods from psychology as an experimental science were used beyond the laboratory in order to address issues of practical relevance to the needs and problems of people. This led to the development of psychotechnics and applied psychology, which grew rapidly from the beginning of the 20th century.

The Origins and Developments of Applied Psychology

Drawing from the study of individual differences and an emphasis on the measurement of mental functions, psychology began to focus on everyday issues and questions. Many of the early applications of psychology were developed in the US, often by psychologists who had studied with Wundt (see Benjafield, 1996). As mentioned earlier, Wundt's student Cattell spent much of his career developing measures of individual differences in order to better understand individuals' adaptation to their contexts. This led in 1890 to his introduction of the term "mental test," thus establishing the ground for the development of one of the most important psychological techniques. At around the same period, G. Stanley Hall (1844–1924), also heavily influenced by Wundt and a visit to Germany, began to research children's development through the use of questionnaires. In the 1880s he initiated what became known as the Child Study Movement which aimed to apply scientific methods to the investigation of children to discover the normal laws of child development. This movement led to links between psychologists and teachers, and in this way psychology became strongly embedded in the American educational system. Also around this time, Lightner Witmer (1867–1956), professor of psychology at the University of Pennsylvania, founded the first psychological clinic to treat children and adolescents with educational, psychological and behavioural problems. This clinic was founded at the University of Pennsylvania where Witmer is also credited for being the first person to define an area called "clinical psychology."

At about the same time as psychology was beginning to be applied to everyday problems of a mental and developmental nature, Hugo Münsterberg and Walter Dill Scott (1869–1955), both students of Wundt, played key roles in early applied psychology. Münsterberg had an important role in the development of applied psychology, especially clinical, forensic and industrial psychology (Moskowitz, 1977). He studied a range of relevant problems both in the laboratory and in real-life contexts; these included monotony, fatigue and attention, and social influences at work, as well as individual differences and their importance for selection and vocational guidance. Although his early career developed in Germany, he became Professor at Harvard University and in 1898 was elected President of the American Psychological Association (APA). In 1913 he published *Psychology and Industrial Efficiency*, considered a landmark in the establishment of applied psychology. Walter Dill Scott is perhaps best known for his work in applying psychology to advertising, researching methods of social control, human motivation and suggestibility.

Meanwhile, in Europe, a major contribution to the development of the mental testing movement was made by the French psychologist Alfred Binet (1857–1911) who invented the first useable intelligence test, and developed concepts such as Intelligence Quotient (IQ) and Mental Age (MA). Binet and his colleague, the psychometrician Théodore Simon (1872–1961), developed a series of tests to measure and operationalise the concepts of IQ and MA which had a profound and significant influence on the school context. The contributions by the Swiss neurologist and psychologist Edouard Claparède (1873–1940), to education, vocational guidance and personnel selection, testing and classification were also central for the development of psychological technology or what became known as psychotechnics in Europe. This was a productive period for these developments to which numerous other psychologists contributed in many other countries of Europe.

In parallel to this applied research an effort was made to define and conceptualise applied psychology, and a start was made with its institutionalisation. In his pioneering work, William Stern defined applied psychology as "the science of psychological facts that are relevant for their practical utility" (Stern, 1903, p. 4). From the start, applied psychology was not conceived of as the mere application of theoretical models formulated in experimental psychology. Aiming to provide responses to real-life needs, applied psychology promoted its own study, analysis and research of applied problems. It developed concepts, tools and technologies that in many instances represented rigorous and relevant contributions to society, and can therefore be considered as basic science (Roe, 1996).

Mainly in the European tradition, applied psychology emphasises a contextualised individual not in a laboratory world of stimuli, but in real-life specific contexts, such as the school, the factory, the hospital, etc. The focus is on the adaptation of the person to environments that are not only natural but are also social and constructed by humans, and thus can be changed. The focus of applied psychology is on the processes of adaptation of persons in their different real-life contexts and in redesigning these environments to make them more appropriate for people's lives. It aims to identify and measure relevant psychological differences for this adaptation and to develop tools and technologies that help individuals to change themselves and their environment for a better adaptation and well-being in interaction with their contexts (see Carpintero, 2002, 2006). An important factor in the development of applied psychology was its institutionalisation beyond the walls of the university, through organisations and institutions both national and international.

Institutionalisation of Psychology

Towards the end of the 19th century and the first decades of the 20th century psychology began to be institutionalised outside universities through national and international organisations across Europe and in the US. This institutionalisation occurred in different ways and helped to promote research and application of psychology in different fields, as well as communication and knowledge sharing among psychologists. The formation of national and international psychology associations created the opportunity for wider academic and professional exchange, while the creation of institutions with a focus on applied psychology allowed for research and practice in this new field.

The first national psychology association, the American Psychological Association (APA), was founded in 1892, with G. Stanley Hall as its first President, at a time "when the new experimental psychology was still in its infancy in America" (Evans, Sexton & Cadwallader, 1992). This was followed in 1901 in Europe by the formation of two national associations, the Société Française de Psychologie (SFP) and the British Psychological Society (BPS). This latter was formed to "advance scientific psychological research and to further the cooperation of investigators in the different branches of psychology" (Lovie, 2001, p. 96; and see Knight, 1954). A few years later the Deutsche Gesellschaft für experimentelle Psychologie was founded in 1904, and the Societa de Psicologia Italiana in 1910. From the beginning these associations were more focused on scientific and academic perspectives; the professional focus emerged only gradually in the course of the 20th century.

At the same time, there was an emerging interest in establishing and promoting international relations. Already at the first International Congress of Psychology in Paris in 1889, a permanent international congress committee was formed in order to ensure the continuation of International Congresses and to provide some form of organisation for international psychology. This international committee, subsequently named the International Congress of Psychology, continued to organise congresses and by 1905 had grown in membership to 76, representing 16 countries (Rosenzweig, Holtzman, Sabourin & Bélanger, 2000). In 1932 at the 10th International Congress of Psychology, the congress committee formed an Executive Committee of seven members, with the Swiss psychologist Edouard Claparède as Executive Secretary. This led, finally, to the creation of the International Union of Psychological Science (IUPsyS) in 1951, with national psychology associations from 20 countries as members; IUPsyS is a union or federation of national psychological association members and now has 82 national members. It continues to organise the International Congress of Psychology every four years.

Claparède had earlier played another important role in the process of internationalisation, leading the organisation of the First International Conference on Psychotechnics, in Geneva in 1920, where the International Association for Psychotechnology was founded. Following a name change this became the International Association of Applied Psychology (IAAP), an organisation with individual members from over 80 countries and which organises the quadrennial International Congress of Applied Psychology. In their study of the early developments in this process of internationalisation, Carpintero and Herrero (2002) have analysed the Congresses of IAAP and have identified interesting trends. Their observations confirm that applied psychology originated not just as the application of previously existing theory, but also as a means to find solutions to people's practical problems. Its main aim was "the study of human subjects behaving in concrete situations (business, schools, hospitals, traffic ...) as conscious and purposeful agents" (Carpintero & Herrero, 2002, p. 51). Thus, attention was paid to specific characteristics of individuals (age, gender, social class, family, group, etc.) and to the particular contexts where they behave and live (school, hospital, industry, etc.), as well as to socially and historically relevant factors. Moreover, "the needs for practical results and useful interventions have always been put above theoretical orthodoxy" (p. 51).

However, at the same time other forms of institution began to emerge with a focus on applied psychology. As mentioned above, in 1897 Wundt's student Witmer founded a clinic to treat children and adolescents with mental and learning problems (Routh, Del Barrio & Carpintero, 1996). Other early institutions of this period are the Bureau of Vocational Guidance at the Civil Service House in Boston opened by the school counsellor and founder of vocational psychology, Frank Parsons, in 1908, and the Jean Jacques Rousseau Institute for education founded by Claparède in Geneva, Switzerland, in 1912. The second decade of the century saw the creation of a number of other new centres which brought together applied psychologists. These included the Institut für Industrielle Psychotechnik at the Technische Hochschule Charlottenburg, in Berlin, Germany in 1918, the Central Psychological Occupations Office of the Roman-Catholic Trade Union in Utrecht, the Netherlands in 1918, the British Health of Munition Workers Committee formed during the First World War in 1916 and which became the British National Institute of Industrial Psychology under the directorship of Myers in 1921, the Institute for Professional Guidance created in 1926 by E. Mira in Barcelona and many others.

Thus, during the final decade of the 19th century and the early decades of the 20th century important developments took place in applied psychology. These built upon the success and progress of psychology as an experimental and differential science, and were driven by the conviction that psychology has to contribute to the solution of relevant demands and problems that individuals, groups and societies experience in their lives and that occur in different contexts and settings. The new "paradigm" of psychology was successful in producing and "selling" the great value of scientific psychology to provide reliable and effective services contributing to the solution of human and social needs and demands. At the same time, the new approach progressively unveiled the poor psychological services provided by practitioners such as phrenologists, physiognomists, characterologists, mesmerists, mediums and mental healers among others, who offered so-called psychological services "before there were psychological laboratories and scientific psychologists" (Benjamin & Baker, 2004).

The Profession of Psychology in Context

The Emergence of Psychology as a Profession

The profession of psychology began to emerge during the first half of the 20th century with the consolidation of the practice of applied psychology not only by psychologists working in universities but also by those working in institutions or as independent practitioners. Like applied research, the work of professionals addressed the human problems that were prevalent in society, such as fatigue, accidents, vocational choice, worker productivity, employee selection, learning and education, mental retardation, mental illness and so on. These were all related to major trends of the time, for example industrialisation, development of transportation, warfare, demographic trends, the introduction of general education, health care reform, etc. The institutions in which professional work was carried out and in which future psychologists were educated had a strong influence on this. They were instrumental in defining the roles that psychological professionals performed vis-à-vis their clients, developing preferences regarding the knowledge and methods to be used, and developing the rules of conduct that would over time be incorporated into codes of ethics.

It is important to note that the process of professionalisation in psychology has resulted in a remarkable degree of differentiation. Unlike the medical profession, psychology did not develop a generic form of the profession and a series of specialised forms (e.g. general practitioner alongside neurologists, urologists, ophthalmologists), but rather a series of parallel forms – each for a particular field of practice and with a typical professional role. These forms have become known under a variety of names, including clinical psychologist, school psychologist, industrial psychologist, counselling psychologist, forensic psychologist, traffic psychologist and sports psychologist. In this respect psychology resembles engineering with its branches of chemical, civil, electrical, mechanical engineering, etc. It is like a plant that has many branches but lacks a common stem, yet has common roots – in a shared foundation of scientific knowledge and methods. As a result, substantial diversity has remained in approaches to the same problems, particularly in the clinical field. Together with the differences between countries in the array of professional forms, which also reflect philosophical and linguistic traditions, this represents one of the factors that make psychology hard to understand for outsiders.

The diverging development of psychology with many branches and in each of them a progressive specialisation, has not remained without debate among psychologists. For instance, about the middle of the 20th century Robert I. Watson (1954) stated: "Psychology is the profession – not clinical psychology, not counselling psychology, not industrial psychology. To be sure, there is room for specialisation within the profession, but there is one profession, not several" (p. 2). Some years later, Lévy-Leboyer wrote of psychology "bursting into a myriad of specific subfields with not much in common" (1992, p. 281), though she also considered this diversity to be a strength of the discipline. The situation today is described by Peiró as a "dynamic tension between . . . centrifugal and centripetal forces" (Peiró, 2014, p. 232). On the one hand there is a unified psychology, science or profession, with various subdisciplines or different professional psychologists in different fields, while on the other hand there are strong forces which drive some of these to join other disciplinary fields or professions.

It is not surprising, then, that the development of the psychological profession, out of a completely new and emergent science, and claiming to be applicable to a wide range of human problems that were formerly provided for by other professions, has taken many decades. It required considerable efforts for psychologists to convince the public, other professions and officials of their capacity to effectively diagnose, clarify and solve particular problems. We could quote many examples of enduring competence disputes between psychologists and those practising older professions. An illustration is the dispute about the competence of testing the fitness of car drivers between psychologists and physicians. In many areas of practice it took more than half a century before the psychological profession became established and acquired a place among the already existing professions.

An interesting question is when psychology reached a stage where it could be called a profession and what its status is today. We will try to answer this question with the help of insights from the sociology of professions. Allsop et al. (2009) define a profession as formed by "practitioners who have achieved a degree of closure around an area of work and are governed through a regulatory body and associations that exercise varying degrees of control over knowledge creation, knowledge transmission and work performance." (p. 489). This implies a collective demarcation of an occupational area or field of practice. Regulation is justified to protect the interest of the public and the clients, although it can also serve to protect the members of the profession (see Chapter 8; Freidson, 1994, 2001). The control exerted tends to regulate the education of professionals, access to the profession and registration as a recognised professional. Control is also intended to guarantee good practice, standards and quality of service and compliance with an ethical code. Moreover, the activities that characterise the profession have to be recognised and identified by outsiders. Professional associations are crucial for the development of the profession and play a critical role in the control of boundaries and normative issues. They also display member socialisation strategies aiming to promote professional ties and loyalties to the profession, and contributing to its identity, good image and reputation.

Similar features as mentioned by Allsop et al. (2009) that are considered distinctive for a profession have been identified by other authors (e.g. Brante, 2011; Evetts, 2011). We mention the following:

1. the activities of its members are based on and grounded in scientific knowledge, and research is the privileged way of obtaining relevant knowledge;
2. access to the profession is granted on the basis of education by an established institution, such as a university or polytechnic school;
3. there exists a professional association with primary aims to enhance the level of competence of its members and maintain the integrity of its members by means of a code of ethics, thereby guaranteeing the quality of professional services and the protection of the public;
4. the profession has a clear identity and is publicly recognised.

To better understand the background against which *EuroPsy* has developed, we will consider in more detail how these features emerged and developed in the case of the profession of psychology.

Science as the Ground of Professional Practice

As indicated above, in the early years the applications in psychology were justified by the claim that they were grounded in scientific knowledge. Great care was taken to distinguish these applications from those of pseudoscientists who offered different kinds of psychic services. However, the relationship between science and practice within psychology is not always straightforward, and it soon became clear that the services rendered by psychology for the benefit of clients and the solution of human problems were not merely the application of scientific knowledge gained in experimental research. Using the methods of science, applied psychologists often carried out research to find adequate solutions to meet the needs of people in specific contexts and situations. Their work also led to the development of techniques, such as tests and clinical interventions, and to the emergence of psychological technologies that provided the scientific basis for assessment and intervention. In that way they broadened the scope of psychology as an explanatory (or basic) science and established psychology as a technological or artificial (Simon, 1969) science (Roe, 1996). This does not mean that different groups of psychologists always agreed about what constituted proper research and how the relationship between psychological science and practice should be defined. Some of the tensions became played out within national psychological societies, which were initially dominated by scientists, with subsequent developments such as broadening of their scope, splitting and creating new associations.

Although in some countries professional associations emerged earlier (e.g. NIPP, the Dutch Association for Practising Psychologists which was founded in 1938), the creation of professional associations in most European countries only started after the Second World War. This was also the case in the US where it took until 1945 before the APA bylaws were changed to include profession as the object of the Association "the advancement of psychology as a science, a profession, and as a means of promoting human welfare" (cited in Benjamin & Baker, 2004, p. 75; and see Capshew & Hilgard, 1992, for a detailed account of the transformation of APA following the Second World War). In many countries professional and scientific associations exist alongside each other as separate organisations, while in others they are integrated. In spite of occasional tensions, positive relations are usually maintained, as professionals generally agree about the importance of science as the basis of their activity, and the scientist-practitioner model of training and practice is widely accepted in European countries. This originated at the Boulder Conference on Graduate Education in Clinical Psychology that took place in 1949 in Boulder, Colorado, at which a model for education was agreed upon that included training in research as well as practice (Raimy, 1950; Benjamin & Baker, 2000; Peterson & Park, 2005). The scientist-practitioner model with its commitment for psychologists to be trained both as researchers and as practitioners or clinicians has had a long-lasting influence on psychology education across the western world.

However, Allsop et al. have pointed out that in spite of this, when comparing psychology to medicine and engineering,

> psychology does not have a knowledge base that is recognised internationally, and not all professional bodies in countries in this study define the knowledge base of psychology in the same way. For example, in France, psychologists tend to draw on psychoanalysis, while in the UK and Canada, there is a stronger link with the biomedical and scientific disciplines that may include cognitive behaviour therapy, psychological testing or sector specializations such as educational or industrial psychology (Allsop et al., 2009, p. 493).

This observation underlines the fact that psychology is both a natural and a social science, and that its knowledge base is only partly shared across the world. This fact, and the variety of epistemologies and conceptions of science that psychologists embrace, does not weaken the assertion that many psychological interventions and technologies are reasonably well grounded in science and thus benefit from scientific knowledge and research.

Access to the Profession on the Basis of Education by an Established Institution

Most of the early education of psychologists focussed on scientific knowledge and scientific research methods, as obtained through academic study. Psychology as a field of study took many years to develop. Initially being part of the field of philosophy, it was increasingly recognised as a separate field of study with its own experimental methods and empirically founded theories. Its growth is reflected in the growing number of new chairs dedicated to psychological subjects, a trend that was visible all over Europe. For most of the first half of the 20th century, university education remained largely theoretical and research oriented and it was only gradually that it took on a more applied or professional focus.

As the body of specialised and technological knowledge grew and the practice of psychology expanded, it became clear that professional education and training were required. This led to the gradual adoption of courses of psychological assessment and intervention, typically aimed at specific work settings (e.g. schools, industries, clinics) in university education. In most of Europe, psychology as an independent field of study – primarily dedicated to theory and research in basic and applied science, but extended with professional courses – was established during the second half of the 20th century. The development of psychology as a technology and the dissemination of techniques and tools that had been shown to be valid and effective, were very important for the status of psychology as a profession. It meant that psychologists could distinguish themselves from those lacking such a knowledge base, and it provided the basis for competent and accountable practice (Poortinga & Lunt, 1997; see also Chapter 8).

While university education in Europe built on long-standing national or regional traditions, which differed noticeably across countries, there was substantial influence of models from the US – such as the scientist-practitioner model – in the years after the Second World War. Interesting to note is the testimony of the British psychologist H.J. Eysenck about a visit to the US to obtain information on establishing clinical psychology as a profession in England. During this visit he learned that clinical psychologists were subordinate to psychiatrists; their aim was mainly to use psychotherapy and psychoanalysis, and their main tools for diagnosis were projective tests. On the basis of his observations Eysenck decided to "initiate a kind of training in clinical psychology which was in many ways the exact opposite to the kind of training that was popular in the United States" (Eysenck, 1990, p. 6).

With the growth of higher education in the second half of the century, the number of faculties and institutes where psychology was being taught grew exponentially. In some larger countries like Germany, the United Kingdom or Russia, psychology also made its way into polytechnic schools that subscribed to the principle of psychology as a science-based profession but did not offer training in psychological research. Although there have been many changes in university structures and curricula over time, the requirement of having an academic education in psychology to start working as a psychologist was nonetheless widely shared. In Chapter 4 we will discuss how the education systems of different countries and regions of Europe gradually converged and common standards emerged.

A Professional Association Aiming to Enhance the Competence and Maintain the Integrity of its Members, Guaranteeing Quality and Protecting the Public

Part of the process of institutionalisation described earlier, was the creation of psychological associations that had already started by the end of the 19th century. In the course of the 20th century all European countries established at least one psychology association, either focused on science, the profession or both. These national associations have contributed to the professionalisation of psychology and typically have sections for branches of psychology such as educational, organisational, clinical and traffic psychology. In some countries there are also associations for more specific areas such as counselling, addiction or political psychology. We note that there is also an increasing number of international associations, and European associations working, for example, in the professional areas of education, addiction, neuropsychology, as societal and client demands and needs become regional as well as national, and as psychologists engage increasingly in collaborative activity across borders.

The activities of these national associations are largely oriented to keeping members informed about new developments, raising their competence by further training and continuing professional development, setting standards and promoting the interests of psychology and psychologists. Associations often publish journals and organise conferences, to distribute knowledge about psychology and raise the profession's level of expertise. In addition, they may also provide information to the public about the activities of their members, keep registers of their members' qualifications and some of them control the professional conduct of members by means of an ethical code. Many are also involved in contacts with national governments and local authorities to improve the conditions under which psychologists operate and render their services to society, serving in some countries the function of trade union. Increasingly national psychology associations have taken on a role in regulating professional practice with the purpose of raising its standards and guaranteeing the quality of services and protecting clients.

A significant development for the advancement of psychology in Europe has been the foundation of an overarching European association, the European Federation of Psychologists Associations (EFPA[1]). This organisation was created in 1981 by national psychologists associations from 12 countries, and was originally limited to professional psychology (Freeman & Steyaert, 2011; Poortinga & Lunt, 2011). As we will describe later, the federation grew to 36 national members by 2013 and broadened its scope to include the science and education in psychology. EFPA added significantly to the status of psychology as a profession, by promoting the collaboration among psychologists within and between countries, and by offering European standards for psychologists' education, ethical conduct, etc. In countries where more than one national association existed, EFPA promoted the creation of national networks or federations. It supported national associations in developing and strengthening their own codes of ethics (Lindsay, Koene, Øvreeide & Lang, 2008).

Professional ethics was an important issue for EFPA. As early as 1990 it set up a Task Force with the goal of producing a common ethical code for psychologists in Europe. As Lindsay et al. (2008) point out "there was concern that a psychologist disciplined in, say, Portugal could move to the UK without this being known" (ibid p. 10). As the realisation of a common code seemed to be impossible, efforts were directed towards a Meta-Code of Ethics (1995, revised in 2005) which provided a framework to enable all European countries to meet a standard in relation to ethical conduct and protection of the public and psychologists' clients. Meanwhile EFPA has gone further and developed a Model Code

[1] The organisation was founded in 1981 as the European Federation of Professional Psychologists Associations (EFPPA) and changed its name in 2001 to the European Federation of Psychologists Associations (EFPA) to reflect its wider goals. The acronym EFPA will be used hereafter, except for referencing requirements.

(EFPA, 2013b) that is meant to induce greater congruence between national codes of ethics.

A Clear Identity and Public Recognition

It has taken much time to develop a clear public image of the psychological profession – and there is still need for further work. In everyday life, psychologists are too often seen as clinical professionals only (which ignores their role in schools, industry, traffic, law enforcement, sports, etc.) or they are confused with psychiatrists. This may be explained by the wide range of professional activities of psychologists, and differences in the profile of psychology across countries. National psychologists associations work with governments, other agencies and the media endeavouring to increase awareness and understanding of the identity and work of psychologists. Despite the diversity within psychological science and the profession, psychologists themselves tend to share an image of their profession and a sense of identity. This is based mainly on psychology's foundation in science and research, and in the commitment of the profession to the well-being of people and welfare in society.

National associations continue to devote efforts to making governments aware of the specific nature of psychology as compared to other professions, and the need to protect the public from services that may seem to be psychological but are offered by persons without the proper scientific education and without a binding commitment to a rigorous code of ethics. As a result, many countries in the industrialised world have some form of legal recognition of psychology. In most European countries there exists a legal protection of the title and/or the professional activities of psychologists. EFPA has been active in this area since the late 1980s (see Matefi & Häring, 1993; Pulverich, 1997; Lunt, Baneke, Berdullas, Hansson & Nevalainen, 2001). At the time of writing (2013) EFPA is developing a Model of a Psychologists Law, which is meant to encourage governments of European countries to adopt the same principles for recognising the psychological profession and protecting the public.

Growth and Diversification of the Profession of Psychology

We now move to look at the development of the psychological profession in its societal context. From this perspective the way in which psychology has developed – in research, education and professional work – and the diversity it exhibits today are anything but accidental. Rather they reflect the societal conditions and the political, economic and technological developments that took place during the 19th and 20th centuries.

In the late 1800s when scientific psychology was founded, Europe was politically divided into major zones of influence, with Germany, Austria–Hungary, Britain, France, Russia and the Ottoman Empire as major players. It was a time when Britain, the Netherlands, Spain, Italy, Portugal were important colonial powers, and the US was still an emerging country thriving on immigration. Europe was engaged in a deep transformation bringing industrialisation, urbanisation and new infrastructure to some areas (particularly Germany and Britain) and leaving others with agricultural societies. There were clear distinctions between the North–West and Europe's Southern and Eastern areas.

The interest in psychology, the way it was financed and taught, and its adoption by authorities and citizens differed widely and the way in which psychology – and its applications – developed reflects the changes that followed.

World War I meant a huge military engagement, involving 65 million mobilised men from 27 countries, resulting in an unprecedented destruction and followed by a dramatic rearrangement of the map of Europe. It opened specific niches for psychology, such as testing of army recruits and officers or clinical work with survivors who had incurred neurological damage. The same holds for the demographic and technological changes, and the new economic developments, including the economic depression of the late 1920s, in the period to follow. Opportunities arose in education for the general population (which had only begun to spread around the turn of the century), traffic, new industrial jobs, work with the unemployed and so on. World War II had an even more dramatic impact, not only because of the vast military confrontations and the enormous human toll incurred by genocide that was carried out by the Nazis and their allies, but also the long-term division of Europe into a Western and Eastern part and the "struggle between Western democracies and Soviet totalitarianism" (Judt, 2005; and see Marquand, 2011). The division by a deadly "iron curtain" that effectively separated large parts of Europe from each other brought widely contrasting political and economic systems, and exposure to very different patterns of cultural dominance – from the Soviet Union in the East and the United States in the West. This situation continued until 1989 when Communist rule collapsed, resulting in the demise of the Soviet Union, independence for the countries of Central and Eastern Europe, and new wars in the Balkans.

The effects of the Second World War and the impacts of the East–West divide on psychology – and other scientific professions – are hard to overestimate. They range from the way in which (and by whom) psychology was taught, to the topics on which psychologists could and could not work, the institutional frames in which this happened, the way in which psychology was financed, and the forms of practice. We should also mention the direct effects on the lives of psychologists, many of whom were forced to migrate or suffered from oppression. In several Eastern European countries (e.g. Russia, Romania, Czechoslovakia) psychology was completely forbidden or severely suppressed during certain periods, which sometimes meant that it was continued underground (see for Eastern Europe, e.g. Roe, 1995). In Western Europe, the former influence of German psychology was almost completely eradicated, and psychology was largely rebuilt on the basis of American doctrines. Of course, all this was moderated by the mastery of German and English languages, and occurred in interaction with national and regional traditions and needs. Other developments taking place simultaneously had an influence on psychology as well. Among them are the spread of democracy, the emergence of the welfare state, economic growth and restructuring, technological advances and increasing global trade. The greater concerns of governments for the well-being and health of citizens, more opportunities for education, life style changes associated with secularisation, greater income and more leisure time that resulted from this generally stimulated the demand for psychological services.

There are similarities across countries in the factors that have shaped the psychological profession in Europe to date. For instance, clinical and health psychology have clearly profited from support by governments embracing the welfare state, particularly in countries with long-lasting social-democratic governments, providing comprehensive social security systems and public provision under what became known as the Scandinavian "model" in the Nordic countries (see Sejersted, 2011; Brandal, Bratberg & Thorsen, 2013). Work and organisational psychology has grown strongly in all countries where industry and business were promoted, but with different emphases in countries that stressed industrial productivity and innovation, worker protection or workplace democracy. The level of trade unionisation also played a role in this development. School psychology has benefited in countries where general and special education were high on the agenda, and where legislation was enacted for provision for pupils with special educational needs or disabilities (e.g. UK). We could mention several other examples, including the influence of demographic changes on the relative attention given to developmental and geronto-psychology, of growing consumption on marketing psychology, of increasing leisure time on sports psychology and of growing affluence on the psychology of addiction. The devastating and long-term effects of wars and dictatorial oppression on the physical and mental health of populations have strengthened the psychology of trauma and stress.

However, there are also differences between countries, which made such general trends work out quite differently. First of all, political and economic differences can explain why psychology grew at different rates. For instance, countries in Eastern and Southern Europe with dictatorial regimes tended to constrain psychology, keeping the numbers of students and university staff small. In countries with democratic governments that were witnessing long-term economic growth, participation in higher education grew and new generations of students had almost unlimited opportunities to study social and behavioural sciences, including psychology. Due to this and the acceptance of the welfare state, with its extended care for people's well-being and health, psychology became the fastest growing profession in many of the Western European countries. However, countries also differed in their economic and social structure, as well as in their institutions, which implied different needs and opportunities for psychology. For instance, psychology developed more in industrial and service economies than in agricultural economies. National employment services and health services were favourable for the adoption of psychology, as were tripartite systems of labour relations. There were many other factors, including geography, culture, religion and education that contributed to the development of psychology in the different countries, giving each country a particular professional profile. This helps to understand why counselling psychology is quite common in Great Britain, community psychology in Italy, transport psychology in Hungary and engineering psychology in Russia – to mention a few examples.

The overall effect of the broader context on the psychological profession in Europe cannot be understood without considering the course of history. Apart from the fact that all later developments built on what had happened in earlier decades, there are specific effects of the political processes that changed the map of Europe in the second half of the 20th century (see Judt, 2005). Several countries in Western Europe established relationships with the US and began embracing models and practices from American and British psychology – particularly the Netherlands, Belgium and the Scandinavian countries, which adopted English as a second language early on. Other European countries (e.g. France, Italy) kept more of their own traditions, being more selective in their adoption of Anglo-American ideas. For decades the countries of Central and Eastern Europe largely followed models from the Soviet Union, but mostly dropped these after the fall of the Iron Curtain. They reconnected to former traditions and began looking for alternatives – with particular interest in Western countries, with which they began collaborating after entering the European Union. We will discuss the role of the European Union in the following section.

European Integration

Of particular importance for the more recent development of the psychological profession in Europe has been the establishment of the European Union (originally the European Communities, 1957) and its evolution into an economic and political partnership of Member States that currently covers 28 European countries with a total population of more than 500 million people. The EU emerged out of the European Economic Community (EEC) which was established by the Treaty of Rome (1957) as an economic union of six Western European countries (Belgium, France, West Germany, Italy, Luxembourg and the Netherlands) with the aim to promote collaboration and avoid conflict between its members. Over time more countries entered, including – after 1989 – countries of Central and Eastern Europe that had been part of or were controlled by the Soviet-Union.

The EU has its legal base in treaties between the Member States, and is built around the concept of a Single Market (formerly the common market), which guarantees the free movement of people, goods, services, and capital (the four freedoms). It has gradually evolved into an organisation that spans many common policy areas, from competition and employment to education and human rights. Economically, the EU has become a major player in the world. In 2009 it generated 28% of the nominal Gross World Product (GWP) and 21% of the Gross World Product corrected for purchasing power (GWP-PPP). In 2012 its GWP-PPP amounted to $15,700 trillion, the highest of any political entity in the world, and about $2 trillion more than the United States. The EU has had a tremendous influence on its Member States, not only in economic respects, but also in promoting equal rights, social cohesion, education, innovation and so on. Its origins lay in a vision and a set of values, and an ideal of "a common *European* identity, reflecting common European values, a common European civilisation and a common commitment to the European project" (Marquand, 2011, p. 43). It has become the major engine of legislation, with two-thirds of all national laws finding their origin in EU directives and other legislation. It promotes coordination, collaboration and joint action between Member States in all policy domains.

The EU is of interest for psychology in a number of ways. First, because EU policy-making affects the foundations of psychology as a profession – that is scientific research, education, association and recognition (see above). Second, because it directly regulates facets of the professions that are connected to the four freedoms of mobility. Third, because it has an influence on various sectors in which psychologists operate, promoting greater transparency and congruence. And fourth, because it offers opportunities for psychology to present itself at the European level and to influence policy-making, before it reaches the national level.

Although the EU fosters transatlantic relations, its very activities imply that European countries share views and practices with each other, and no longer orient themselves primarily towards the US. The focus is on collaboration and on developing approaches and standards that meet the needs and values of Europe. This applies to all policy domains, ranging from employment and social rights to the natural environment and health. It also affects the areas of scientific research and education, in which the EU has launched several programs aiming to develop collaboration and setting up a common infrastructure. Psychological research as such is not a focal area in EU research but psychology has profited from the so-called "Framework" programs which have allocated several billions of Euros to policy-relevant research on issues related to innovation, environment, governance, education, employment, health, etc. The recently announced Horizon 2020 Research and Innovation Programme commits almost 80 billion Euros over the next 7 years with a major commitment to address societal challenges. As we shall see in Chapter 4, the EU has strongly stimulated collaboration in the field of education, sponsoring the development of common curricula and joint degrees, and the mobility of teachers and students, for example through the Erasmus programme. The EU has also supported the "Bologna Process," which aims to develop a common European space for higher education, involving the majority of countries in Europe, and projects to harmonise educational structures and curricula (e.g. the so-called "*Tuning* projects," one of which has focussed on psychology, see Chapter 4). These activities regarding research and education are important because they strengthen the foundations of the psychological profession in Europe.

There are also impacts of the EU on the other foundations – association building and public recognition – but to understand these we first need to discuss the way in which the EU offers a new playing field for the professions and gives them an opportunity for representation and influence that did not exist before. We refer here to the establishment of the European Institutions, that is, the European Commission, the European Council, the European Parliament, the Economic and Social Committee, the European Court of Justice and several others, all operating at a supra-national level. These institutions are creating a new space for organisations of stakeholders such as professions, industries, consumers and patients to express their views and interests, provided that they are indeed organised at the European level and do adequately represent the stakeholders.

EFPA's Role in Fostering Greater Integration

Along with many European bodies representing other professions, EFPA has welcomed this opportunity and confirmed its role as representative organisation for psychology. In fact, EFPA redefined its role and gave European representation and lobbying the highest priority. It revised its structure and embraced many of Europe's specialist psychology associations as Associate Members (Roe & Freeman, 2011). As it is becoming more involved in European policy-making and is recognised by European institutions as the voice of psychology at the European level, EFPA can better support its Member Associations in promoting psychology at the national level. It is able to work with the Member Associations in a coordinated way, when it comes to specific actions regarding education, professional training, ethics, etc., as can be seen in the following chapters. Its new position enables EFPA to put more force behind projects that were started in earlier decades, when the EU was still emerging. The development of the Model Code of Ethics and the Model of a Psychologists Law, mentioned above, are examples of this.

Returning to the foundations of the psychological profession, it will now be clear that the EU has created an opportunity for EFPA to establish itself at the European level as an institution that supplements and reinforces the national associations of psychologists. Apart from the fact that EU funding was obtained early in the process of developing *EuroPsy*, the EU has also created the conditions for developing the European Certificate in Psychology. EFPA has built on this and taken responsibility for its implementation and for introducing it in all countries represented by its Member Associations. This considerably enhances the possibilities for EFPA and its Member Associations to raise the competences of psychologists and to promote high standards and a strong and common Code of Ethics. Its position also allows EFPA to emphasise the coherence of the profession and to promote the collaboration among psychologists across the borders of specialties and countries. As we will see in Chapter 9, *EuroPsy* is very instrumental in this respect. The intention is that these activities will help to develop a common identity of psychologists in Europe, and to enhance the image of the profession.

We mention briefly here the issue of mobility, a topic that has been on the agenda of the EU for many years. In the course of its existence, there have been multiple occasions on which the EU has issued directives aiming to promote the mobility of professionals by facilitating the mutual recognition of their qualifications by the Member States, most recently in 2005 (Directive 2005/36/EC). Psychology was not included in the list of professions with automatic recognition, for which sectoral directives had been issued between 1977 and 1993 (see also Chapter 2). The directive has been updated in 2013 and with the introduction of Common Training Frameworks, semi-automatic recognition of psychologists' qualifications may become a reality within the next few years. This means that *EuroPsy* may have an instrumental role in the future in this respect. We will expand on the European Qualifications Directive and the expected changes in Chapter 9.

We would like to close this section by emphasising that the expansion of the EU, the growth and transformation of EFPA and the change in its activities – including the development and implementation of *EuroPsy* – have happened over a period of more than two decades (Roe & Freeman, 2011). Some European countries have been part of the EU and have been able to benefit from this for longer than others, but with the welcoming approach that the EU – and EFPA – takes to newcomers, this difference is quickly vanishing. Of note is the European Union's "extraordinary capacity to attract new members . . . a long line of countries on its periphery has applied successfully for membership, not because anyone forced them to but because they thought they would be better off inside" (Marquand, 2011, p. 35). The same holds for EFPA.

Psychology Among the Professions

To properly understand the position of the psychological profession in Europe, it is important to realise that it is one of many professions, some of which are much older and were institutionalised much earlier, like lawyers, architects, midwives, physicians and pharmacists. Among them are also new professions, which emerged during the past few decades and of which the status is still contested, for example, coaches, mediators, management consultants and informatics professionals. Although some professions had founded

European associations in earlier decades, many have more recently established themselves at the European level, realising the opportunities that the EU and its Single Market are offering. This is worth noting, because psychologists can collaborate with other professional associations on several issues to promote shared interests, such as the recognition of requirements for continuing professional development in the context of the EU Qualifications Directive. However, there is also room for conflicts to emerge, for example regarding the demarcation of professional roles and competences between psychologists and physicians, or psychologists and psychotherapists with lesser qualifications.

Issues regarding the demarcation of professions and of collaboration versus conflict are not likely to diminish in the years ahead. On the contrary, the increasing permeability of borders, particularly in knowledge-based professions, will make such issues more prevalent. Cross-teaching, knowledge sharing via bibliographic databases, and interdisciplinary research infuses the work domain of psychologists with elements from that of biologists, physicians or economists, and vice versa. With multidisciplinary approaches becoming more popular, we should expect that professions will increasingly address the same problems from different angles and sometimes perform overlapping activities. The issue may become more pressing where the psychological profession borders on new professions, such as coaching, management consultancy or project management, which draw their knowledge from a broader and poorly bounded knowledge base. Such new professions may enter into areas that psychologists (or other professionals) consider as "theirs" and use new strategies of professionalisation, including self-credentialing and endorsement by corporate clients to mark and defend their professional territory (Muzio, Hodgson, Faulconbridge, Beaverstock & Hall, 2011).

As psychologists often work together with other professionals, either as independent (liberal) professionals or as employees within the same or collaborating institutions, they may encounter problems of identity and loyalty. For instance, school psychologists, work and organisational psychologists or health psychologists, may ask themselves what is and is not psychological in their work, what they are expected to do, and what they should not do as psychologists – also in ethical respects. As we shall see in later chapters this underlines the importance of *EuroPsy* as a source of guidance.

Conclusion

Psychology as a science has a relatively short history of almost 150 years. Given its relevance to human and societal challenges, applications of psychological science developed almost from the start. The psychological profession emerged later and developed very rapidly as societies developed in complexity and challenge. Towards the end of the 20th century, countries in Europe had made significant developments in psychology education and profession at a national level; this had resulted in considerable differences. This provided the impetus for the foundation of EFPA in 1981 and the initiatives for *EuroPsy* which started in 1998. Both of these were strongly supported by the increasing significance of the European Union. In the next chapter we describe the creation of *EuroPsy*: how and why it happened.

2 The Creation of *EuroPsy*

This chapter describes how the awareness of differences in national systems of education and qualification inspired European policy-makers to search for greater comparability and convergence, and how a project to develop a common qualification for psychologists initiated by European psychologists and funded by the EU resulted in *EuroPsy*. At the start of the project (1998), psychologists were educated according to national systems and norms, and qualifications were not recognised beyond national borders. A decade later, when *EuroPsy* was established (2010) the situation had changed significantly. Although a great deal of difference still existed, there was a single standard for future education and training that was recognised all over Europe. The first section of this chapter provides the rationale for *EuroPsy* looking at some features of the period leading up to the start of the project. This is followed by an analysis of the European context which happened to provide a fertile ground for the development of the *EuroPsy*. We include developments associated with the growing integration of Europe, such as the growth of the European Union (EU) and more widely the commitments of European Ministers of Education towards harmonisation and collaboration leading up to the Bologna Agreement. The third and major part of the chapter provides an account of the *EuroPsy* projects undertaken from 1999 to 2004, the trialling of *EuroPsy* in six countries between 2006 and 2009, and implementation by EFPA in 2010.

Rationale for *EuroPsy* and Early Initiatives

Europe is probably best known for its multifaceted diversity (Lunt, 1998; Lunt & Poortinga, 1996; Peiró & Lunt, 2002). Not only do we see a diversity of languages, cultures, histories, religions and ideologies; Europe also reveals a rich variety of higher education systems, with different intellectual traditions, varying structures and organisation of degrees, nomenclature of qualifications, traditions of professional education, training and practice, and assumptions about pedagogy, learning and assessment. This diversity is reflected in the dissimilar requirements, paths, standards and organisation of professional formation for psychologists that existed across European countries in the period prior to the projects that led to *EuroPsy*. Thus, Newstead and Makinen (1997, p. 5) noted that "there appears to be surprisingly little consistency in the manner of teaching, the length of courses, or even the content of the syllabus" (see also Chapter 4).

Despite attempts by the European Community to promote mobility across countries in Europe, mobility for psychologists was minimal. This was in part due to language differences and the fact that each country imposed its own requirements for psychologists' education and training, and in part to a lack of trust and will to collaborate on mutual recognition. Le Bianic and Svensson (2008) point out: "A good mastery of national languages is a precondition for professional practice, and psychologists usually practise in human-service organisations locally situated and strongly nationally defined and regulated" (p. 568). At the time, the UK was a net importer of psychologists who applied to work in the country, mainly because of the language factor, as English was increasingly seen as lingua franca and because there was a shortage of psychologists on the labour market. Still, the UK recognised very few psychologists with qualifications from other countries as having equivalent qualifications and almost all applicants were required to have (or gain) compensatory experience such as supervised experience, a research project or an aptitude test (see also Hall & Lunt, 2005).

The understanding that something had to be done about the diversity and fragmentation in education and training was certainly one of the factors that played a role in the foundation of the European Federation of Professional Psychologists Associations (EFPPA) in 1981. There was an increasing awareness that the growing opportunities for mobility in the countries of the European Economic Community would have an impact on the professions, and a realisation that collaboration would benefit the profession, both nationally and at European level. Roe and Freeman (2011) remind us that "the long-term aims as spelled out in the Statutes of 1981 were to exchange information, establish common standards and to promote legal registration in the Member Associations."

EFPA addressed the question of the quality of education and common standards early on, and in 1986 formed a Committee on Training and Education in Psychology (COTEP). Its goal was to compare standards for education and training of psychologists across the member associations of EFPA, and to derive a common view of standards for the future. Its short report, titled *Optimal Standards for the professional training in psychology* was published in 1990 and unanimously endorsed by the 20 Member Associations of the Federation at the General Assembly in July that year. It stated:

> EFPPA ... fully recognises that the content and form of training in professional psychology in each country will inevitably reflect its own legal, educational, and professional traditions. However, to encourage international cooperation among professional psychologists and to assist member associations in their efforts to develop professional training and practice in their own countries, EFPPA is publishing the following statement which describes the optimal standards for training required for independent professional practice (EFPPA, 1990)

The document was an attempt to produce a broad framework with some core elements, such as length of training, location in university base, theory and practical application, with which all member associations could agree, even if that agreement implied an aspiration rather than a description of the actual situation and reality in their country. In fact, it was accepted that the optimal standards were just that. Nevertheless, the agreed statement provided a very important starting point for further development, although it had no formal status and was nothing more (nor less) than a rather broad goal, aspirational rather than prescriptive, setting out optimal rather than minimal standards.

Table 1. Extract from Optimal Standards for the Professional Training in Psychology (EFPPA, 1990)

1. Preparation for autonomous practice of psychology comprises at least two parts, a core programme concerned with knowledge and skills relating to psychology as a scientific discipline (broad introduction) and an advanced programme concerned with knowledge and skills necessary for autonomous practice in a chosen field of applied psychology.
2. Both of these should be provided within a university or IHE (Institution of Higher Education).
3. The two components should last at least six years with at least half the time devoted to the core programme.
4. Entry to independent or autonomous practice should be restricted to those who have completed both components.
5. Research methods are essential and students should have the experience of conducting an original and independent research project.
6. National associations should ensure training is consistent with codes of practice and ethical standards.

As may be seen from the extract above (Table 1), the standard provided by the COTEP report played an important role within EFPA as it became used by psychology associations in countries to enhance the quality of education and training for psychologists in their country. The standard involved a university education of at least 6 years, with a restriction of entry to independent practice as a psychologist to those suitably qualified. The Committee was well aware at the time that the majority of countries in Europe did not meet the standard. However, proposing that it should be seen as an optimal standard was of strategic significance as it provided a goal that the profession of psychology throughout Europe could strive for.

Aware of the increasing emphasis within the European Union on mobility and evaluation of qualifications, and the challenges for psychologists in relation to this, in 1994 EFPA set up a further Task Force focusing on the content of the psychology curriculum across European countries. The Task Force reviewed previous literature and initiated a questionnaire-based survey in Europe. In a report on this work Newstead and Makinen (1997) commented on how difficult it was to obtain a coherent picture of psychology teaching in Europe. Most of the available information was in the form of articles, reports, and chapters in edited books that each described a single European country (e.g. Nixon, 1990; Prieto, Fernandez-Ballesteros & Carpintero, 1994; Schorr & Saari, 1995; Sexton & Hogan, 1992, Fowler, 2006). These sources provided limited insights and were hardly a sufficient database to permit systematic comparisons. Nevertheless, the scattered body of information allowed Newstead and Makinen (1997) to conclude that there was considerable variation in how psychology education and training were being organised in Europe.

Differences existed in the duration of programmes (from four to six years), methods of teaching, the length of courses, etc. The main distinction in their article is between three overall patterns of education and training. The first of these patterns is labelled as *Five Year Specialist/Continuous Specialist*. Throughout such a programme, found for example in Finland and Sweden, the education is aimed at a single professional field, such as clinical/health or education. In the second pattern, *Five Year Generalist/Continuous Generalist*, the study starts with a general study of psychology and provides specialisation in a specific field towards the end of the programme, usually in a separate phase. This was the most common pattern, found in a majority of countries. The third pattern of education and training was labelled as *Three plus Three/Discontinuous Specialist*; here students follow a three-year general programme after completion of which they enrol in a new programme, sometimes at a different university, where they specialise. Examples of this third pattern were reported for Greece, Ireland and the UK. Since the number of students post-Bachelor programmes in these countries tends to be limited due to a form of numerus clausus, many students in a country like the UK would terminate their studies after three years, that is, the Bachelor degree in psychology. On completion of the three year programme these graduates might enter the labour market and undertake a range of very different roles, though not working as a psychologist. With all three patterns, qualification as a psychologist would be obtained only at the end of the longer programme of study, and it might take five years or six years to qualify for work as a psychologist. These differences meant that psychologists qualified under a system in one country were unable to practise in another country, despite the fact that the knowledge base and the main professional activities (e.g. assessment, intervention, evaluation) were very similar between European countries.

Newstead and Makinen (1997) also provided an overview of the percentage of time devoted to various areas of psychology during the first three years of study. Although the information was sketchy, they concluded that there was a great deal of similarity in the content of curricula at the level of "undergraduate, or theoretical foundation for psychology." A common set of core areas including psycho-nomics (or experimental psychology), developmental psychology, biological psychology, social psychology and individual differences (or personality psychology) was covered in all countries, although the percentage of time spent on each of these areas might differ substantially. A notable feature in all programmes was the time devoted to methodology, taking up between 10% and 20% of the curriculum.

A parallel activity of EFPA coordinated by a Task Force on Legal Matters derived from a questionnaire-based survey of legal regulations for psychologists across EFPA member countries (Lunt, Baneke, Berdullas, Hansson, & Nevalainen, 2001; Matefi & Häring, 1993; Pulverich, 1997; and see Lunt, 2000). The emphasis was on the legal regulation of the profession of psychology in various European countries. A large variation was found to exist; there were countries where the title (and in some cases the practice) of psychologists was regulated by statute and other countries where there was no form of regulation for either the practice or the title of psychologist. It should be noted that most member associations of EFPA have now, at the time of writing (2013), achieved some form of regulation of psychologists. This regulation does not, however, specify any curriculum content, although in some countries the title of psychologist is protected and regulated by government and is defined by a governmental body which sets requirements which may include some broad specification of the curriculum.

In the course of the 1990s, EFPA set up a number of other Task Forces in fields such as clinical psychology, health psychology, psychotherapy, educational psychology, forensic psychology, organisational psychology, traffic psychology which attempted over the years to provide a general map of the field of training and practice in particular areas across a number of European countries. However, this was not an easy task as there had been no comprehensive mapping of qualifications regarding professional practice which might facilitate mobility and comparability.

Outside EFPA, another organisation, the European Network of Organisational and Work Psychologists (ENOP) had embarked on a similar exercise in the field of work and organisational psychology (W&O) as early as 1987. The first so-called "Reference Model" was discussed in ENOP at its symposium in 1993, and in a special session at the 6th European Congress of Work & Organisational Psychology in Alicante, Spain that year. Further comments were solicited from associations and interest groups in the various countries of Europe, as well as from readers of the journal *The European Work and Organisational Psychologist*. A revised model, established at the ENOP symposium in 1994, served as the basis for a survey of the state of play with regard to the teaching of W&O psychology in Europe. This survey identified the common core of W&O psychology and the variations across the curricula of the different universities (Roe, Coetsier, Lévy-Leboyer, Peiró & Wilpert, 1994; ENOP, 1998). This proved to be a demanding task, as one of the ENOP members, Bernhard Wilpert, observes:

> We gravely underestimated the difficulties involved in such an exercise. To come up with a relatively final result took us more than eight years with various iterations of surveys, discussions, and verifications (Wilpert, 1999, p. 220).

The final version of the Reference Model "defines a standard for the basic training in W&O psychology, that is to say, the minimum requirements that curricula should meet in order to be considered as providing the necessary academic preparation for professional work and research in W&O psychology . . ." (ENOP, 1998, p. 1). The Model specified four dimensions: educational objectives, fields of study, type of science, and depth of specialisation. These were brought together in a multi-dimensional matrix which was used to structure the curriculum, and provide minimal standards. The educational objectives were defined as:

- orientation,
- knowledge of explanatory theories,
- knowledge of technological theories,
- diagnostic skills,
- intervention skills,
- professional competencies,
- research competencies.

The ENOP model provided a useful framework for early discussions about *EuroPsy,* not least because there was significant overlap in membership of ENOP and the *EuroPsy* team. However, the activities of ENOP were restricted to the field of W&O psychology and did not affect psychology education and training at large. Moreover, there remained a substantial degree of inertia and path-dependency in national systems of education and training, with professional psychology rooted firmly in national contexts of practice, legislation and professional custom, with the result that "unfortunately there ha(d) not been significant progress in promoting the mobility of psychologists across Europe" (Hall & Lunt, 2005, p. 720).

The European Context: A Fertile Ground for *EuroPsy*

In 2002 Peiró and Lunt wrote:

> Psychology in Europe is now at a crossroads where there is some awareness about the benefits of integration at a European level . . . but there is still a long way to go . . . in this process of integration, the diversity currently existing in Europe may be seen both as a threat and as an opportunity (Peiró & Lunt, 2002, p. 169).

As already mentioned in Chapter 1, this diversity reflected long and strongly held traditions of different national histories, languages, politics, economies and religions which contribute to the unique and multifaceted complexity in which European integration was and is occurring. Although it may appear to some that greater European integration has a compelling logic (or even inevitability), there is a substantial ambivalence at the level of the Member States, which seek collaboration with the European partners and at the same time try to maintain the status quo and pursue national interests. This is often perceived as a tension between the pressures of Brussels[2] for greater convergence and the tendency of national governments to strive to retain their national identity, and the consequent balance between pressures for regional integration versus the pulls of nationalism.

In this context, we consider two major developments, one by the EU, the second by national Ministers of Education across European countries which have had a significant impact on higher education and which provided a fertile ground and background support for the development of *EuroPsy*. The first development originates from the start of the European Economic Community back in 1957 which made the bold claim that "Freedom to work anywhere in the European Community is one of the basic rights laid down by the Treaty of Rome." An ambitious statement that appeared hard to implement, and in fact is still at the stage of a work in progress through a series of Directives which aim to facilitate recognition of qualifications, and professional mobility. Of equal significance is the second development, the commitment by national Ministers of Higher Education in European countries, who created the Sorbonne and Bologna Ministerial Agreements which have now been signed by 47 countries in Europe. We will look at these two developments in some detail since they provided a frame for the creation of *EuroPsy*, and a context that encouraged greater collaboration and promoted strategies to seek convergence. We also mention briefly some other aspects of the "fertile ground" on which *EuroPsy* grew.

European Community and Qualifications Directives

Free movement of people across the borders of European countries posed a major challenge, given the very diverse education, qualification and professional recognition systems. Already during the 1960s in the early years of the implementation of the Treaty

---

[2] As unofficial capital of Europe, and the administrative centre of the European Union, Brussels is frequently used as a shorthand to signify the European Union, Commission or other European political institutions.

of Rome, there was an idealistic and ambitious goal to *harmonise* the structure and content of professional education and training systems of the six European countries. This took the form of what was referred to as a vertical approach to recognition of qualifications, (i.e. harmonisation of qualifications profession by profession), and required negotiation of virtually identical patterns of education for each profession across the member states. The result was the creation, as from 1977, of so-called "Sectoral Directives" which required member countries to guarantee, for that profession, the "right of establishment" that is the right to work across the countries of the European Community (EC). Harmonisation requires that the rules which apply in one country apply in all of the others and the Sectoral Directives therefore specified a common set of minimum standards on training and qualification requirements for the particular profession to apply across the countries of the EC. The process of harmonisation involved a detailed comparison of the education and training systems of different countries for a particular profession, followed by a lengthy process of consultation, negotiation, and compromise in order to establish a European Standard for each profession.

As might be expected, these attempts to harmonise qualifications proved to be enormously time-consuming and complex (e.g. the Architects' directive took 17 years to agree before being adopted in 1985), and the task began to look impossible. According to McPherson (1988):

> the slow progress was partly of course due to the technical problems of harmonising what were often quite heterogeneous systems of training and practice. However, possibly the main reason was that free movement and right of establishment was a political goal for which few professions expressed much enthusiasm. Many of the negotiations showed a lack of urgency (p. 354)

Sectoral Directives were achieved for seven professions only (architect, dentist, doctor, midwife, nurse, pharmacist and veterinary surgeon), with agreement for those professions across all Member States of the content of courses, minimum length of study and training, and skills that a graduate in the field should possess. With the realisation that this challenge was ultimately unrealistic, the task of extending the process of harmonisation to other professions was abandoned by the EC/EU. Instead, there was a gradual awareness within the European Commission that *equivalence* of qualification was more important than *equality or harmonisation*, and that a more feasible approach would be required.

As Haaksman (1990) pointed out:

> in comparing study courses and professional skills, equivalence is more important than equality. In other words credentials evaluation should be based on mutual trust and respect rather than suspicion and pedantry . . . the acquired skills should be comparable. The thing that matters is: equivalence in its most literal meaning (p. 25).

A new approach was developed which took the form of a system of *mutual recognition* based on *equivalence* rather than *harmonisation.* This resulted in the General Directive 89/48/EEC (Mutual Recognition of Higher Education Diplomas), which was published in draft form in 1985, introduced on December 21, 1988 and took effect in January, 1993. It aimed to introduce a system for the recognition of qualifications of those professions to which access is in some way regulated or restricted by the State and which require at least three years' university level training. In countries where the profession of psychologist was regulated by law, psychologists were covered by the General Directive. These countries were required to develop procedures for evaluating the equivalence of qualifications, and facilitating recognition of competence and thus mobility (Lunt, 1998, 2002).

The principle of mutual recognition on the basis of *equivalence* was formally introduced in 1989, and was followed over the next 15 years or so by a number of amendments and new Directives, as the EC struggled to find ways to achieve free movement within the Single European Market. Although based on joint decision-making in the European Council, this was essentially a top-down process. Yet, it relied on individual Member States creating the mechanisms to evaluate equivalence and having the will and the mutual trust and respect to accept the quality of education and training gained in other member states. The first general system Directive (89/48/EEC) was followed by a second general system Directive (92/51/EEC), amended by Directive 1999/42/EEC, and finally all Sectoral and General Directives were repealed and subsumed under the Directive 2005/36/EEC.

Directive 2005/36/EC sets out three systems for recognition of qualifications: (a) automatic recognition for the seven professions for which training conditions had already been harmonised (the sectoral professions) (though problems can arise with changes in practice over time which may be appropriate in one member state, yet require negotiation across the EU), (b) the general system for other regulated professions, including psychologists, and (c) recognition on the basis of professional experience for certain professional activities (e.g. the craft, commerce or industry sector). Under the general system, mutual recognition should be automatic where there is sufficient commonality of education and training. Where there are significant differences in the education and training, the Directive requires that recognition be granted by the Member State after compensation in the form of either an adaptation period or an aptitude test. The Directive has recently been modernised (2013) with the aim of accelerating the mobility of professionals in the EU's Single Market. It currently provides for automatic recognition if a professional meets the requirements of a Common Training Framework and introduces a European Professional Card, issued in the home country and linked to a European database, to speed up the recognition process. More information on this will be given in Chapter 9.

It is important to note that the Directives are established in a legislative process that involves the European Commission, the European Parliament and the European Council (Ministers of the Member States). Once established, the Directives must be transposed into national law by the governments of the Member States. This is typically done through designated competent authorities authorised by the governments (see Chapter 9). Under the Directive 2005/36/EC psychologists qualified in one country in the European Union should be able to travel to another European Union country and have their qualifications recognised or, at least where the qualifications differ significantly, take an examination or undergo a period of adaptation. The numbers of psychologists who have made use of the opportunities for having their qualifications recognised have remained small (some 3,000 in the decade up to 2012), partly due to issues of language. These numbers may grow in the future.

Agreements Made by Ministers of European Countries

Alongside these political developments within the EU, a longer-standing and broader system of recognition processes was evolving. Ever since the foundation of the Council of Europe, an international organisation promoting cooperation between all European countries (not to be confused with the EU) in 1949, study abroad for students across Europe has been recognised as an important element of European integration. This became manifested through EU programmes such as Erasmus (see below) and was embodied in the Lisbon Recognition Convention,[3] signed on April 11, 1997, which was an international convention of the Council of Europe (then 40 member states) developed in collaboration with UNESCO. This Convention aimed to ensure that qualifications and periods of study gained in one country would be recognised in another. Mechanisms included the use of the Diploma Supplement, which was intended to provide descriptions of qualifications in an easily understandable form, and the establishment of national and European information centres in the European Union (NARICs, i.e. National Academic Recognition Information Centres and the ENIC, i.e. the European Network of Information Centres).

The Lisbon Convention was a direct forerunner of moves initiated by Ministers of Higher Education in Europe that led in 1998 to the signing of the Sorbonne Agreement, and a year later in 1999 the Bologna Agreement. These were to have a major impact on systems of higher education across Europe – the European Union as well as other countries of Europe.

In 1998 at a conference organised at the Sorbonne to commemorate the 800th anniversary of the University of Paris, the ministers of four countries (France, Germany, Italy, UK) signed the Sorbonne Agreement, entitled the Joint Declaration on Harmonisation of the Architecture of the European Higher Education System and invited governments and institutions to harmonise their university provision.

> Progressive harmonisation of the overall framework of our degrees and cycles can be achieved through strengthening of already existing experience, joint diplomas, pilot initiatives and dialogue with all concerned (Sorbonne Declaration, 1998).

We note, in passing, the use here of the term and concept "*harmonisation*," which had already been dropped by the EU. We note also that this had, significantly, been softened a year later in the Bologna Declaration to the term "*convergence*." A year after the Sorbonne Declaration, the group of four ministers had expanded to the 29 who signed the Bologna Declaration (or Agreement, as it is frequently named), in June, 1999, as a "pledge by these countries to reform the structures of their higher education systems in a *convergent* way" (Bologna Declaration p. 1, current authors' italics). As Neave (2003) points out, the Sorbonne term "architecture" remains central to the Bologna Declaration and "harmonisation and architecture mean essentially the same thing, namely convergence around common practices and therefore standards" (p. 157) (see also Kladis, 2003; Lunt, 2005). This reform was to be achieved by creating a European Higher Education Area (EHEA) by

[3] In full, The Convention on the Recognition of Qualifications concerning Higher Education in the European Region.

2010 in order to improve both the quality and the international attractiveness and competitiveness of higher education in Europe. The EHEA was also intended as a means to promote greater convergence of higher education systems, and to encourage mobility both of students and of faculty.

The Bologna Declaration set in motion a series of initiatives that have already led and continue to lead to greater convergence of university programmes for psychology. In Chapter 4 we will describe some of these developments and show how they are facilitating the acceptance of the *EuroPsy* system across Europe. Significant among the initiatives arising from the Bologna Process is the so-called *Tuning* initiative, which aims to create agreed benchmarks for subjects, including psychology, across Europe (Chapter 4, see p. 72–74).

Other Initiatives

Another important initiative in education was the Socrates programme of the European Commission. This ran from 1994 to 1999 (and Socrates II from 2000 to 2006) and aimed to improve competence in European languages, strengthen the European dimension in education and promote cooperation and mobility. Linked to this, the Erasmus[4] programme, an early EU initiative launched in 1987 to promote student mobility, has also had a major impact on student mobility, and therefore also on systems for recognising study periods abroad by different European countries. The Erasmus programme supports EU students (as well as academic and administrative staff) spending an internship/study period between 3 and 12 months in a different European university as part of their recognised degree, and since its inception has involved over 2 million students, with over 4,000 students involved at any one time. Linked to this, the Erasmus Mundus programme, which supports the creation of joint Master's programmes through consortia of universities, has extended the reach of the initial Erasmus programme to include non-EU students and staff, with the goal of globalising European education and attracting talent from other regions in the world.

These and many other developments at the wider European level linked with a growing political pressure for European integration show how a fertile ground for the *EuroPsy* project had been created in Europe. European aspirations to create an integrated and competitive European Higher Education Area (EHEA) combined with the EU's commitments to greater cross-border mobility led to awareness amongst national governments and thence psychology associations that cooperation was important. Project funding was also an important element of the initial *EuroPsy* initiative.

The *EuroPsy* Projects

The concrete origins of the *EuroPsy* Certificate lay in a project submitted in 1998 for funding within the EU Leonardo da Vinci programme. This programme, created in 1995 as

[4] European Community Action Scheme for the Mobility of University Students.

part of the European Commission's Lifelong Learning programme, was set up to fund, and continues to do so, practical projects in the broad field of vocational education and training in order to increase mobility, to develop innovative practices and to share best practices. EU funding programmes provide considerable opportunities, while also imposing clear direction, priorities and objectives, requirements and constraints. Bernhard Wilpert, a leading international work and organisational psychologist and a partner in the first Leonardo project reflects with insight on the genesis of what came to be known as the two *EuroPsy* Leonardo projects, and "the constraints and opportunities under which the research process itself took place" (Wilpert, 2002). He mentions a number of factors as particularly relevant for international collaborative research; these include pressures external to the research team, team composition in terms of personality match, time constraints, resource availability, theoretical and methodological competence and power differentials in the team, different interests pursued by team members, and group dynamics. All of these factors certainly played their part through the Leonardo projects which demanded a careful balance between purpose and direction on the one hand, and compromise and negotiation on the other. The first project (1999–2001) developed a European framework for psychologists training (EuroPsyT), while the second project (2001–2004) built on this to create the benchmark for psychologists' education and training based on professional competences, the *EuroPsy* (see also Lunt, 2008, 2011).

Leonardo Project 1 and a Shared Model of the Curriculum

It is worth considering here the statement of aims and objectives developed for the first Leonardo project (Table 2). These aims and objectives were carefully formulated in order to meet the requirements and priorities of the Leonardo da Vinci programme. After all, the rhetoric of the programme provided the political legitimacy for the ambitious goals of the *EuroPsy* projects.

Preparatory work to submit the bid included the creation of a project team[5] of partners (individuals) from different European countries, representing different types of organisations (universities, professional bodies, employers' organisations, other organisations). Each partner was expected to create a national network to be used for consultation and dissemination; there was an expectation that this network should be as broad and diverse as possible and include representatives of universities (e.g. Deans of psychology faculties), national psychology societies/associations, and other relevant stakeholders such as national and European students' associations, employers, training organisations, government bodies and so on.

Participation in the project was by personal invitation, a decision that proved highly effective, since invitations were to individuals on the basis of their competence and experience. Team members were therefore not bound to represent the viewpoint of a particular

[5] The project team for the bid involved 15 partners from the following 12 European countries: Denmark, Finland, France, Germany, Greece, Italy, Netherlands, Norway, Spain, Sweden, Switzerland, UK. EFPA was also involved as a partner through the then EFPA President (see Appendix 2 for names).

Table 2. Aims and objectives of Leonardo 1 project

Leonardo Project 1

April 1999–April 2001

The project aims:

- to develop a framework of knowledge, skills and competencies for training psychologists across Europe which may in future, if deemed appropriate, provide the basis for a future European Diploma for Psychologists. The level of focus is the level at which psychologists are deemed qualified for independent practice as psychologists;
- to produce a detailed comparison of university training curricula and professional patterns of training from individual member states;
- to carry out wide consultation with a range of stakeholders;
- to facilitate mobility of psychologists across member states through the creation of a common framework;
- to develop new models of professional training based on competencies and underpinning knowledge;
- to make more transparent systems for mutual recognition.

The specific objectives of this project are to:

- promote a high uniform standard of professional practice based upon the core knowledge, skills and competencies identified by the curriculum comparison;
- strive towards agreement among national authorities on a common basic framework for a specification of the knowledge, skills and competencies required by psychologists, using a new approach which involves specification in outcome terms;
- develop a system to credit modules gained in different member states as part of a future Diploma qualification;
- enhance the quality of education and training in professional psychology across the member states;
- facilitate free mobility of psychologists within the European internal market.

organisation. Furthermore there was hardly any turnover in project membership, as tends to happen with appointments by associations which are for a limited time period. The commitment of the team members to a common goal was an important asset given some of the challenges of the initiative, and the duration of the project. Although the project involved EFPA as a partner, this was not an EFPA project, a feature which probably proved a benefit at the time, given the complexity and political sensitivities of the task. It is testimony to the strength of the project team that the majority of the early partners are active in implementation of *EuroPsy* today.

Also required by the Leonardo specification was an explicit statement of areas of impact, again useful in the political context in which the project was embedded. The project proposal identified the following five main areas of impact: universities, consumers, the psychological profession and associations, employers and individual psychologists. A concern with all these groups has continued to inform the direction of *EuroPsy* development. The proposal also required identification of beneficiaries, stated in the proposal as practising psychologists, students and graduates, the European public, employers and national professional associations. As it turned out, these requirements which were inspired by demands of the funder proved useful both in the formulation and thinking prior to the project, and also throughout the project, and indeed its implementation as the team negotiated the progress of *EuroPsy*.

Following the successful bid for funding during 1998, work started on EuroPsyT in 1999. As mentioned above, the Leonardo da Vinci funding programme brought significant requirements, which included wide stakeholder involvement (beyond that of universities and professional associations, which could be said to have particular stakes in the project), consultation and dissemination, and the development of a product (preferably innovative and contributing to mobility). These requirements, however, contributed to the momentum of the project, which, given the limited funding available for research activity, was important for the progress of the work within the two year period available. Thus the requirements and time deadlines of the Leonardo grant for interim reporting, financial reports and the final report created the necessary pressures to drive activity.

The process of EuroPsyT involved a number of different activities. Considerable use was made of electronic communication, including setting up and maintenance of a website. The project team met face to face on six occasions, normally for a two day meeting or workshop organised to undertake detailed comparisons, trial frameworks, discuss different patterns of education and training, and undertake the complex task of developing a framework with which the different stakeholders could agree. The project involved a detailed exercise of collection and comparison of documentation on curricula, training requirements and professional requirements at national level. Confirming the findings of earlier work such as that of Newstead (1994), the project team found considerable diversity in patterns of education and professional formation across countries. Consultation both nationally and at European level was a key activity, and each partner undertook extensive consultation exercises in their own country in order to develop a product that could have wide support at European level. Finally, and related to consultation, dissemination at national, European and international level proved an important activity: Presentations were made regularly at national conferences, and each year at all major European and international conferences during the life of the project. This activity has continued to the present time.

After extensive consultation and negotiation to bridge all the diversities across European countries in structure and length of education and professional training of psychologists, the first project ended with the final report submitted in June 2001 and the publication of *EuroPsyT: a framework for education and training for psychologists in Europe* (Lunt et al., 2001). Timing was auspicious and the EuroPsyT was submitted to, and accepted by, the General Assembly of EFPA in July that year. EuroPsyT introduced significant features of a common curriculum framework which included:

- the requirements for a minimum of a 5 year academic programme and a 1-year period of supervised practice,
- a framework based on the Bologna cycles (a 3 year first cycle, a 2 year second cycle plus a year of supervised practice),
- minimum standards of length of education and training and broad composition of the curriculum,
- a framework organised according to perspectives of individuals, groups, systems.

A schema was developed for the first phase of education and training for psychologists (see Appendix 5) and for the second phase (see Appendix 6), and a framework of core standards in terms of ECTS[6] (Appendix 7). It will be noted that the first phase provides a basic and broad education in psychology theories and techniques, and does not lead to any occupational qualification of competence for independent practice. Under the Bologna system, the first phase corresponds to the Bachelor level. In EuroPsyT the second phase describes the university education that prepares (though does not qualify) the student for independent practice as a psychologist, and corresponds under the Bologna system to the Masters level. The third phase for EuroPsyT is the year of supervised practice, which is required by *EuroPsy* prior to entry into independent practice. Although this may be seen as a 3 year plus 2 year plus 1 year structure (3 + 2 + 1), it is acknowledged that other structures of education and training exist (e.g. the integrated 5 or 6 year programme) and are equally valid. EuroPsyT made a commitment to respect diversity provided that the common standards agreed by the project would be met. Already in EuroPsyT the team accepted the usefulness of an analysis of professional competence in terms of outputs and the commitment to further work on the development of a specification for competences at European level.

On completion of EuroPsyT, there was general agreement that further work was needed to develop a useable certification system (a Diploma qualification), and a second bid was therefore prepared for funding from EU, which awarded a second Leonardo grant for a project from 2001 to 2004.

Leonardo Project 2 and the Development of Competences and a Certificate

There was a strong rationale for the second Leonardo project, following the success of EuroPsyT in developing a framework for psychologists training across Europe and given developments external to the project in the wider EU. EuroPsyT provided the framework; what was needed in order for it to achieve practical success was a more detailed specification of the Diploma or Certificate qualification.

Looking again at the challenges for recognition of qualifications across the EU, four options existed, at least in theory. The first was harmonisation of education and training programs, which, as discussed above, has proved to be neither feasible nor desirable. The second option involves reciprocity agreements, usually forged between professions in different countries, jurisdictions or regions (see Hall & Lunt, 2005), such as those already existing for psychologists across Nordic countries. These are immensely complex and require considerable trust and a degree of similarity between systems. The third option was mutual recognition. This requires both trust and respect between countries, and robust and credible mechanisms of implementation. The final option was some form of certification involving an agreed standard and additional testing, and award of a certificate recognised at European level. This was the option aimed at in the second Leonardo project. However, considerable discussion was required as to the nature of the certification.

[6] European Credit Transfer and Accumulation System (ECTS) is a standard unit used for comparing the study hours of students across the EU. One academic year corresponds to 60 ECTS (equivalent to 1500–1800 hr of study). It has been used to enable recognition of periods of study in different countries.

Table 3. Aims and objectives of Leonardo 2 project

Leonardo Project 2

November 2001–November 2004

The projects aims:

- to elaborate the EuroPsyT framework, consult on it, test it, draft the terms of reference for a European Diploma (including the institutional aspects) and prepare a plan to implement it.

The specific objectives of the project are to:

- prepare the ground for a European Awarding Body with contacts to appropriate existing assessment and awarding organisations in each of the partner countries;
- sustain, enhance and extend the network of partners so as to ensure that the network continues after the end of the project;
- extend the influence of the network to reach other countries, including pre-accession states;
- test a set of standards of competence for a high level profession as a pilot, and show that it is a practical basis for defining professional competence; this will have wide implications for transnational mobility, transparency of qualifications, the design of professional qualifications, etc. across all professions and sectors, well beyond psychology;
- disseminate the results of the project to other professions in all the partner countries, and more widely in Europe, to encourage them to move towards similarly specified Europe-wide qualifications;
- hold an international conference to share the findings and products of the project.

Certification could take the form of a full syllabus, examination and qualification arranged at European level; or the form of a standard or benchmark that enabled comparison of existing qualifications; or it could provide accreditation or certification of individual countries' qualifications. For various reasons, it was agreed that the option of a standard or a benchmark at European level was most appropriate. The aims and objectives for the second project are presented in Table 3.

The proposal listed a number of outcomes. These included taking over the EuroPsyT website and keeping it up-to-date, strengthening the partnership by holding 9 workshop meetings of the international partners over the 3 years with a full agenda, working papers and notes, producing a detailed model of the European Diploma (with specification of knowledge, skills and competences, assessment guidance, institutional framework), consulting on this model, and a dissemination and implementation plan.

The project team for Leonardo 2 built substantially on that for the first project.[7] Of the 15 individuals taking part in the first project, 9 continued into the second project. The process of Leonardo 2 involved similar activities to those of Leonardo 1: maintenance of the website, workshops and 13 face to face meetings plus a number of subgroup meetings for particular purposes; development of working documents and wide consultation on the Diploma; dissemination through articles and conference presentations at national, European and international level. Early on in the project (already in January 2002) a subgroup had produced a draft of a Diploma with draft regulations, and guiding principles to inform

[7] The team submitted for the bid involved 15 partners from 11 countries: Denmark, Finland, France, Germany, Greece, Italy, Netherlands, Norway, Spain, Sweden, UK. A partner from Hungary joined subsequently. EFPA was involved as a partner (see Appendix 3 for list of names).

the work. These formed the basis for the final product and were the subject of intense and at times controversial debate, negotiation and compromise.

There were a number of issues that reflected the very different traditions pertaining in European countries at the time and which elicited debate and required negotiated compromise. One major issue at the time concerned the use of competences, a development that was new to many countries. Another was the creation of a balance between an input and an output approach. However, the most controversial issue was the question of contexts of practice: Should psychologists on initial qualification be considered qualified in all (any) contexts, or should they be limited to one professional context for which they have been prepared by specialisation in education and training? This again reflected fundamental differences in education and training of psychologists in different countries. A further issue of considerable debate focussed on the concept of "revalidation." Should a psychologist be qualified for life or should there be a formal requirement for Continuing Professional Development (CPD) and revalidation? These issues were never taken to the vote, though they were hotly debated and invariably compromise was finally reached.

In the event the project required an extension of time and lasted three and a half years (November 2001 to April 2005). Key to the *EuroPsy* were a number of guiding principles (see Table 4) which set the frame for the whole endeavour and proved instrumental in helping to move the project forward. They, too, were subject to debate and negotiation, but the whole project team was committed to the central goals of high quality and facilitating mobility.

Specification of professional competences provided an innovative and acceptable way forward for setting the standard. This also provided an important basis for structuring the period of supervised practice, and a clear rationale for its requirement.

The product *EuroPsy the European Diploma in Psychology* (Lunt et al., 2005) accompanied the final report to the Leonardo da Vinci Programme, and was launched and accepted by EFPA at its General Assembly in Granada in 2005 at which point the project was formally handed over to EFPA to take forward. The product consisted of a set of Regulations (EFPA, 2013a, see Appendix 4) and a definition of the Register of *EuroPsy* psychologists, and relevant procedures for issuing certificates. It also included a set of appendices outlining (a) the EuroPsyT framework of minimal standards, (b) competences and competence profiling, (c) an exemplar of the *EuroPsy* certificate and application form, (d) supervised practice and (e) continuing professional development. These have been used to guide the implementation of *EuroPsy* since 2005, and the Regulations provide the ultimate authority concerning the *EuroPsy*.

Despite the existence of the product (at the time called European Diploma),[8] and the widespread consultation exercises undertaken throughout the projects, the Diploma existed in 2005 as a paper product only. Time limitations had not permitted field-testing during the Leonardo projects, and it would have been irresponsible to launch such a product with little notion of how it might work in practice or the kinds of challenges and difficulties that might emerge during implementation. Following acceptance of *EuroPsy* by EFPA in

[8] The name Diploma was changed to Certificate during the implementation period, given the ambiguity implied by the term "diploma" and its usage both at European level and by some countries.

Table 4. Principles underpinning *EuroPsy*

Guiding principles

The principles aim to:

1. promote the availability of adequate psychological services across Europe. Every citizen and any institution should be able to obtain psychological services from a competent and qualified professional and the system should help to achieve this objective;
2. protect consumers and citizens in Europe through the assurance of quality and protect the public against unqualified providers of services;
3. contribute to mechanisms to promote the mobility of psychologists by enabling them to practise anywhere in Europe, provided that they have the proper qualifications;
4. ensure that the *EuroPsy* is awarded on the basis of: (a) demonstrated completion of an academic curriculum in psychology of sufficient scope, (b) demonstrated competence in the performance of professional roles during supervised practice, (c) endorsement of European (as well as national) ethical standards for psychologists;
5. ensure that the *EuroPsy* system is fair and avoids favouring or disfavouring psychologists on the basis of national or other differences in educational or professional background, and that it recognises high service quality as a prevailing principle. This implies that the *EuroPsy* will not pose specific requirements concerning the structure or format of the academic education, or the nature and organisation of the internship for professional practice;
6. guarantee the qualification for psychological practice at an entry level to the profession as well as beyond;
7. endorse a commitment to the active maintenance of competence. For this reason the *EuroPsy* is awarded for a limited time period, and shall be renewed again for a limited period of time, on the basis of evidence of continuing professional practice and professional development;
8. respect national regulations for psychologists which are already in place.

2005, there was agreement to testing out the working of *EuroPsy* in six countries through a pilot or so-called "experimental garden" project as a means to explore implementation and assess feasibility issues. Six countries were chosen to achieve a range of national contexts which might throw up different challenges, and the Leonardo project group became the *EuroPsy* Steering Group set up to trial the working of a European Awarding Committee (EAC) and to oversee the pilot.

EuroPsy Pilot Projects

The six countries (Finland, Germany, Hungary, Italy, Spain and the UK) were chosen from among the countries which had participated in the Leonardo projects. The selection aimed to achieve maximum diversity in system, viz: Finland (a Nordic country), Spain and Italy (large and southern countries), Hungary (a country from former Eastern Europe), Germany (a large country with strong structures), UK (a country with a long history of developing professional qualifications, and using competences). At this point, there was no longer EU funding and EFPA itself took responsibility for encouraging the experimental project, and negotiating that activities be supported by EFPA Member Associations.

In practical terms, the aim was for the pilot group of six countries to stimulate the creation of a provisional National Awarding Committee (NAC) in the country and to trial the implementation of *EuroPsy* in that country. The Steering Group would serve as a simulation of a future EAC, and have a role in advising, taking lessons from the experience and identifying aspects of the system that might need further attention. A large number of operational procedures required development and testing. The *EuroPsy* report needed to be translated, and guidelines, forms and protocols developed in each country. Each of the six pilot countries formed a NAC, which began the work of marketing, evaluating individual applications, keeping records and developing a Register system. Arrangements for evaluation of supervised practice were set up in each of the pilot countries, with forms and protocols for recording professional experience. The competence framework proved useful both as a structure for supervised practice, and as a framework for evaluating the competence of already qualified psychologists through transitional or grand-parenting arrangements. The transitional EAC (the Steering Group) and the pilot group met regularly over the experimental period, while at national level the EFPA Member Association and the NAC undertook the task of a simulation of the whole *EuroPsy* process. Again, the processes took much longer than might have been anticipated, revealing very useful lessons in each country. The pilot group worked purposefully over a two and a half year period between June 2006 and March 2009 to try out the *EuroPsy* system, with each country identifying different challenges, and different ways of implementation.

The pilot project brought up many of the issues which had proved challenging during the course of the development of *EuroPsy*, but the process of addressing these now at a more operational and practical level allowed for new insights and fresh compromises. Some of the main challenges are identified here:

- *Supervised practice*. Supervised practice turned out to pose a major challenge, though also an important opportunity for enhancing the quality of psychologists' standards of work through *EuroPsy*. Given the diversity of practice (some countries have well-developed systems of supervised practice requirements, while other countries have no such requirements), developing a definition of supervised practice, a definition of supervisors, evaluation of supervised practice (or equivalent for grand-parenting, or transitional arrangements to recognise experienced psychologists) proved to be significant challenges. One country, Spain, used this challenge as an opportunity to develop the education and training for psychologists, and introduced competence evaluation as part of supervised practice for new cohorts of psychologists in training (see Chapter 6 and Lunt & Peiró, 2012).
- *Competences*. Again, the challenge reflected the diversity of practice and tradition. While some countries (e.g. UK, and see Bartram, 1996) had already introduced competences into the requirements and evaluation of the education and training for psychologists, for a number of countries this proved to be an entirely new approach. Devising formats for recording competence acquisition and evaluation was a challenge (see also Chapters 5 and 6). Overall the challenge that emerged was how to promote the dissemination of the competence model as a shared view of the work and the roles a psychologist has to perform. It was important that both the newly qualified applicants for the certificate and their supervisors should develop a familiarity with the competences model as a way of understanding the work done and the roles of psychologists. This shared view of

the competence model is a challenge that *EuroPsy* has to achieve progressively. It is one that is supported by the Bologna process and moves at a wider European level requiring universities to specify learning outcomes for different levels of degree (see also Chapter 4).

- *Fields or contexts of practice.* As mentioned earlier, this was an issue that had challenged *EuroPsy* throughout the two earlier projects, again reflecting the very different traditions of education and training across European countries. While a compromise decision had been reached in the Regulations, the use of a field labelled "Other" which might cover contexts that applied in one country and not in others was controversial, and remains so to this day.
- *Specialisation.* A number of countries had well-developed systems of psychologists' specialisation. During the development of the Diploma, general proposals had included the development of Advanced Diplomas (Certificates), to reflect these developments, and to build on work that had already been undertaken in the field of psychotherapy (PT) by a Standing Committee of EFPA. The original proposal was for Advanced Diplomas which would build on the Basic *EuroPsy* Diploma. In the implementation phase the idea of Advanced Diplomas was developed through the creation of Specialist Certificates, intended to build on the basic *EuroPsy* Certificate, and reflect expertise in particular specialist fields. The development of Specialist Certificates was not trialled in the Pilot period, though this has been taken up by EFPA as a central strategic objective in its recent activity plan, and is of key importance to the development of *EuroPsy*.
- *"Grand-parenting" and transitional arrangements.* The use of a period of grand-parenting (or transitional arrangements) proved unfamiliar to some. Still, it emerged as an important practical mechanism for evaluating equivalence during the pilot period, although, in the event, with mixed usefulness. Some of the experimental garden countries used transitional arrangements or grand-parenting to give automatic recognition for those already qualified as psychologists, thus trialling registration though not evaluation of individual qualifications. Others took the opportunity to develop a system to record the professional experience of experienced psychologists using the competence framework to evaluate qualified psychologists as a means to develop systems for recording work experience. However, it was important that each country develop procedures both to evaluate applicants made on the basis of transitional arrangements (i.e. those already qualified) and to evaluate newly qualified and qualifying psychologists, who would be evaluated against the *EuroPsy* framework.
- *Continuing professional development.* As mentioned, this proved to be another requirement unfamiliar to a number of countries, and the appendix in the Regulations was found to be insufficient for the development of a robust recording system.
- *Revalidation.* Linked with continuing professional development, the notion of revalidation is only recently being introduced into professional discourse, and remains unfamiliar to some countries. Not surprisingly, it also proved to be controversial.

- *Psychology curriculum. EuroPsy* provides a very general framework for the psychology curriculum. National Awarding Committees have been asked to provide a list of the universities with psychology curricula which meet the *EuroPsy* specification. This list might serve the purpose of a form of accreditation or at least recognition in relation to *EuroPsy*, such that graduates from these programmes are automatically recognised as meeting the educational requirements. It was noted that the different European countries continue to have very different arrangements for accreditation of university programmes, despite the efforts of organisations such as ENQA (see Chapter 4).

The immediate conclusion from the pilot project was that despite numerous practical difficulties the *EuroPsy* system (the product, the structure and the process) was feasible and could be implemented in the six countries, and that implementation could be adapted to fit different contexts and meet different local circumstances.

Implementation and Further Development

Following completion of the pilot project early in 2009, EFPA organised its first Implementation Workshop in Brussels in January 2009, and since that time has made significant and successful efforts in the implementation phase. One important part of the *EuroPsy* system which was not trialled during the pilot project was the Register and the infrastructure and systems required in the EFPA Head Office in Brussels for the registration of holders of the *EuroPsy* Certificate. This was developed as part of the EFPA implementation process during the course of 2009 and enabled the system to be launched in January 2010. Annual *EuroPsy* Info Days provided a forum to support EFPA Member Associations in implementing *EuroPsy* locally, and in creating a NAC and systems needed for local qualifications scrutiny, and, crucially the development of promotional activities in order to encourage take-up. At the time of writing 20 EFPA Member Associations have set up NACs and been approved to issue *EuroPsy* Certificates.

Specialist certificates for recognition of advanced competence in certain areas (see Chapter 3) were not included in the initial pilot period. However a Specialist Certificate in Psychotherapy (PT) was established after a parallel field test conducted by the EFPA Standing Committee for Psychotherapy. For the Specialist Certificate in Work and Organisational Psychology (W&O) a different procedure was followed. A detailed proposal for such a certificate, including a system of competence development and assessment that extended the ideas of *EuroPsy*, had been developed by a Working Group of the European Association of Work and Organisational Psychology (EAWOP) in 2006–2007. The fact that some members of the EAWOP Working Group had also been involved in the Leonardo projects, and early experiences with the development of the ENOP Model had been used in developing the EuroPsyT framework, appeared conducive to a high degree of compatibility between the Specialist Certificate in Work and Organisational Psychology and *EuroPsy* as well as to good collaboration with EFPA during the pilot test. An updated version of the proposal was presented to EFPA in 2009. Upon the request of EFPA, EAWOP conducted a pilot test of the specialist certificate in five countries (Finland, Italy,

Norway, Spain and the UK) in 2012–2013. After the report of the pilot was completed, the Specialist Certificate in WOP was established by the EFPA General Assembly in 2013. As a side-product a model was also established for future specialist certificates.

Conclusions

In this chapter we have described the process of developing *EuroPsy* (the *why* and the *how*) up to its initial implementation, and located this in the broader context of some key developments in Europe which were taking place over the same time period. One reason for emphasising the aspect of process has been to provide a historical account of how *EuroPsy* came about, and the time required for its successful completion. A second reason has been to provide colleagues, including those outside Europe, with a document that they may wish to consult when launching similar projects. The developments in the European context provided a fertile ground for the growth of *EuroPsy*, not only politically but also substantively as they had influence on higher education programmes across European countries. The European Union played an instrumental role, both in funding the early projects, and in the use of its own drivers and resources to support particular initiatives. Finally EFPA took over the *EuroPsy* product and supported the next phase of implementation, and the launch of *EuroPsy* in 2010 as well as the introduction of specialist certificates.

3 What Is *EuroPsy*?

In the previous chapter we addressed the questions of why and how *EuroPsy* was created. In this chapter we look at the implementation of *EuroPsy* and consider the question what it is and what it implies. It can best be described as a certification system that has been established with the purpose of defining, regulating, and developing the profession in the interest of the clients of psychologists and the profession itself. *EuroPsy* helps to make clear what professional psychology is, and what should be expected from qualified psychologists in terms of expertise, competence, professional conduct and maintenance of expertise. We begin with a description of the nature and scope of *EuroPsy* in terms of its legal status, geographic reach and target groups. Next, we describe the logic and content of *EuroPsy,* in terms of the guiding principles and the requirements of the certificates. After describing the organisational and procedural aspects of the *EuroPsy* certification, we discuss how *EuroPsy* matters for students, psychologists, clients, employers and other professionals. We also expand on the role of *EuroPsy* in a longer-term and global perspective.

Nature and Scope of *EuroPsy*

A distinguishing feature of *EuroPsy* is that it is not enshrined in national or European law, but derives its legitimacy and strength from the consensus of 36 national associations of psychologists, organised in EFPA, the European Federation of Psychologists Associations. These national associations represent more than 300,000 psychologists serving a population of more than 740 million people. Over 90% of these psychologists live in the 28 EU countries, and serve a population of over 500 million people. The list of countries is included in Appendix 1. The formal basis of *EuroPsy* is constituted by the Regulations of *EuroPsy*, which are established by the General Assembly of EFPA and require at least 2/3 of the votes for change and ratification. These Regulations were first established in 2009 and were updated in 2011 and 2013 (see for the latest version: http://www.europsy-efpa.eu/regulations, and Appendix 4). The logo and name of *EuroPsy* are legally protected: *EuroPsy* is a registered trademark in all European countries.

It should be clearly stated that although it provides European psychologists with a distinct qualification mark, *EuroPsy* does not provide a license to practise in any country. It does not replace or alter any existing national licensing or certifications system. However, the fact that it has been developed by a team of experienced leaders in psychology across European countries, following wide consultation, and that it is supported by psychologists' organisations from all over Europe, gives *EuroPsy* the potential to fill a noticeable gap in legislation at European level. This gap arises from the fact that the psychologists' profession is not one of the sectoral professions in the European Directive on the Recognition of Professional Qualifications (Directive 2005 EC/36) (see Chapter 2). As has been pointed out in consultations with the European Commission and the European Council, as an agreed European framework, *EuroPsy* will provide a strong base for defining a Common Training Framework for psychologists in the context of the envisaged modernisation of the directive. In this way, *EuroPsy* may promote mobility of psychologists and exert an influence on national legislation in the EU member states. As part of its strategic plan, EFPA is currently developing a model of a Psychologists Law that can help national governments to bring national legislation into line with *EuroPsy*.

It is important to note that *EuroPsy* certification is intended for European psychologists, that is, those who have received their academic education and professional training in any of the 36 European countries represented, and that an application for certification can only be made after the national EFPA Member Association in the country of education and/or practice has become a participant in *EuroPsy* and has a recognised National Awarding Committee. By 2014 the number of participating countries has grown to 20 with several other countries making preparations for participation (see Appendix 1). It may take some more years before the remaining countries will all be involved. For the near future *EuroPsy* will not be available for psychologists from these countries.

EuroPsy is not only intended to apply in most of Europe but also to cover the psychological profession in all its forms and levels of differentiation or specialisation. Thus, it pertains to psychologists in schools, work organisations, health care, transportation, police and the military, courts and prisons, public administration, etc. Although there are differences in content of psychologists' education and training – between countries and areas of practice – the requirements posed by *EuroPsy* are comparable for all areas of practice. However, for specialised (in contrast to basic) practice higher standards apply and are reflected through the development of Specialised Certificates.

The focus on the psychological profession, that is, on the way in which psychologists render services that aim to better understand and solve human problems by utilising scientific knowledge and methods, has an important limitation. This is that *EuroPsy* does not address the work of those whose professional role is to teach psychology or conduct psychological research, even though by tradition they are also called psychologists. Although they include highly qualified people with advanced academic titles and unique insights into what psychology is, they are – from an occupational perspective – not practising psychologists, but teachers and researchers. Becoming a qualified teacher, whether at a university or another institution, requires a different set of competences than those that are required to become a qualified practising psychologist. Psychology teachers show much greater similarity with teachers of, for example, sociology, pedagogy, medicine or statistics in this respect. The same holds for researchers in psychology, who need comparable competences as researchers from other social and biological sciences. Thus, although psychologists, psychology teachers and psychology researchers have for long had overlapping careers, and although the psychologist's role may involve elements of teaching and research, the work of psychology teachers and researchers is not covered by *EuroPsy*.

Whether separate European certification for psychology teachers and researchers is needed, is a question to be addressed in the future.

The Logic and Content of *EuroPsy*

EuroPsy is based on the idea that a person must meet a series of minimum standards in order to be considered qualified to practise as a psychologist. These are standards regarding education and training, professional ethics and continuing professional development (CPD); having a Bachelor or Masters degree in psychology is not sufficient to guarantee adequate practice. The *EuroPsy* standards serve as a benchmark for evaluating the qualifications of psychologists. Individuals who have demonstrated that they meet the standards are eligible to receive a *EuroPsy* Certificate, which is valid for a certain number of years. Since professional qualifications should be maintained by continuing practice and professional development, the certificate must be renewed (or revalidated) after a number of years. There are two types of standards, namely for entry into the profession and for practice as a specialist. Accordingly, there are two types of certificate: a *EuroPsy* Basic Certificate and a *EuroPsy* Specialist Certificate. The requirements for obtaining these two types of certificates, and for renewing them, are described below.

To inform the public *EuroPsy* uses a Register with the names and contact details of all holders of *EuroPsy* Certificates. The Register can be consulted through the Internet and allows clients, employers and authorities to quickly identify who is deemed to be a qualified and trustworthy psychologist. By doing this it enhances transparency in the market of psychological services, and promotes the availability of adequate psychological services across Europe. Through its websites in different countries and languages, *EuroPsy* also provides information for clients who might wish to make a complaint against a psychologist in the case of suspected misconduct. In this way it leads to a better protection of consumers and citizens in Europe. Altogether, *EuroPsy* is a vehicle for quality assurance and protection of the public against unqualified providers of services.

Requirements for the *EuroPsy* Basic Certificate

Crucial for understanding *EuroPsy* is the distinction between education as an input to professional learning and competence as an outcome of it. In order to practise independently as a psychologist evidence of both input and output is needed. Thus, *EuroPsy* combines an input model and an output model (Bartram & Roe, 2005). The input model describes the minimum educational requirements in terms of curriculum content. The output model describes the competences that must have been acquired during initial – that is, dependent and supervised – practice. In this section we present the overall requirements and the models on which they are based. Further details are presented in Chapters 4 and 5.

Educational Requirements

Since psychology is a science-based profession, *EuroPsy* requires psychologists to be educated at a university or similar academic institution. The length of the education should be

Table 5. Minimum requirements (in ECTS) for education for independent professional practice in psychology

Phase	Component	Individual	Group	Society	Total
1st Phase: (Bachelor or equivalent)	Orientation	The curriculum should include orientation to psychology, its sub-disciplines and areas of professional activity			Min 125
	Theoretical courses and practical exercises	Min 60	Min 20	Min 20	
	Academic skills	Academic skills training should be included			
	Methodology		Min 30		Min 45
	Nonpsychology theory		Min 15		
					Total 180
2nd Phase: (Masters or equivalent)	Theoretical courses, seminars, assignments, etc.				Min 60
	Internship/stage/Placement		Min 15–30		Min 30
	Research project/thesis		Min 15–30		
					Total 120
3rd Phase	Supervised practice		Min 60		Total 60
					Total 360

at least 5 years, which – under the prevailing "Bologna system" (see Chapter 4) – implies a Bachelor and a Masters Degree in psychology. *EuroPsy* uses a curriculum framework and minimum standards to evaluate the content of a psychologist's education. It is important to note that *EuroPsy* does not prescribe any particular curriculum but respects existing differences in academic programs across countries and institutions, as long as the common requirements are met. It acknowledges that such differences reflect the cultural and philosophical diversity of Europe as well as the unique way in which psychological research and teaching have developed in different countries. The curriculum framework makes a number of essential distinctions – between types of content and educational objectives – which allow for analysis of the curricula through which psychologists are (or have been) educated. The minimum standards allow for evaluation as to whether these curricula have a comprehensive composition in terms of covering the various content categories. The standards are expressed in European Credit and Accumulation Transfer System (ECTS) units, which are widely used across Europe (see footnote Chapter 2, p. 38). One ECTS unit is equivalent to 25–30 hours of teaching/study time; there are 60 ECTS in an academic year. The ECTS system has been developed in order to compare the different higher education systems pertaining in European countries and to provide a standard measure of study load (1 year = 60 ECTS units). The framework and requirements are summarised in Table 5; more detail is given in Chapter 4. It should be noted that in terms of ECTS units the educational requirements are the same for all psychologists and that there is no differentiation between fields of psychology.

Supervised Practice

EuroPsy also requires psychologists to have at least 1 year of supervised practice, before they are able to start to practise independently. This is needed to develop the work role and to integrate what has been learned during academic education into the competences that are required to render services to clients in an effective, science-based and ethically acceptable way. Supervised practice typically occurs after completion of the university education, although there are also countries where it is partially (or completely) integrated into the curriculum. Either way, the period of supervised practice should have a length of 12 months (or be equivalent to 60 ECTS).

EuroPsy does not merely assess the length of the period of supervised practice, but evaluates its outcomes in terms of the competences that the psychologist has acquired. For this purpose it uses a competence model, which serves as the output model referred to above. The competence model comprises 20 professional competences, grouped in six categories, that are specific for the work role of psychologists, and nine enabling competences that relate to professional practice in general. These competences are listed in Table 6.

As is the case with academic education, *EuroPsy* acknowledges that the actual supervision process and the profile of competences acquired by psychologists vary greatly. To a large degree such variation reflects the professional settings in which psychologists operate. For instance, a school psychologist counselling parents, a work and organisational psychologist advising the management of a business firm, and a clinical psychologist providing psychotherapy to individuals with mental illness do, in fact, perform different roles and need different competences. Their work may also be affected by how services tend to be provided in the country. Nonetheless, there are certain similarities in how psychologists do and should operate. *EuroPsy* therefore describes the competences in generic terms, but requires that they be evaluated with respect to a particular area of practice, such as clinical/health, education (or development), work and organisation. *EuroPsy* currently distinguishes specifically these three areas of practice and uses a fourth broad category to group other areas of practice. However, the list of recognised areas of practice is likely to grow over time. *EuroPsy* relies on the supervisor to assess the specific competences with reference to the requirements in the area of practice. Chapter 5 provides more information on the competences and the way in which they are assessed.

Since supervision is a critical process in becoming a psychologist, *EuroPsy* pays due attention to the requirements that supervisors should meet and to the way in which the process should be organised and documented. This is a domain in which countries and areas of practice show considerable differences, and where important developments are taking place. More information about supervision and its various aspects are given in Chapter 6.

Professional Ethics

A cornerstone of the psychological profession, worldwide, is the commitment to professional ethics. *EuroPsy* therefore requires every psychologist to make a formal commitment

Table 6. Primary competences of psychologists

Primary competences	Description
A. Goal specification	Interacting with the client for the purpose of defining the goals of the intervention or service that will be provided
1. Needs analysis	Gathering information about the client's needs by means of appropriate methods, clarifying and analysing the needs to a point where meaningful further action can be taken.
2. Goal setting	Proposing and negotiating goals with the client, establishing acceptable and feasible goals, and specifying criteria for evaluating goal fulfilment at a later time.
B. Assessment	Establishing relevant characteristics of individuals, groups, organisations and situations by means of appropriate methods.
3. Individual assessment	Carrying out assessment by means of interviewing, testing and observation of individuals in a setting relevant for the service demanded.
4. Group assessment	Carrying out assessment by means of interviewing, testing and observation of groups in a setting relevant for the service demanded.
5. Organisational assessment	Carrying out assessment by means of interviews, surveys and other methods and techniques which are appropriate for studying organisations in a setting that is relevant for the service demanded.
6. Situational assessment	Carrying out assessment by means of interviews, surveys and other methods and techniques which are appropriate for studying situations in a setting that is relevant for the service demanded.
C. Development	Developing interventions, services, or products on the basis of psychological theory and methods for use by the clients or psychologists.
7. Service or product definition and requirements analysis	Defining the purpose of the service or product, identifying relevant stakeholders, analysing requirements and constraints, and drawing up specifications for the product or service, taking into consideration the setting in which the service or product is to be used.
8. Service or product design	Designing or adapting services or products in accordance with the requirements and constraints, taking into consideration the setting in which the service or product is to be used.
9. Service or product testing	Testing the service or product and assessing its feasibility, reliability, validity and other characteristics, taking into consideration the setting in which the service or product is to be used.
10. Service or product evaluation	Evaluating the service or product with respect to utility, client satisfaction, user friendliness, costs and other aspects which are relevant in the setting in which the service or product is to be used.
D. Intervention	Identifying, preparing and carrying out interventions which are appropriate for reaching the set goals, using the results of assessment and development activities.

(continued on next page)

Table 6. (continued)

Primary competences	Description
11. Intervention planning	Developing an intervention plan that is appropriate for reaching the set goals in a setting relevant for the service demanded.
12. Direct person-oriented intervention	Applying intervention methods that directly affect one or more individuals in accordance with the intervention plan, in a setting relevant for the service demanded.
13. Direct situation-oriented intervention	Applying intervention methods that directly affect selected aspects of the situation in accordance with the intervention plan, in a setting relevant for the service demanded.
14. Indirect intervention	Applying intervention methods that enable individuals, groups or organisations to learn and take decisions in their own interest, in a setting relevant for the service demanded.
15. Service or product implementation	Introducing services or products and promoting their proper use by clients or other psychologists.
E. Evaluation	Establishing the adequacy of interventions in terms of adherence to the intervention plan and the achievement of set goals.
16. Evaluation planning	Designing a plan for the evaluation of an intervention, including criteria derived from the intervention plan and the set goals, in a setting relevant for the service demanded.
17. Evaluation measurement	Selecting and applying measurement techniques that are appropriate for effecting the evaluation plan, in a setting relevant for the service demanded.
18. Evaluation analysis	Conducting analyses in accordance with the evaluation plan, and drawing conclusions on the effectiveness of interventions in a setting relevant for the service demanded.
F. Communication	Providing information to clients in a way that is adequate to fulfil the clients' needs and expectations.
19. Giving feedback	Providing feedback to clients, using appropriate oral and/or audio-visual means, in a setting relevant for the service demanded.
20. Report writing	Writing reports as to inform clients about the results of assessment, service or product development, interventions, and/or evaluations, in a setting relevant for the service demanded.

to conduct professional activities in accordance with the code of ethics of the national association of psychology in the country of practice. This implies that the psychologist subjects herself[9] to the ethical regime of the national association, which makes it possible for clients or members of the public to make a complaint, for this to be investigated and for sanctions to be applied if and when appropriate. *EuroPsy* also asks the psychologist to submit a pledge, stating that she subscribes to the principles of professional conduct set

[9] Throughout the book, "she" is used to refer to the psychologist, "he" to the psychologist in training or student, and "they" as a generic term.

Table 7. Overview of requirements for the *EuroPsy* certificate

Requirements
> 6 years of professional education and training (in total)
> 5 years academic education (matching the requirements)
> 1 year supervised practice (with competence development and competence ratings)
Declaration on ethical behaviour
Obligation of CPD

out in the Meta-Code of Professional Ethics of EFPA (EFPA, 2005). These principles are: respect for a person's rights and dignity, competence, responsibility and integrity. The Meta-Code is superordinate to the ethical codes of EFPA's national Member Associations, and until now the single common standard for professional ethics in Europe. EFPA has recently developed a Model-Code of Ethics, based on the same principles, which is meant to become the new standard for professional ethics. More information on professional ethics and the *EuroPsy* requirements are given in Chapter 8.

Continuing Professional Development

One of the guiding principles of *EuroPsy* is that psychologists should be committed to actively maintain their competence through their professional practice and CPD. There is no requirement for evidence of CPD when psychologists apply for *EuroPsy* for the first time, except for experienced psychologists wishing to enter on the basis of transitional arrangements. However, as is the case with other academic professionals, psychologists are expected to stay abreast of new research, to attend conferences, to take part in seminars and workshops, to follow additional training, etc. *EuroPsy* recommends a minimum number of hours per year, and requires evidence when applying for revalidation of their *EuroPsy* certificate. Keeping a logbook of pertinent activities and evidence of participation are also required (see Chapter 7).

Overview

Table 7 (above) presents an overview of the requirements for the *EuroPsy* Basic Certificate, which constitute minimum requirements for independent practice as a psychologist.

Requirements for the *EuroPsy* Specialist Certificate

EuroPsy Specialist Certificates can only be obtained by holders of a *EuroPsy* Basic Certificate who meet a number of additional requirements. At the time of writing (2013) there are two specialist certificates, namely for Psychotherapy and Work and Organisational Psychology. More specialist certificates are likely to be developed in the future. The additional requirements vary somewhat with the specialty but the "Standard Requirements

Framework for Specialist Certificates" which was developed by EFPA in 2010 and confirmed in 2013 lists the following general requirements:

- Postgraduate study of at least 400 hr (16 ECTS).
- Post qualification experience and training of at least 3 years.
- Supervision during this time of at least 150 hours (i.e. on average 50 hours a year).
- Supervised practice of at least 500 hours.
- Submission of a logbook to evidence the specialism (optional).

The specific requirements for the specialist certificates in psychotherapy and work and organisational psychology can be found in the *EuroPsy* Regulations (http://www.europsy-efpa.eu/regulations). An additional requirement for the *EuroPsy* Specialist Certificate in Psychotherapy is at least 100 hours of personal development (personal therapy). The *EuroPsy* Specialist Certificate in Work and Organisational Psychology requires more postgraduate study, namely at least 2,400 hours (90 ECTS) of which 1,600 hours (60 ECTS) should be devoted to courses and 800 hours (30 ECTS) to applied research or assessment or intervention. Given the variation in education and training across Europe, there are countries with early differentiation or specialisation (e.g. as part of the Masters degree), where a maximum of 30 ECTS acquired in the basic curriculum may be waived, leaving minimally 60 ECTS for the postgraduate study. The requirement for supervised practice (called "coached practice") is 1,200 hours, that is, 400 hours per year. This certificate also requires evidence of the competences, following the *EuroPsy* competence model.

Revalidation Requirements

According to the current Regulations (EFPA, 2013a) all *EuroPsy* certificates expire after 7 years, unless they are revalidated. The logic behind this rule is that people's expertise and competence decay unless they are actively maintained. *EuroPsy* poses three requirements for revalidation, namely:

1. Maintenance of professional competence by means of practice as a psychologist for a certain number of hours (400 hr per year averaged over a period of not less than 4 years, during the past 7 years).
2. Continuing Professional Development: *EuroPsy* recommends a minimum of 80 hr per year, and requires that psychologists show explicit evidence of 40 hr per year (during the past 7 years) of recognised professional development activities.
3. A renewed pledge regarding ethical conduct, referring to the code of ethics of the national association of psychology in the country of practice and the Meta-Code of EFPA.

For psychologists with a *EuroPsy* Basic Certificate, these requirements apply to practice as a psychologist in their recognised area of practice. For psychologists with a *EuroPsy* Specialist Certificate (who are also required to hold a *EuroPsy* Basic Certificate) the requirements apply, in principle, to their specialised practice.

Organisational and Procedural Aspects of Certification

European and National Level

EuroPsy as a certification system has been created and is maintained by EFPA and its national Member Associations. As already mentioned, the formal basis for *EuroPsy* is provided by the EFPA Regulations on *EuroPsy* (EFPA, 2013a), which are established by the General Assembly of EFPA. The fact that a 2/3 majority is needed to change the Regulations (as is the case with the EFPA Statutes) indicates the importance that is attached to *EuroPsy*. The responsibility for *EuroPsy* Certification has been assigned to a European Awarding Committee (EAC), which is composed of psychologists from different countries who represent the main areas of psychology and work as practitioners and/or at universities. This body delegates the actual handling of applications and the awarding of *EuroPsy* Basic Certificate to National Awarding Committees (NACs). These NACs are appointed and administratively supported by the national Member Associations participating in *EuroPsy*. There is a similar arrangement for each Specialist Certificate: a Specialist European Awarding Committee (S-EAC) and Specialist National Awarding Committees (S-NACs) at the national level. The specialist committees are connected to those for the basic certificate, through a linking member. It is important to stress that the highest authority regarding the awarding of *EuroPsy* certificates rests with the EAC. This body has the power to withdraw the authority for awarding *EuroPsy* from a NAC if it does not act in agreement with the *EuroPsy* Regulations.

In carrying out its tasks, the EAC collaborates with the Executive Council of EFPA, which has the power to initiate changes in the *EuroPsy* Regulations by making proposals to the EFPA General Assembly. For consultation on strategic matters, a small informal group consisting of the President of EFPA, the Chair of the EAC and an EC member of EFPA, called the *EuroPsy* Coordination Group, has been established. The preponderance of activities related to the processing of applications and issuing of *EuroPsy* certificates occurs within operational triangles involving NACs, Contact Persons at the Member Associations and the EFPA Head of Office. In cases of violation of a national code of ethics, the Member Association's Ethical Committee will be involved. An overview of the *EuroPsy* organisation structure is provided in Figure 1.

Apart from the various awarding committees, whose tasks are spelled out in the *EuroPsy* Regulations, the EFPA Head Office and the national Member Associations also play important roles. They maintain the information and communication infrastructure for *EuroPsy*, including *EuroPsy* related websites in different languages and the *EuroPsy* Register with the names and some further information on all *EuroPsy* Certificate holders. They provide information and answer questions regarding *EuroPsy*, manage the flow of documents, meetings and finances, and issue *EuroPsy* Certificates.

Application Process

A psychologist who wishes to obtain a *EuroPsy* certificate starts the application process by completing an application form that can be downloaded from the national *EuroPsy* website in the country of (actual or intended) practice. The form requires information on the applicant's university education and supervised practice, specifying the professional

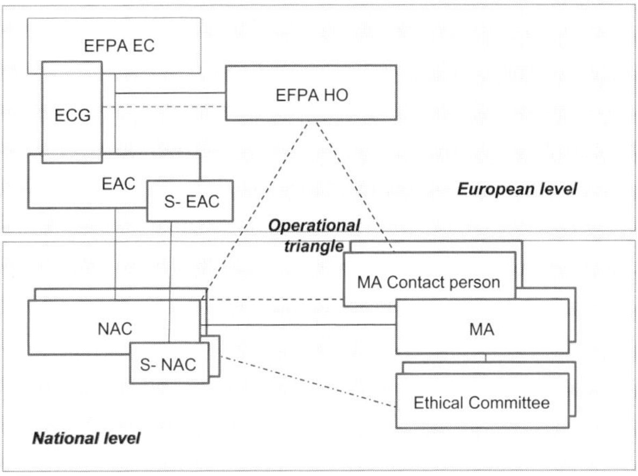

Note.

EFPA EC	=	EFPA Executive Council
EFPA HO	=	EFPA Head Office
ECG	=	*EuroPsy* Coordination Group
EAC	=	European Awarding Committee
S-EAC	=	Specialist European Awarding Committee
NAC	=	National Awarding Committee
S-NAC	=	Specialist National Awarding Committee
MA	=	Member Association

Figure 1. Overview of the *EuroPsy* organisation structure.

competences and contexts within which she has worked under supervision to qualify for independent practice. The applicant sends the form to the NAC together with authorised reports by her supervisor(s) and a pledge regarding ethical conduct. Next, the NAC evaluates the application, examining the applicant's education, supervised practice and competences. It decides whether the applicant meets all the criteria, and if so, in which area of practice the candidate is qualified for independent practice. The NAC can ask the applicant to provide additional information. If the country where the application is made differs from the country where the psychologist was educated, the NAC may need to obtain the advice of the NAC in the country of education. This will cost additional time and will only work if a NAC has already been established in that country.

After the NAC has been able to evaluate all information, the applicant will be informed of its decision on whether to award or not to award the *EuroPsy* Certificate. In the first case she will receive a copy of the requested *EuroPsy* Certificate and her details will be entered into the *EuroPsy* Register. The *EuroPsy* Regulations specify the dates within which applicants should be informed about the need for additional information and the acceptance or rejection of their application. The processing of an application and the act of entering a psychologist in the *EuroPsy* register and issuing a *EuroPsy* Certificate are contingent on the payment of a fee set by the national Member Association.

When a NAC decides not to award the requested certificate, the applicant will be informed about the grounds that lead to this decision. If the applicant accepts the decision, she may undertake additional education or professional training, to compensate for any noted deficiencies. However, the applicant may also lodge an appeal against the NAC's decision. This should be done with the national Member Association in the country concerned, providing the grounds for the appeal. According to the *EuroPsy* Regulations, the association will establish an independent advisory committee, consisting of at least three experts, to examine the appeal. This committee will rule on the appeal and provide a written judgment within 60 days. If the appeal is rejected the applicant may direct herself to the EAC for further appeal.

During the initial years of implementing *EuroPsy*, transitional arrangements apply and the application requirements for those already qualified as psychologists differ from those mentioned above. The *EuroPsy* Regulations (Article 38) state

> Applicants, who before this date have been licensed to practice independently as a psychologist by a national licensing body recognized by the European Awarding Committee, and/or meet the requirements and conditions of practice as a psychologist in their country of practice can substitute listing of their supervised practice as a psychologist, with a record of their work history after they were qualified for independent practice as a psychologist. In these cases evidence of at least 3 years or the equivalent, within the past 10 years, of independent practice as a psychologist, and evidence of current competence and continuing professional development needs to be provided.

For this purpose another application form needs to be completed, which can also be found on the national *EuroPsy* website. Transitional arrangements apply for limited time periods. For the *EuroPsy* Basic Certificate this is 3 years after the establishment of a National Awarding Committee in a country. For any *EuroPsy* Specialist Certificate it is 3 years after the establishment of the Specialist National Awarding Committee. In the latter case, applicants to the *EuroPsy* Specialist Certificate can apply for the *EuroPsy* Basic Certificate for an additional 2 years.

Register and Certificates

When a psychologist has been found to meet the *EuroPsy* requirements and the required fee has been received, her name and additional details (work or home address of the registrant, the university education, the country of practice, the context of practice and the place and date of authorisation by the NAC) is entered in the *EuroPsy* Register. This is a database that can be consulted online via the Internet. Following this registration, clients and employers can find the psychologist's details and recognise her as a holder of a *EuroPsy* certificate. At the same time a printed certificate is provided in the English language as well as in the local language of the country where the application was made (see Figure 2 for an image of the Basic Certificate). Both the Register and the printed Certificate indicate for which area of practice the psychologist is considered qualified to practise independently, and for how long. Some further qualification details can also be found on the back of the printed certificate.

EuroPsy
European Certificate in Psychology

Date of issue:
Registration number:

This is to certify that

First name Last Name

having demonstrated the required scientific knowledge and professional competences, and having agreed to abide by the principles of professional conduct set out in the Ethics Meta-Code of the European Federation of Psychologists' Associations (EFPA) and pledged to act in accordance with the national code of ethics of the country of practice

meets the requirements to be called

Registered EuroPsy Psychologist

and is hereby considered qualified for independent practice as a psychologist, within the professional context(s) specified in the EuroPsy Register, and below, in any European Country in which the EFPA Member Association has accepted the EFPA Regulations on EuroPsy, in as far as there are no restrictions from national regulations in the country concerned.

We, the undersigned, have satisfied ourselves that the said evidence is in accordance with the EFPA Regulations on EuroPsy concerning the award of the EuroPsy Certificate in Psychology, approved by EFPA on July 10, 2011.

This Certificate is valid until

Specified context:

Chair of the National Awarding Committee

Member of the National Awarding Committee

Figure 2. Certificate for Registered *EuroPsy* Psychologist.

A psychologist's infringements of national law or code of ethics can have consequences for her *EuroPsy* registration. Her record will be removed from the Register when a court of law or a national committee has imposed a sentence or measure against the holder that prohibits her from exercising the profession of psychologist, such as removal from a national register or withdrawal of a national license. A record may be marked as "suspended" when a court of law or a national committee has imposed a sentence or measure that suspends the holder's right to exercise the profession of psychologist. The mark suspended will be removed when the period of suspension ends.

How *EuroPsy* Matters

The general aims of *EuroPsy* have already been mentioned:

1. Protection of consumers and citizens in Europe by providing quality assurance and protection against unqualified and ethically questionable practice.
2. Promotion of the availability of adequate psychological services across Europe by creating transparency and raising standards.
3. Promotion of the mobility of psychologists (and clients) in Europe.

In this section we will move beyond these general aims and explain how *EuroPsy* matters for different categories of people – those who are recipients of the services of psychologists, those who will be or are professional psychologists as well as those who employ psychologists, or work with them.

Clients

The *EuroPsy* Register is a useful resource in the vast world of psychological service providers and helps clients to find a qualified psychologist to consult. It provides reassurance to know that a significant European organisation such as EFPA is collaborating with national psychologists associations from all over Europe to guarantee that psychologists meet trustworthy standards of qualification and professional conduct. The fact that it is easy to find out whether psychologists are *EuroPsy* certified, at the basic level or as specialists, helps clients to find an appropriate psychologist and ensures that there is an opportunity to complain in case something goes wrong. This can be done regardless of the country where one lives or where the psychologist practises. The main tool for clients is the *EuroPsy* Register, which can be found on the Internet – through the website of EFPA (http://www.europsy-efpa.eu/search) or on the national *EuroPsy* website. The Register can be searched on the basis of country, town, area of practice, specialisation, language, gender and the psychologist's family name. The search results in a list of psychologists with contact details. In the near future this will be extended with practice details and referrals.

The Register is not the only source of information for clients. Clients may also consult the *EuroPsy* website in their own country, which uses the national language, or the *EuroPsy* website of EFPSA (the European Federation of Psychology Students

Associations) to gain further information about *EuroPsy* or to find an answer on frequently asked questions.

Students

Of the curricula in psychology offered by universities and other institutions throughout Europe, many but not all meet the requirements of the curriculum framework and minimum standards of *EuroPsy*. Students who study psychology with the intention of becoming a psychologist therefore need to check whether the curriculum of their university matches these standards and will be recognised when they apply for *EuroPsy*. Studying this comprehensive curriculum implies that the student has undergone an appropriate scientific education and training, and guarantees that the necessary knowledge, skills and basic competences are acquired. This is the first step to prepare for getting a *EuroPsy* Certificate.

After graduating at the Master's level from a university with a recognised curriculum students should complete a year of supervised practice. Arrangements for this process will vary across countries. In some countries, this means that they should find a supervisor, a qualified senior psychologist who agrees to monitor and guide their work (for further detail see Chapter 6). The year of supervised practice is a learning period during which the graduate becomes introduced to and becomes familiar with all aspects of the psychologist's role, including interactions with clients, colleagues, managers, etc. In addition to practical, financial, and legal matters, special attention is paid to ethical aspects of the work. A major objective of this period is to acquire the required (professional as well as enabling) competences through learning-by-doing. This implies performing particular tasks, such as conducting an intake interview, administering tests, making a treatment plan, counselling a client, giving training, etc. Which competences should be acquired follows from the *EuroPsy* list of competences (see Chapter 5). The role of the supervisor is to help in planning this work, providing feedback, and – at the end of the period – making an assessment of the acquired competences.

As soon as the supervised practice year is completed the *EuroPsy* application can be submitted. For this, the *EuroPsy* application form must be used and the required documents (university degrees, supervisor report, signed statement on ethical conduct) must be submitted. If all requirements are met, and the required fee has been paid, the applicant will receive the *EuroPsy* Basic Certificate and be included in the *EuroPsy* Register. From this moment on everyone can see that a young psychologist is fully qualified. Registration is a clear mark of distinction in the eyes of clients, employers, colleagues and the public at large.

It is important to know that students need not undertake their whole study and supervised practice at the same place, in the same country. As long as the curriculum meets the *EuroPsy* requirements, it is possible, and indeed strongly encouraged by the EU, to move to another university or another country and follow the year of supervised practice there. Crossing borders is also possible at any time afterwards, since the *EuroPsy* Certificate is valid across all European countries participating in *EuroPsy*.[10] Of course, working in another country is dependent on one's language capability, as good mastery of the local language is essential to practise as a psychologist. Language is therefore one of the features in the *EuroPsy* Register, that clients can use to find a psychologist.

Junior and Senior Psychologists

Psychologists who have completed their studies in the past and who have worked for a number of years may wonder whether they should apply for *EuroPsy* and what the costs and benefits are, compared to their current situation. The main added value of *EuroPsy* would be that of having an additional recognition of their qualification, at European level that complements the recognition they have obtained at the national level. This is something that raises their visibility and standing in the eyes of clients, employers, and authorities, as well as their reputation among colleagues. It is most relevant for psychologists working in an environment where there are also colleagues from other countries. Apart from gaining a distinction of quality and professional ethics, it may also be important to exhibit the commitment to CPD that is inherent in *EuroPsy*. For some, this aspect of taking the profession very seriously is the most important reason to apply for *EuroPsy*.

A second benefit of *EuroPsy* is the competitive advantage that it may give in comparison with other professionals. This is particularly appealing for psychologists who work in areas where there is a strong competition with other professionals, such as psychotherapy, human resources management or organisational consulting. They will therefore mainly be interested in obtaining a *EuroPsy* Specialist Certificate. The competitive advantage would ultimately translate into higher chances of attracting clients or being employed, greater job security and higher income.

A third benefit of a *EuroPsy* Certificate, appealing both to less experienced and to senior psychologists, is that of being better equipped for mobility. Here, one should not only think of psychologists crossing borders but also of clients and employers. Although it does not currently provide automatic recognition, *EuroPsy* is helpful in obtaining recognition of one's qualifications for psychologists migrating to other participating countries or providing cross-border services (see above). Clients are also increasingly mobile, particularly in the European Union, and may find it attractive to gain the services of *EuroPsy* certified psychologists rather than those with a local certification only – particularly if they are able to use additional languages. In a similar way *EuroPsy* may make psychologists more attractive for foreign employers operating in their country.

An important point to clarify is that *EuroPsy* can be obtained by all psychologists in a country regardless of whether they are a member of the national association that is involved in administering *EuroPsy* in the country. Thus, *EuroPsy* is a public service that is available for all psychologists and does not require membership of any association. Those considering application must take into account that associations tend to give a

[10] It should be noted that *EuroPsy* does not provide a license to practice psychology nor automatic recognition; this is determined at national level. For EU countries this may change with the modernisation of the Qualifications Directive.

discount on the application fee to their members, implying that the application fee for nonmembers may be somewhat higher. Moreover, for any application, participation in *EuroPsy* implies a commitment to the code of ethics of the association and submission to its disciplinary procedures. In some countries where there are more than one psychologists association, initiatives have been taken to develop a common ethical code for all psychologists – a process supported by the EFPA Model Code of Ethics (EFPA, 2013b) that EFPA has recently developed.

Employers

While *EuroPsy* certification is still at an early stage, there are a number of reasons why it is of interest for employers of psychologists. First, the possession of a *EuroPsy* Certificate can start to play a role in the recruitment and selection of psychologists, particularly for international organisations employing staff from European countries. In this context *EuroPsy* is a standard that distinguishes psychologists holding a *EuroPsy* Certificate from those with only a national psychologist's certificate, or without any certificate. Applicants with *EuroPsy* Certificates can also be compared with holders of other certificates. For example, the *EuroPsy* Specialist Certificate in Psychotherapy allows for a distinction between psychologists specialised in psychotherapy and psychotherapists with a European Certificate for Psychotherapy. This latter certificate is issued to professionals who vary in disciplinary backgrounds and length of education. The education it requires is equivalent to 2 years of study, of which part is dedicated to psychotherapy. For some types of jobs employers may prefer to hire these professionals, for others they will prefer psychological staff with a *EuroPsy* Specialist Certificate because of its clearer profile, higher qualification standards and guarantees for competent practice at a specialist level.

Having a basic or specialist *EuroPsy* Certificate may also become a factor in decisions about the placement of psychologists, for example, in expatriate assignments. Holders of *EuroPsy* Certificates have qualifications that are more widely recognised than holders of national certificates, similar to the case of for example, engineers, specialists in clinical chemistry and laboratory medicine, informatics professionals or maintenance professionals.

EuroPsy further matters to employers because of the association with CPD required for revalidation of the certificates. Of course, this is a sound way to assure maintenance of a high level of professional expertise among the psychological staff.

Other Professionals

Psychologists often do not work alone; many of them collaborate with other professionals in the same institution and in other organisations. It can be envisaged that as time goes by other professionals will recognise the *EuroPsy* Certificate as a quality standard for competent psychologists. The *EuroPsy* Register is for them an important tool. This will take time. The main advantage in the short term will be the fact that it is becoming easier to identify the higher qualifications of psychologists with a *EuroPsy* Certificate. This is particularly important for those who refer patients or clients to psychologists, that is, in the clinical domain. For them the *EuroPsy* Register is an instrument to identify and contact psychologists whose expertise and professional responsibility can be fully trusted. This works at the level of the *EuroPsy* basic Certificate as well as that of the *EuroPsy* Specialist Certificates.

EuroPsy in a Long-Term and Global Perspective

From the viewpoint of EFPA and its Member Associations, *EuroPsy* is a tool for the long-term development of the psychological profession – in Europe. *EuroPsy* promotes a standard to ensure that psychology students are properly educated and prepared for practice in a wide range of contexts, it stimulates supervision by well-trained supervisors according to proven methods, it underlines the ethical component of professional practice, and it encourages CPD practices all over Europe. In addition, it creates convergence regarding key facets of the profession without pressing for complete harmonisation, thus endorsing the diversity that is needed to serve the people of Europe in accordance with local circumstances and cultural traditions.

Although it might be argued that the logic of *EuroPsy*, and perhaps components of the system, could well be applied to psychology in other parts of the world, it was never the intention of its designers to export it to other regions of the world. The present view is that psychological science should be sensitive to the diversity in the human ecology and human behaviour across the globe, and that psychological practice should be responsive to the socioeconomic and political context in which it is conducted. While it may be said that the region of Europe has a degree of homogeneity, even here it is essential to respect diversity and social and cultural context. As Silbereisen and Ritchie suggest, "psychology education and training must address the diversity of the human existence and its possible manifestation in different principles and mechanisms across societal and cultural borders" (Silbereisen & Ritchie, 2014, p. 7). Psychology as a profession should therefore show a certain degree of variety responding to local contexts. What makes sense in Europe, that is, the set of standards known as *EuroPsy*, with agreement about certain key elements but also room for diversity, may not fully meet the current needs of, for example, Africa, Asia, Latin-America, the Pacific or North America. Only a bottom-up process involving various parts of the world that take sufficient time will show how and where *EuroPsy* and other systems for developing psychology will meet.

Conclusion

EuroPsy has been developed as a standard or benchmark for psychology in Europe. Building on this, EFPA has developed *EuroPsy* as a certification system which forms the basis for the European Register of *EuroPsy* certified psychologists. This means that it is possible for anyone to check the credentials of psychologists in Europe, thus leading to improvement of standards and protection of the public. *EuroPsy* does not imply harmonisation of qualifications or university education, but rather an agreed framework or standard which the 36 national Member Associations of EFPA have signed up to. At the present time,

EuroPsy does not yet provide a tool for mobility, but the goal is that it should provide the foundation for the Common Training Framework proposed by the EU, and that it should become the mechanism for evaluating equivalence of qualifications. In the next chapter we consider the curriculum and professional training for psychologists, and the ways in which *EuroPsy* has had an impact on the education for psychologists.

4 *EuroPsy* and the Psychology Curriculum

As with all professions, the most crucial part defining the psychological profession is education. After all, the education provides the basis for the knowledge and expertise, and to a large extent for the identity of the profession. In this chapter we will look at how *EuroPsy* has defined the educational programme for psychologists. Given the diversity in educational structures across European countries noted in the previous chapter, it is obvious that reaching an agreement about the education of psychologists that would be acceptable throughout Europe, would not be an easy task. However, the process was greatly facilitated by the structural harmonisation of higher education in Europe that took place while *EuroPsy* was being constructed. In this chapter we will describe the major changes in the European context and explain how these have helped to create a common educational framework as part of *EuroPsy*.

We start with an overview of the developments at the European level, with an emphasis on the Bologna Declaration of 1999, and its progressive implementation in subsequent years. We discuss the Bologna process and the creation of the European Higher Education Area (EHEA) and look at European standards for quality assurance, qualification frameworks, the common credit system ECTS, and competences. In the second section we discuss a specific Bologna initiative, the *Tuning* project, which aimed to set benchmarks for university subjects of study, and we consider the issue of benchmarking in psychology. In the third section we present the *EuroPsy* framework and standards, and discuss how their adoption has benefited from the Bologna process. We clarify how this has helped to complement the traditional input orientation (the student as the recipient of a set of courses) with an output orientation (the demonstration of ability to act competently by the student). In the next section we consider some of the challenges of *EuroPsy* in relation to accreditation. In the final section we look at convergence and divergence in the education and training for psychologists across Europe, and the possible impact of *EuroPsy* on this.

The Bologna Process

When *EuroPsy* was developed, Europe was witnessing a number of important changes. Among them were the rapid expansion of the European Communities (from 2002, the European Union), mainly due to the entry of former Communist Countries, and the drive towards a higher level of integration that would help the realisation of the four freedoms (or rights) mentioned in Chapter 1 – the free movement of people, goods, services and capital. An important event regarding higher education was the signing in 1999 of the so-called "Bologna Declaration" by the ministers of education (or their representatives) from 29 European countries. This declaration is a short document spelling out a preference for a joint structure of degrees (without reference to content) with the intention to create a EHEA,[11] which would promote mobility, attract students and staff from Europe and other parts of the world, and be internationally competitive (http://www.ehea.info/). Noteworthy is the fact that the ideas expressed in the declaration were appealing to many in Europe. The signatories were not only ministers from the EU member states but also from other European countries, and in the years to follow many other countries would join (now 47).

Bologna Declaration and EHEA

The Bologna Declaration of 1999 became of great historic significance. It set into motion a process of convergence in the structure of university programmes across Europe and even beyond (Reichert, 2010; Adelman, 2009; Birtwistle & McKiernan, 2008; and see Keeling, 2006). In order to facilitate mobility of professionals between countries a system was envisaged of easily comparable degrees, and a Diploma Supplement in which additional educational credits can be specified. The Bologna Declaration involved six key thematic objectives:

1. adoption of a system of easily readable and comparable degrees;
2. adoption of a two cycle system (undergraduate and graduate). This has now been extended to three consecutive cycles: the undergraduate cycle (Bachelor) lasting a minimum of 3 years, the graduate cycle (Master) of 2 years (or 1 year), and the Doctorate cycle;
3. establishment of a system of credits (the European Credit Transfer System or ECTS) as a common students' workload measure and as a means of promoting student mobility. In this system, 1 ECTS point is given for a study load equivalent to a certain number of study hours, usually 25–30 hours;
4. promotion of mobility for students, teachers, researchers and administrative staff;
5. promotion of European cooperation in quality assurance with a view to developing comparable criteria and methodologies of teaching and learning assessment across European countries;
6. promotion of the European dimension in higher education, in relation to curricula, interinstitutional cooperation, mobility schemes and integrated programmes of study.

Prudently, the Bologna Declaration balanced its drive towards greater European integration with an acknowledgement of European diversity:

> We hereby undertake to attain these objectives – within the framework of our institutional competences and taking full respect of the diversity of cultures, languages, national education systems and of University autonomy – to consolidate the European area of higher education. To this end, we will pursue ways of intergovernmental cooperation, together

[11] The Bologna Agreement aimed to create a EHEA by 2010; this is sometimes referred to as European Higher Education Space (EHES).

> with those of nongovernmental European organisations with competence on higher education (Bologna Declaration, 1999, p. 2).

The original Declaration has achieved momentum through what is referred to as the "Bologna Process," by which the political goals of increasing convergence, mobility and the competitiveness of the European higher education system have been pursued. The Process involves a series of biennial meetings at high ministerial level where progress is reviewed through "Stocktaking" reports and specific goals are set for the next 2-year period. The first such conference took place in 2001 in Prague; the ninth one will take place in 2015 in Yerevan, Armenia. Considerable investment of time and funds has been made to push forward the Process, including the formation of a "Bologna Follow-up Group" (the BFUG) steered by a Bologna Board, and numerous specific project groups. Although the Bologna region extends far beyond the 28 countries of the European Union, and is formally independent of the EU, the EU plays an important role in the Bologna Process and is the major funder of Bologna projects and initiatives. As a consequence, the EU has correspondingly major influence over the Process (Lunt, 2005; Lunt & Peiró, 2012).

Although the Bologna process has no legal status as an agreement or treaty, and is rather seen as a binding commitment, it has succeeded in achieving a high degree of convergence and it is arguably one of the most powerful drivers for change in education in the history of Europe and indeed beyond Europe (Reichert, 2010; and see Adelman, 2009, 2010). At the moment (2013) the Bologna process involves 47 European countries and is supported by the European Commission. Several international organisations participate as consultative members, including the Council of Europe, the UNESCO European Centre for Higher Education, the European University Association, the European Association of Institutions in Higher Education, the European Students' Union, the European Association for Quality Assurance in Higher Education, the Education International Pan-European Structure, and Business Europe. The majority of participating countries have now implemented structural reforms to their degree system to create the Bologna two (three) stage system, and are committed to the use of ECTS and the Diploma Supplement to support recognition of study periods in different countries. The various Bologna related activities pertain to student and staff mobility, a common framework of qualifications, and shared approach to quality assurance in the design and delivery of university degree programmes. These activities have been crystallised in policy documents and recommendations, which have been implemented by the countries involved. At the 7th Ministers' Conference in Budapest-Vienna in 2010, the EHEA was officially launched, and since then further plans have been developed. At the eighth Ministers' Conference in Bucharest 2012 a new work plan was accepted with a focus on a more structured approach to the organisation of the work, the results of which will be reviewed in 2015.

Quality Assurance

Given the Bologna commitment to improve the competiveness of the EHEA, a major initiative involved quality assurance (QA) and enhancement, and the development of an overarching European framework or standard for QA. There are various international networks of quality assurance agencies; overall, these appear to be largely comparable and transparent (Aelterman, 2006; Hall & Altmaier, 2008). As part of the Bologna implementation, ENQA, *the European Association for Quality Assurance in Higher Education*, was asked in 2003 to develop an "agreed set of standards, procedures, and guidelines on QA." The *Standards and Guidelines for Quality Assurance in the EHEA* known as the *European Standards and Guidelines* (ESG; ENQA, 2005) were published by ENQA in 2005 in cooperation with a number of other associations with a similar interest in the quality of higher education (European Universities Association, European Association of Institutions of Higher Education and the European Student Unions). Membership of ENQA consists mainly of national agencies concerned with accreditation and quality assurance of education programmes in higher education. A *European Quality Assurance Register for Higher Education* (EQAR) has been established for national agencies that have *National Qualifications Frameworks* (NQFs) which substantially comply with the ESG. The ESG, agreed in 2005, covered internal and external quality assurance of higher education institutions, and made a commitment to a framework of agreed standards and guidelines with an emphasis on subsidiarity, with reviews being undertaken nationally where possible.

The internal quality assurance standards prescribe that a higher education institution should have policies and procedures in place to assure the quality of their education programmes and they should have a quality enhancement policy. There are numerous further requirements, such as clear procedures for regular review of programmes, for assessment of students and for public and objective information about the programmes being offered. The external quality assurance standards (the assessment of which falls to an external quality assurance agency) should take into consideration the internal quality procedures that are in place in an institution. Other standards specify clarity of criteria on which evaluations should be based, follow-up on recommendations for action resulting from evaluations, and advance notice of the length of the period in a review cycle. The standards for external review also specify summary reviews of evaluations and assessments, thus providing overall information on the quality of institutions and subject areas in a country. A major objective of external quality assurance is to safeguard standards in higher education; this implies accreditation of programmes and institutions (see below). Finally, there are standards requiring that the external quality assurance agency (or agencies) in a country should be recognised by "competent public authorities" and have an established legal basis. The agencies should be independent, that is they should have autonomy in their operations and their conclusions and recommendations should be free from interference by universities or ministries of education.

It is important to note that the ESG do not demand total compliance, rather that the term "substantial compliance" is being used. There may be local differences in the way an agency carries out its task of quality control and differences in local traditions of education. Hence, it is generally agreed that a quality assurance system should allow for some imprecision and that there is a need for flexibility (e.g. Amaral & Tavares, 2009). Moreover, international agencies do not have any authority to force national compliance with rules and regulations. Even the EU, despite its influence through financial support of ENQA and similar organisations, does not seek to impose standards on a country.

Officially the EU maintains the principle of "subsidiarity" which implies that a more central government or administration should only be responsible for tasks which cannot be performed adequately at a more local level. At the same time, if a country wishes to be part of the community of countries that recognise each other's education programmes it has to meet common standards. For example, the EQAR register is voluntary, but a screening procedure with an independent review is applied to examine whether the European standards are being upheld by a national agency seeking entry in this register. In this way, European agencies achieve convergence without a demand for uniformity or harmonisation.

Accreditation

Related to quality assurance, accreditation amounts to the official recognition of an educational programme, or even of an entire institution as meeting certain quality standards. Replacing earlier systems of state authorisation for educational programs, accreditation systems started to be introduced in Europe in the late 1980s. Accreditation is performed by independent assessment committees on behalf of national governments, and entitles a university or other institution to offer a certain educational programme or programmes at a certain level. Traditionally universities were exempt from assessment and evaluation; they relied on public trust to the effect that they would be providing education of high quality. Although education programmes are rarely closed down because of lack of quality, nowadays quality control agencies in various European countries quite frequently demand improvements, which are mandatory with closure as the ultimate sanction. During the last few decades several countries in Europe have introduced quality controls that amount to accreditation (e.g. Rauhvargers, 2004). Amaral and Tavares (2009, p. 5) have argued that there is an overwhelming movement towards state approval schemes, mentioning Austria, Germany and Norway as examples.

European Frameworks of Qualifications

As part of the development of a system of comparable degrees, two different qualification frameworks have been developed within Europe, the first by the BFUG in 2005, the second by the European Union in 2008 as part of its efforts to promote life-long learning. Both are relevant here, and both promote the use of learning outcomes and competences, aiming to guide the development of NQFs. Although the two frameworks were developed separately and in parallel, they have been made compatible and their implementation has been coordinated.

A strong feature of the EHEA is the *Qualifications Framework of the European Higher Education Area (QF-EHEA)* developed in 2005 by the BFUG. This is a common European reference framework which links countries' qualifications systems together, and uses learning outcomes to show what a learner knows, understands, and is able to do on the basis of a given qualification. It aims to serve as a translation device to make qualifications more readable and comprehensible across different European countries, and as a framework to help countries in restructuring degree awards in higher education. Using the so-called Dublin[12] descriptors, this framework provides generic descriptors for each of the three cycles (Bachelor, Master, Doctorate), based on learning outcomes and competences. The Dublin descriptors are internationally acceptable descriptors developed jointly by stakeholders across Europe. In the Biennial Bologna meeting in 2007, Ministers emphasised their importance, and committed signatory countries to developing their own national qualification frameworks based on the QF-EHEA:

> Qualifications frameworks are important instruments in achieving comparability and transparency within the EHEA and facilitating the movement of learners . . . they should also help HEIs to develop modules and study programmes based on learning outcomes and credits, and improve the recognition of qualifications as well as all forms of prior learning. (London Communiqué, May, 2007).

The Dublin descriptors provide broad and generic learning outcomes for first, second and third cycle awards, and have proved to play a key role in the development of the Bachelor/Masters structure of higher education across Europe. An example from the first cycle is:

> have the ability to gather and interpret relevant data (usually within their field of study) to inform judgements that include reflection on relevant social, scientific or ethical issues;

from the second cycle:

> have the ability to integrate knowledge and handle complexity, and formulate judgements with incomplete or limited information, but that include reflecting on social and ethical responsibilities linked to the application of their knowledge and judgements;

and from the third cycle:

> are capable of critical analysis, evaluation and synthesis of new and complex ideas.

Although the descriptors are broad and generic, they provide an attempt to articulate the differentiation between the three cycles in terms of knowledge and understanding, applying knowledge and understanding, making judgements, communication and learning skills, and emphasise the use of learning outcomes throughout.

In parallel with this Bologna initiative, the European Commission developed its *European Qualifications Framework for Lifelong Learning (EQF)*, which was adopted by the EU in 2008. According to its website, the EQF is meant to act as a translation device to "better understand and compare the qualifications levels of different countries and different education and training systems" (http://ec.europa.eu/education/lifelong-learning-policy/eqf_en.htm). The EQF provides a set of eight reference levels, covering all sectors of education and training, each defined in terms of three parameters: what a learner knows;

---

[12] Within Europe, documents are frequently labeled according to the location of the meeting where they were developed/agreed, in this case Dublin.

what a learner understands; and what a learner is able to do. Given its focus on lifelong learning, in this approach the duration of formal study is not a parameter for recognition. EQF is meant to reflect learning outcomes (skills, competence and knowledge), regardless of the way in which these outcomes were acquired.

One of the stipulated objectives is to enable international sectoral organisations which are associations of national organisations (like EFPA) to relate their qualifications to the common set of reference levels, and to make it easier for students, employers and other stakeholders to understand the qualifications of workers wherever they trained and qualified. The EQF is also meant to facilitate cooperation and the exchange of good practice. The QF-EHEA (Bologna) and the EQF (EU) have been coordinated as follows:

EQF	Bologna QF-EHEA
Levels 1–4	Pre-tertiary education
Level 5	Short cycle
Level 6	Ist cycle (Bachelor)
Level 7	2nd cycle (Masters)
Level 8	3rd cycle (Doctorate)

ECTS

In order to facilitate mobility, comparability and recognition of periods of study in other countries, the *European Credit Transfer and Accumulation System* (ECTS) was set up initially to provide a standard for recognition of the credits earned by students outside of their own university when participating in the ERASMUS exchange scheme set up by the EU (and see footnote Chapter 2, p. 38). ECTS credits are now used widely across European countries by national organisations to express the workload of a course or some other part of a university education programme. A year of full-time study amounts to 60 ECTS credits. Since this workload across European countries ranges from 1,500 to 1,800 hours, one ECTS credit corresponds to between 25 and 30 hours of study. The common 3-year Bachelor study and the 2-year Masters study in the Bologna scheme typically amount to 180 and 120 ECTS credits, respectively.

The ECTS system has been elaborated further to serve as a system of credit accumulation and transfer that can accommodate all learning outcomes. If all teaching processes and learning outcomes are expressed in ECTS units this will facilitate evaluation and validation of qualifications as well as student mobility. Learning achievements of an individual person can be entered on a Diploma Supplement that provides a listing of all learning outcomes recognised by a higher education institution.

Competences

Both the QF-EHEA and the EQF have a focus on learning outcomes and by analogy competences. It should be noted that competence is thought of in a broad and generic sense, as is illustrated with the following definitions in the EQF (European Parliament, 2008):

> "Learning Outcomes" means statements of what a learner knows, understands and is able to do on completion of a learning process, which are defined in terms of knowledge, skills and competence.
>
> "Knowledge" means the outcome of the assimilation of information through learning. Knowledge is the body of facts, principles, theories and practices that is related to a field of work or study. In the context of the EQF, knowledge is described as theoretical and/or factual.
>
> "Skills" means the ability to apply knowledge and use know-how to complete tasks and solve problems. In the context of the EQF, skills are described as cognitive (involving the use of logical, intuitive and creative thinking) or practical (involving manual dexterity and the use of methods, materials, tools and instruments).
>
> "Competence" means the proven ability to use knowledge, skills and personal, social and/or methodological abilities, in work or study situations and in professional and personal development.

As mentioned above, the EQF defines eight reference levels, defined through knowledge, skills and competence. In Table 8 we provide the description of the two highest levels. The learning outcomes of Level 7 are meant to correspond to the Bologna second cycle. In other words, these are the learning outcomes expected for students who have graduated from a Masters programme in psychology. The levels are defined in terms of the three parameters of knowledge, skills and competence, with skills presuming knowledge, and competence presuming knowledge and skills. A relevant clause in the EQF description of Level 7 is that graduates should be able to manage "contexts that are complex, unpredictable and require new strategic approaches." This description is reminiscent of the practice of the professional psychologist who is often faced with situations that are unique and for which no prescribed approach or strategy is available.

The learning outcomes of level 8 reflect the level of the doctorate, and will be discussed later in this chapter and in Chapter 10.

Tuning Educational Structures in Europe

A specific Bologna initiative, called "*Tuning* Educational Structures in Europe" was launched in 2000 in the context of the need for compatibility and comparability of degrees across Europe and the needs of students and employers for transparent and reliable information as to what a degree qualification stands for in practice. The *Tuning* initiative built on experiences gained through the Erasmus and Socrates programmes, using ECTS and the qualification frameworks as these were developed. The name "*Tuning*" was chosen

Table 8. Levels 7 and 8 in the EQF (Recommendation of the European Parliament and of the Council, 2008, p. 6)

EQF level	Knowledge	Skills	Competence
1. *Learning outcomes relevant to level 7* (corresponding to 2nd cycle i.e. Masters)	1. Highly specialised knowledge, some of which is at the forefront of knowledge in a field of work or study, as the basis for original thinking or research. 2. Critical awareness of knowledge issues in a field and at the interface between different fields.	Specialised problem-solving skills required in research and/or innovation in order to develop new knowledge and procedures and to integrate knowledge from different fields.	1. Manage and transform work or study contexts that are complex, unpredictable and require new strategic approaches. 2. Take responsibility for contributing to professional knowledge and practice and/or for reviewing the strategic performance of teams.
2. *Learning outcomes relevant to level 8* (corresponding to 3rd cycle i.e. Doctorate)	Knowledge at the most advanced frontier of a field of work or study and at the interface between fields	The most advanced and specialised skills and techniques, including synthesis and evaluation, required to solve critical problems in research and/or innovation and to extend and redefine existing knowledge or professional practice.	Demonstrate substantial authority, innovation, autonomy, scholarly and professional integrity and sustained commitment to the development of new ideas or processes at the forefront of work or study contexts including research.

to reflect the fact that it was not seeking harmonisation of degree programmes, or prescriptive and mandatory curricula, but rather looked for convergence and a shared understanding, seeking "common reference points" (González & Wagenaar, 2003, 2008).

The *Tuning* initiative aims to offer a concrete approach to implementing the Bologna Process at the level of higher education institutions and subject areas. It is based on a Europe-wide methodology to design, develop, implement and evaluate study programmes for each of the Bologna Cycles in different subject areas. The methodology involves the formation of a small team of experts in a field or discipline and widespread consultation of students, university staff and other relevant stakeholders to identify important skills and competences. *Tuning* uses a common approach across the different subject domains, specifying the content and learning outcomes for the Bachelor degree (EQF level 6), the Master degree (EQF level 7) and the Doctorate degree (EQF level 8). This results in reference points for each subject, providing a benchmark which national higher education institutions may use for planning curricula.

Benchmarking provides a means for the academic community to describe the nature and characteristics of programmes in a specific subject or subject area. Subject benchmark statements are used by quality assurance agencies as a source of reference for external evaluation, and provide guidance for higher education institutions in designing new programmes and articulating learning outcomes. They are also used by students and employers seeking information about subject content of different programmes. As a specific example, the UK benchmark statement for psychology (QAA, 2007) identifies the core knowledge domains within psychology for Bachelor level as: research methods, biological psychology, cognitive psychology, individual differences, developmental psychology and social psychology, with a foundation of conceptual and historical perspectives in psychology. In addition the document identifies a wide range of subject-specific skills which the graduate from the Bachelor degree should possess. Increasingly subject benchmarking occurs at international level in order to compare standards of psychology across different countries (e.g. ESRC, 2011). The purpose and benefits of benchmarking include a greater transparency in relation to curriculum content (and associated processes of teaching, learning and research), and a commitment to enhancing quality both nationally and internationally.

The *Tuning* project aims to develop benchmark statements in all major subjects. A coincidence of timing created the opportunity to develop *Tuning-EuroPsy*: reference points for the design and delivery of degree programmes in psychology (Lunt, Job, Lecuyer, Peiró & Gorbeña, 2011). It uses the *EuroPsy* curriculum framework, which was introduced in Chapter 3 as the basis for the reference points, thus supporting *EuroPsy* as a benchmark for psychology in Europe. The *Tuning-EuroPsy* document describes the knowledge and skills that psychology students should acquire and provides generic and specific competences as learning outcomes of the different degree cycles. It also provides information on typical occupations of a graduate in psychology.

The *EuroPsy* Curriculum Framework

EuroPsy defines the requirements for the education of psychologists with the help of the curriculum framework presented in Chapter 3. As discussed in Chapter 2, EuroPsyT provided a framework for education and training of psychologists in Europe, with an input model of broad curriculum coverage for the first phase and second phase, and stipulating minimum standards of length and curriculum coverage. This was complemented in the second Leonardo project by an output model and the specification of competences to be gained substantially through the year of supervised practice. The curriculum framework fits well with the Bologna structure of Bachelor and Masters, which was increasingly being adopted by European countries during the course of the *EuroPsy* project. Thus the standard structure for *EuroPsy* became a 3 + 2 + 1 (6 years) model (Bachelor, Master, 1 year supervised practice), although the project team was committed to respect for diversity and thus to other structures in existence in some countries. One relevant example was the Problem-based learning (PBL) programmes being developed as part of a more integrated professional qualification in a minority of universities in European countries. Here the combination of broad specification of input together with the specification of competences supported some diversity and flexibility. The minimum standard for *EuroPsy* is the completion of a recognised 5-year psychology programme plus 1 year of supervised practice. In order to provide a rigorous and high quality education, the emphasis in *EuroPsy* is on *recognised* psychology programmes.

The requirement for recognition of a psychology programme is that the curriculum meets the *EuroPsy* Standards. Although the recognition is carried out at national level by the National Awarding Committees (NACs) involved in the implementation of *EuroPsy*, it is overseen and moderated by the European Awarding Committee (EAC). In order to be recognised, psychology programmes are required to meet the following criteria:

1. coverage of the specified core components of psychology as indicated in EuroPsyT;
2. focus in the curriculum on psychology both as an explanatory and as a technological (cf. applied) science;
3. focus in the curriculum on individual, group and society in order to achieve a multilevel understanding of professional psychology;
4. inclusion of research competences and completion of a Masters dissertation;
5. a stage or internship placement during the course of university study (and separate from the period of supervised practice).

Most traditional models of university education have placed considerable emphasis on the reproduction of knowledge from lectures and textbooks with the content of psychology programmes geared towards theory, methods, and findings in various fields. Assessments in the form of course examinations mainly asked for reproduction of academic knowledge rather than whether a student could also apply this knowledge. However, this is only one side of psychology, and should be complemented by knowledge and skills related to the application of psychology in assessment or intervention. The working group that developed the *EuroPsy* framework emphasised the importance of both and pointed out the importance of integrating both types of knowledge in professional competences (see Chapter 5). In view of the different didactical requirements involved, it was decided that the 5 years of university education required by the *EuroPsy* Regulations could be based almost entirely on an input model, whereas the subsequent year of supervised practice would be based on an output model (see Chapter 6). The implication of this choice is that a student who has graduated from a recognised psychology programme has met the first requirement of the *EuroPsy* Certificate, and will need a year of supervised practice in order to obtain the Certificate. It should be noted that the actual content of the curriculum and mode of assessment may vary, while fitting the broad framework. As countries adapt to the requirements of the EQFs, university education will increasingly include qualifications descriptors expressed in terms of learning outcomes, and including knowledge, skills and competence.

In a general sense the *EuroPsy* was influenced by and meets the requirements of Bologna initiatives in terms of the two cycle structure of programmes, the use of ECTS, and the focus on competences. However, we note that, while *EuroPsy* benefitted from the Bologna developments, it was a separate initiative that partly predated the Bologna Agreement. Some differences are that the two-cycle structure is not mandatory (see Chapter 2), and it does not support entry to the labour market as a psychologist after the Bachelor or Master qualification, unless additional competences are acquired during a year of supervised practice.

EuroPsy exemplifies a subject-specific convergence within the context of a wider generic convergence created by the Bologna Process. As shown in *Tuning-EuroPsy: reference points, EuroPsy* fits with the EQFs and the associated specification of competences. Although the learning outcomes defined in the EQF are oriented towards later professional practice, the professional competences required by *EuroPsy* are defined in more detail and with reference to psychologists' work settings and work roles. The learning of these competences will largely take place after obtaining the Master Degree, when graduates start performing real-life professional roles. The *Tuning-EuroPsy* makes use of the QF-EHEA, defining learning outcomes for graduates at different levels of education, relates these to EQF levels, and spells out the competences as defined in *EuroPsy* (see Chapter 5).

As regards the European Qualification Framework, the focus of *EuroPsy* is clearly on EQF levels 6 and 7. However, the *Tuning-EuroPsy* includes learning outcomes for Level 8, which correspond to the third cycle specified by Bologna developments, that is, the level of the doctorate. The doctorate is traditionally considered as the PhD with the requirement to develop high level research competencies and to make an original contribution to the further development of science. The study for this type of doctorate is showing signs of change with the introduction of mandatory courses as part of the degree, greater structure and stricter regulations for timely completion. There is also growing interest in the notion of a "European Doctorate" due to collaborations between universities and initiatives to achieve greater comparability and convergence in programmes (e.g. LERU, 2010, 2013). However, a recent development is the application of the doctoral descriptor to professional doctorates. These exist in North America and the UK which both require doctoral level qualification at entry to practice for clinical psychologists (see Donn, Routh & Lunt, 2000, and for further discussion see Chapter 10). It is as yet unclear to which degree this model will spread to other areas of psychology and to other countries. In the context of the *EuroPsy* system the description for Level 8 may be seen as compatible with the Specialist Certificate structure that is currently being developed by EFPA. It may also match the structure and requirements for specialisation under development by countries such as Finland and Norway (see Chapters 3 and 10). This is an area where we expect more developments and where the *EuroPsy* framework provides a robust structure for comparability and equivalence.

At the current time there are continuing debates over equivalence in doctoral education (Scott, Brown, Lunt & Thorpe, 2004), and this level raises important and interesting issues concerning the equivalence and status of academic and professional knowledge. Developments such as European and national qualifications frameworks support the creation of robust structures and criteria for doctoral level qualifications. *Tuning-EuroPsy* (p. 48) refers to third cycle (doctoral or specialisation) degrees in psychology as awarded to students who:

1. have demonstrated systematic understanding of a topic(s) of the science and/or practice of psychology and mastered those skills and methods or research and/or intervention related to such topic(s);
2. have demonstrated the ability to conceive, design, implement and develop a substantial process of research and/or intervention in psychology by developing a

substantial body of work, some of which merits national or international refereed publication;
3. have competences which fit them for employment as professional psychologists in senior positions in psychology and related (e.g. health) sectors, or for a progression to a career in academic research.

These descriptors begin to articulate equivalence in academic and professional knowledge for Level 8, and are important for a consideration of wider international efforts to evaluate equivalence and comparability, and for the development of higher level qualifications for experienced practitioners or professionals (and see Chapter 10).

EuroPsy and Educational Accreditation

The description of the various levels in the EQF amounts to a description of what is deemed desirable. The Bologna Process is based on seeking harmony and convergence between countries, although it has been suggested that quality assurance procedures are implemented in too rigid a fashion (Huisman & Westerheijden, 2010). The implementation by countries of the cycles in higher education, of the ECTS credit system, and of various measures of quality assurance is on a voluntary basis. The wording in the EU and Bologna related documents avoids suggestions of enforced cooperation of countries. An illustration is the almost total absence of the term "accreditation" in the EQF documents (ENQA, 2009; European Parliament, 2008). However, the Bologna Process is exerting pressure towards identical structures and quality assurance processes. If a country does not comply it is likely to be left as an outsider in the European arena. The readiness with which countries have joined the Bologna Process to a considerable extent has to be explained from the desire not to be left behind. As a consequence, quality assurance at the national level tends to amount to accreditation. Nevertheless we note the continued tension between pushes for greater Europeanisation and pulls to retain national decision-making:

> We are facing two difficult-to-satisfy needs to create balance . . . we need to be able to harmonise the structures and mechanisms of European higher education, but at the same time we need to maintain diversity inside Europe in terms of content in order to ensure that we meet the specific needs of the diversity of learners' (Froment, 2003, p. 30).

Considering the objectives of the *EuroPsy* system the question needs to be asked whether the moves towards convergence of structures and national accreditation are sufficient to result in adequate standards for psychology across Europe that meet the *EuroPsy* Regulations. This is a complex issue. First, the Bologna Process can be seen as a welcome development, which is rapidly moving psychology in Europe away from the diversity in patterns of education and training described by Newstead and Makinen (1997) in the 1990s. Similarity of structure helps not only in the enhancement of cross-border mobility of students and professionals, which is the major objective of the European Union, it also helps in comparing educational programmes. Secondly, the move towards accreditation of higher education programmes and institutions within countries on the basis of evaluations and quality assessments is an important mechanism to exclude programmes that do not meet adequate national standards.

However, there are also potentially more worrying aspects related to the adequacy of accreditation mechanisms. Firstly, recognition of national assurance quality agencies is a matter of a national "competent authority," that is, a government office, or a non-government agency designated by the government of a country. International recognition of a national quality assurance agency, notably through registration in the ENQA register of EQAR (see above) is on the basis of an evaluation of the way of working of that agency, that is, on the basis of formal aspects of its functioning, not on the basis of standards of excellence of the programmes or institutions that are accredited by the national agency. It seems likely that with the same formal procedures there can remain substantial differences in the excellence of education programmes across countries. *EuroPsy* is not itself an accreditation system. However, it is likely to play a role as a benchmark for accreditation processes and agencies in Europe. This creates a challenge (to ensure rigorous procedures and high standards across diverse systems) and an opportunity (to raise the quality of education and training across European countries). Strictly speaking, it is still possible that psychology programmes in some countries are evaluated as acceptable, while they do not meet the quality standards aimed at by the *EuroPsy* Regulations.

It may well turn out that this is a temporary concern. The Organisation for Economic Co-operation and Development (OECD), which has successfully conducted international comparative assessments of education programmes at high school level (e.g. the PISA project, OECD, 2009), has launched a pilot assessment to compare higher education programmes in various sciences. In this *Assessment of Higher Education Learning Outcomes* (AHELO) project there will be a quantitative assessment of generic skills (critical thinking, reasoning communication in writing, etc.) and of discipline-specific skills. A quantitative assessment of the latter skills could become a uniform comparison standard to equate the quality of education programmes across Europe (Lunt & Peiró, 2012; Lunt, 2014).

The final answer to the question of adequate standards of accreditation for psychology programmes across countries in Europe depends on the role that the profession of psychology can play in the setting of uniform standards and in the adaptation of such standards over time to reflect new developments in the science and profession of psychology. The General Assembly of EFPA representing the national psychology associations in Europe is the highest authority on matters of *EuroPsy*; although it is obviously not the only player in the field of European higher education in psychology, through *EuroPsy* it has the potential to play a decisive role in setting standards for psychologists' education and services.

The implementation of *EuroPsy* Regulations is delegated to a EAC the members of which are appointed by the EFPA Executive Council. It is the task of the EAC to provide guidance to the NAC in each country and to supervise the proper implementation of the Regulations by these NACs. Each NAC is expected to prepare a list of approved academic programmes in psychology. In principle, it is possible that a NAC does not approve a curriculum that is accredited by the national quality assurance agency of a country. It is also possible that the EAC does not accept a recommendation for approval by the NAC of a country. If the NAC in a country and the EAC approve an education programme, students graduating from that programme will be considered to have met the requirement of 5 years academic education in psychology. If the EAC withholds approval of a programme, each student graduating from that programme will have to show individually that his or her university education meets the *EuroPsy* Regulations. In practice this will mean that a student will have to show evidence of additional education (in the form of ECTS credits).

Despite principles of subsidiarity and the professed authority of national countries over their own education standards, the pressures of the Bologna Process are likely to lead to convergence between countries in the nature and structure of higher education both in general and in particular fields. Pressure towards convergence derives from the interactions between national quality assurance agencies and the ways they influence each other. Moreover, the costs of nonrecognition of a programme are likely to be high in terms of prestige, and also in terms of student registrations. For example, international exchange of students is based on mutual recognition of education programmes; courses followed at an unrecognised programme are likely not to be counted for ECTS credits by the home university of a student.

Generally, conflicts between countries on education standards are likely to be avoided since nobody stands to gain. This also holds true if a conflict were to arise between the NAC in a country and the EAC on the one hand and the national quality assurance agency of that country on the other hand. Although the EAC, or EFPA, does not have any authority over national programmes in psychology, the psychologists in a country and presumably the competent authority on quality assurance will seek to avoid the stigma of inadequate university education. Moreover, the NAC in consultation with the EAC can advise the competent authority in a country on the benchmark standards for higher education programs in psychology reflected in the *EuroPsy* Regulations. However, decisions on psychology education are taken at a number of different levels, both nationally and at European level. The Bologna process requires the Bachelor degree to lead to employability with a specification of learning outcomes which facilitate employment. Responding to this, and to national pressures on higher education funding, some countries may seek to define qualifications nationally at that level and to open up opportunities for employment.

In summary, the ideal of EFPA is to have a strong and independent profession of psychology setting its own standards of quality and competence. The realisation of this ideal will require consistent and continuous effort. In the international arena our profession is one of many players with sometimes convergent and at other times divergent interests. In the implementation of the *EuroPsy* system, EFPA is faced with the potential tension between an inclusive system which recognises as large a number of national systems as possible, and an exclusive system where membership is limited to those countries with the highest level of education requirements. The goal of EFPA is to maximise participation by countries in the *EuroPsy* system, and to support countries in enhancing their education and training in order to meet the standards of *EuroPsy*, thus improving the quality of psychology education and practice across Europe. There is no doubt that *EuroPsy* has already had an impact on some countries, and has succeeded in helping them to raise the level and quality of education and training for psychologists.

Diversity in Psychology Education

In the previous sections of this chapter we considered the development of the EHEA as envisaged in the Bologna Declaration and subsequent extensions. We have also shown how the *EuroPsy* Regulations appear to be in line with these developments. At the same time, we realise that the mechanisms and processes of harmonisation (or even greater convergence) may involve questionable assumptions and ideals. The *EuroPsy* Regulations (EFPA, 2013a) provide a listing of the various subjects that a student has to study with the approximate workload in the form of ECTS credits (see Chapter 3). When the NAC of a country applies for recognition to award *EuroPsy* Certificates the EAC has to consider the total number of ECTS credits and the distribution of such credits in approved university programs. In the *EuroPsy* Regulations substantial conformity to the listing of subjects for the first and the second cycle is required.

Evidence from 20 applications for recognition of NACs mainly from western European countries suggests that there is much conformity in the subject areas of psychology curricula, supporting the earlier finding by Newstead and Makinen (1997). Apparently there is regional consensus in Europe about the subjects that need to be covered in an academic curriculum for psychology. However, this does not imply that there can be no differences in the number of hours dedicated to a particular subject area. It is even less clear whether the correspondence of psychology curricula also implies correspondence in the theories and methods that are presented to students and in the experimental and applied research that they learn about. Countries where students read mainly English language textbooks (the Nordic countries, the Netherlands) tend to share the current mainstream in psychology "made in the US." Indigenous European traditions may be stronger in countries where there are textbooks and a research literature published in the local language, although textbook publishers are increasingly aware of the need to balance the globalising forces (e.g. "made in the US") with adaptations to suit Europe or other regions of the world.

There is considerable variation in the sociocultural and economic contexts of countries across Europe, reflected in ethnic and cultural diversity within and across countries, and in national and regional differences found for psychological variables such as well-being and values (e.g. European Social Survey, 2004; Veenhoven, 2012). The question whether, and if so how, this should have implications for academic curricula in psychology is hardly being discussed. In various countries outside of Europe there are movements towards the indigenisation of psychology (e.g. Adair, 2006; Allwood & Berry, 2006; Sinha, 1997), but the notion of regional or national indigenous psychologies features minimally as an issue within Europe. There seems to be an implicit assumption that when graduating in a second cycle program psychology students from Iceland to Russia and from Norway to Crete know more or less the same about the history of psychology, and are familiar with the same theories, paradigms and methods. We have some reservations about this assumption (Roe, 2014). As a consequence of the implicit beliefs about psychology as being shared, there is no history of arguments on possible implications of cultural diversity across countries for the education of psychologists. As far as we can see the movement towards convergence of formal structures through the Bologna Process does not rule out the possibility that educational content may reflect local circumstances and issues, including local theories and research traditions in psychology. So far quality assurance agencies for higher education operate at a national level and their experiences are mainly limited to curricula within their own country.

To the best of our knowledge there is no country in Europe where the *EuroPsy* Regulations have been rejected by the community of psychologists or by a substantial part of such a community, because these regulations are being seen as encroaching on local traditions of science and practice. This means that the Regulations, including the numbers of ECTS to be devoted to various subspecialties and topics listed in Appendix 7, have become a guiding document for curriculum development. As mentioned, this does not imply any prescription about the concrete theories and methods that are being taught in a curriculum.

Conclusion

The Bologna Process has set in motion a major drive towards harmonisation of higher education programmes. In providing a benchmark of quality in education the *EuroPsy* framework is contributing to this drive. Universities in various countries as well as national quality assurance agencies have started to adopt this framework (also published as the *Tuning* model for psychology). It is to be expected that this harmonisation will extend over more countries as associations of psychologists in more countries seek to participate in the *EuroPsy* system.

Convergence of education programs is necessary to facilitate the mobility of psychologists across Europe, a major goal of the European Union in seeking flexibility of the labour market. Convergence is desirable from the perspective of psychology as a science and profession, and this process is being guided by the *EuroPsy* Regulations adopted by EFPA (2013a). These regulations provide a benchmark for quality assessment of education programmes across Europe and are being used for this purpose by quality assurance agencies in an increasing number of countries.

5 The Competences of Psychologists[13]

In this chapter we will describe the way in which competences are defined and used in the context of *EuroPsy*. In the first section we discuss the importance of competences in developing and assessing professional qualifications, and in safeguarding the interests of psychologists' clients and the public. In the second section we offer a definition of competences and a clarification of their relationship to other notions, such as knowledge and skill. We also describe how competences are acquired through a continuing process of learning-by-doing and consider some alternative ways in which competences can be categorised and used. In the third section we introduce the system that was adopted by *EuroPsy*, which comprises 20 professional and 9 enabling competences. These are all generic and need to be specified when applied to different areas of psychology as well as different specialisations. The fourth section addresses the process of acquiring competences and the ways in which this can be enhanced. It discusses some educational principles and practical arrangements that can promote the process of competence acquisition. In the final section we describe ways in which the process and its outcomes can be documented and evaluated. We point out that post hoc documentation can be complemented or replaced by pro-active documentation, which can considerably support the learning process.

The Need for Definition of Psychologists' Competences

There are a number of reasons for adopting the notion of competence in the context of *EuroPsy*. The first is the need for an operational definition of the "state of the art" in professional psychology that informs psychologists, employers and clients, as well as other professionals and regulators about what represents good practice, that is, what to expect when obtaining services from psychologists. The second reason, related to the first, is quality assurance with regard to the professional activities of psychology, making sure that psychologists are sufficiently competent and do not practise beyond the limits of their competence. This is of importance in the relationship with clients as it defines the accountability of psychologists (Eraut, 1994; Poortinga & Lunt, 1997). The third reason is to promote the professional development of psychologists by giving guidance regarding the training needed for entry into the profession as well as continuing professional development practices. The fourth reason is to inform educators and students with regard to the training needed to become a competent psychologist. In this chapter, we focus on the

[13] This chapter relies considerably on the article Bartram, D., & Roe R. A. (2005). Definition and assessment of competences in the context of the European Diploma in Psychology. *European Psychologist, 10(2)*, 93–102. The tables have been reproduced with permission by the publisher.

system by which *EuroPsy* defines and uses competences. The functions of *EuroPsy* for the purposes mentioned here will be expanded upon in Chapters 6 and 7.

Definition of Competences

The notion of competence is much used in connection with education beyond the classroom, particularly in the workplace (e.g. Cheetham & Chivers, 2005; Malloch, Cairns, Evans & O'Connor, 2011), and in connection with human resources management practices (e.g. Rodriguez, Patel, Bright, Gregory & Gowing, 2002). *EuroPsy* uses a functional view of competence, defining it as "a learned ability to adequately perform a task, duty or role" (Roe, 2002, p. 195). According to this view, competences are acquired through a process of learning-by-doing, in which knowledge, skills, personal values and attitudes become integrated and connected to a particular task, duty or role. Figure 3 presents an architectural model of competence, based on the metaphor of a temple, that displays how competences relate to knowledge, skills and attitudes (KSAs) as well as to other personal characteristics. Competences are displayed as resting on the columns of KSAs. Underlying these are individual dispositions, that is, abilities, personality traits, interests, values, etc. As the dispositions are supposed to be more or less stable, their presence derives from preceding (self) selection. The other elements are seen as changeable and need to be acquired by learning at different stages of education and professional training. What this picture aims to convey is that dispositions represent capabilities for learning; that is, to acquire KSAs, whereas these latter are integrated into complex aptitudes that match the demands posed by tasks, duties or roles in particular work settings. An example for psychology is the integration of knowledge about psychopathology, assessment skills and an empathic attitude into diagnostic competence. The various competences and their constituting elements are added to the person's repertoire of learned capabilities

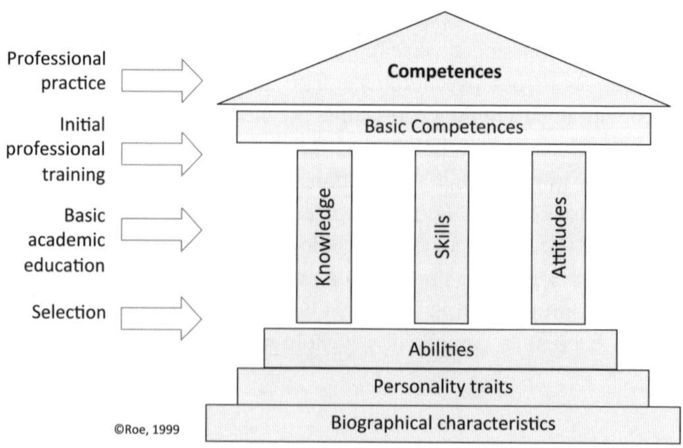

Figure 3. Architectural model of competences (Roe, 1999).

at different stages: most knowledge and skills during basic academic education, many attitudes and basic competences during initial professional education and training, and competences during professional training.

An essential characteristic of competences as defined here is that they are intricately related to a specific work environment and the role the psychologist is expected to perform. Having acquired a certain competence implies that a person masters all relevant KSAs, but also that she is aware of the unique context in which the work is performed, and is able to choose and carry out the appropriate action. What is appropriate is, on the one hand, a matter of "know how," following from the professional knowledge of psychology, and, on the other hand, determined by ethical and legal obligations. Here lies an important distinction with the lower level concepts of knowledge, skill and attitude. A person can have all the knowledge, skill and attitude required for a certain work role and yet not be competent, that is, able to act competently, taking into account all of the profession's expectations and obligations.

At this point, we shall make a note on the distinction between the terms competence and competency (Bartram & Roe, 2005; Whyddett & Hollyforde, 1999). We equate possessing a competence to being able to act competently in a given context, while carrying out a task, duty or role. In contrast, the term competency is often used to designate any attribute of a person that is associated with or contributing to this capability, regardless of whether it is an ability, personality trait, value, knowledge, skill or attitude. Possessing such competencies obviously does not make a person competent. Some form of learning is needed to amalgamate these qualities into the competence to carry out a task, duty or role in the expected manner.

Given this approach, there are of course many competences – as many as there are tasks, duties or roles. This has two important implications. First, one can distinguish between higher order competences, which are broader in scope and smaller in number, and lower order competences, for which the opposite holds. Making an individual treatment plan would be an example of competence at the level of an occupational duty; carrying out a diagnostic interview or administering a personality test would be an example of a task level competence. Roe (2002) defines a special category of low-level competences, which can be part of several high-level competences. Examples of such elementary or basic competences (also sub-competences) would be using spread-sheets or conducting interviews. Second, there is a unique set of competences for every occupational domain, that is, for every area of practice and specialisation in psychology. Thus, the clinical psychologist needs different competences (and associated KSAs) from the work and organisational psychologist. The learning trajectories leading to such competences, although sharing a range of common elements, are different as well. Below we will discuss how *EuroPsy* has dealt with this diversity and what it implies for developing and assessing competences.

Competences in the Psychological Profession

The competences that psychologists should possess have been spelled out in an article by Bartram and Roe (2005). They fall into two major categories, that is, professional (or primary) competences and enabling (or secondary) competences. It is important to distinguish these competences with regard to their content. For describing professional competences we use terms that can also be used to other occupations – which reveals that the psychological profession is one of many professions in the field of professional services, and indicates that there are dimensions on which psychologists can be compared with, for example, psychiatrists, counsellors, social workers or human resources managers. The content is different, however, and is specific for the psychological profession. This also applies to the enabling competences, but to a much lesser degree. They are rather similar across a broad range of occupations.

The professional competences distinguished by Bartram and Roe (2005) are listed and described in Table 9. There are 20 competences in six functional categories, that is, goal specification, assessment, development, intervention, evaluation and communication. This list was originally based on a model of psychologists' professional work as a cyclical series of activities aiming at identifying, clarifying and resolving clients' problems (Roe & Spaltro, 1988). An updated version of the original model is shown in Figure 4. The model describes the flow of the psychologist's activity when confronted with a demand for help by a client. The process starts with activities aiming to determine the goal to be reached, designated as Goal Specification. It includes Needs Analysis and Goal Setting (see Table 9 for descriptions). This is followed by Assessment, which can be differentiated into Individual, Group, Organisational and Situational assessment, and Intervention, which includes Planning and the use of different methods, including Direct Person-oriented or Situation-oriented methods, Indirect methods and Implementation of previously designed methods, which are labelled as Services or Products. This leads on to Evaluation of the effects of the intervention, which includes Planning, Measurement and Analysis, and Communication in the form of Feedback and Reporting. The model includes a category of activities, designated as Development (also referred to Design), which aims at the development of new Services or Products that can be used for Assessment, Intervention, Evaluation or Communication. Typical examples are test development and training design. It has a cyclical structure itself and involves Definition and Requirements Analysis, Design, Testing and Evaluation.

In addition to the 20 professional competences, psychologists should – like people in other professions – be able to organise their practice and function effectively while performing their professional roles. This is reflected in the nine enabling competences, listed in Table 10. It is important to underline the significance of these latter competences. Although they may seem remote from the core of the psychologist's work, they are essential for being able to work as a psychologist – either as employee or independent entrepreneur – and for rendering services in a professionally competent way. Figure 5 divides the enabling competences into two groups, labelled Business Management and Self-Management, and depicts them as supporting the professional competences that were just discussed. The first group includes Professional Strategy, Marketing and Sales, Account Management, Practice Management, Professional Relations and Quality Assurance. The second group includes Research and Development, Self Reflection and Continuing Professional Development.

The descriptions of the competences are clearly generic, that is, they pertain to classes of activities and situations that characterise the psychological profession at a general level. However, as was discussed in Chapter 1, the development of the psychological profession

Table 9. The 20 professional competences of EuroPsy (from EuroPsy Regulations, 2011)

Primary competences	Description
A. Goal specification	Interacting with the client for the purpose of defining the goals of the intervention or service that will be provided.
1. Needs analysis	Gathering information about the client's needs by means of appropriate methods, clarifying and analysing the needs to a point where meaningful further action can be taken.
2. Goal setting	Proposing and negotiating goals with the client, establishing acceptable and feasible goals and specifying criteria for evaluating goal fulfilment at a later time.
B. Assessment	Establishing relevant characteristics of individuals, groups, organisations and situations by means of appropriate methods.
3. Individual assessment	Carrying out assessment by means of interviewing, testing and observation of individuals in a setting relevant for the service demanded.
4. Group assessment	Carrying out assessment by means of interviewing, testing and observation of groups in a setting relevant for the service demanded.
5. Organisational assessment	Carrying out assessment by means of interviews, surveys, and other methods and techniques which are appropriate for studying organisations in a setting that is relevant for the service demanded.
6. Situational assessment	Carrying out assessment by means of interviews, surveys, and other methods and techniques which are appropriate for studying situations in a setting that is relevant for the service demanded.
C. Development	Developing interventions, services or products on the basis of psychological theory and methods for use by clients or psychologists.
7. Service or product definition & requirements analysis	Defining the purpose of the service or product, identifying relevant stakeholders, analysing requirements and constraints, and drawing up specifications for the product or service, taking into consideration the setting in which the service or product is to be used.
8. Service or product design	Designing or adapting services or products in accordance with requirements and constraints, taking into consideration the setting in which the service or product is to be used.
9. Service or product testing	Testing the service or product and assessing its feasibility, reliability, validity and other characteristics, taking into consideration the setting in which the service or product is to be used.
10. Service or product evaluation	Evaluating the service or product with respect to utility, client satisfaction, user friendliness, costs and other aspects which are relevant in the setting in which the service or product is to be used.
D. Intervention	Identifying, preparing and carrying out interventions which are appropriate for reaching the set goals, using the results of assessment and development activities.
11. Intervention planning	Developing an intervention plan that is appropriate for reaching the set goals in a setting relevant for the service demanded.

(continued on next page)

Table 9. (continued)

Primary competences	Description
12. Direct person-oriented intervention	Applying intervention methods that directly affect one or more individuals in accordance with the intervention plan, in a setting relevant for the service demanded.
13. Direct situation-oriented intervention	Applying intervention methods that directly affect selected aspects of the situation in accordance with the intervention plan, in a setting relevant for the service demanded.
14. Indirect intervention	Applying intervention methods that enable individuals, groups or organisations to learn and take decisions in their own interest, in a setting relevant for the service demanded.
15. Service or product implementation	Introducing services or products and promoting their proper use by clients or other psychologists.
E. Evaluation	Establishing the adequacy of interventions in terms of adherence to the intervention plan and the achievement of set goals.
16. Evaluation planning	Designing a plan for the evaluation of an intervention, including criteria derived from the intervention plan and the set goals, in a setting relevant for the service demanded.
17. Evaluation measurement	Selecting and applying measurement techniques that are appropriate for effecting the evaluation plan, in a setting relevant for the service demanded.
18. Evaluation analysis	Conducting analyses in accordance with the evaluation plan, and drawing conclusions on the effectiveness of interventions in a setting relevant for the service demanded.
F. Communication	Providing information to clients in a way that is adequate to fulfil the clients' needs and expectations.
19. Giving feedback	Providing feedback to clients, using appropriate oral and/or audio-visual means, in a setting relevant for the service demanded.
20. Report writing	Writing reports as to inform clients about the results of assessment, service or product development, interventions, and/or evaluations, in a setting relevant for the service demanded.

has led to a marked differentiation of roles over time. As a result, there are nowadays several forms of professional psychology that differ from each other in the type of setting in which psychologists work, the clients and problems they work with, the objectives they try to achieve, and so on. There are also differences in the kinds of theories and methods used, the tools employed, etc. These differences are rather obvious if one considers the work of psychologists in schools, business organisations, clinics and hospitals, traffic environments, the legal systems, the military, and so on. Clients and users also recognise these different roles and the public in general is to an extent, also aware. To promote that psychologists act and perform competently in all these settings, it is necessary to acknowledge

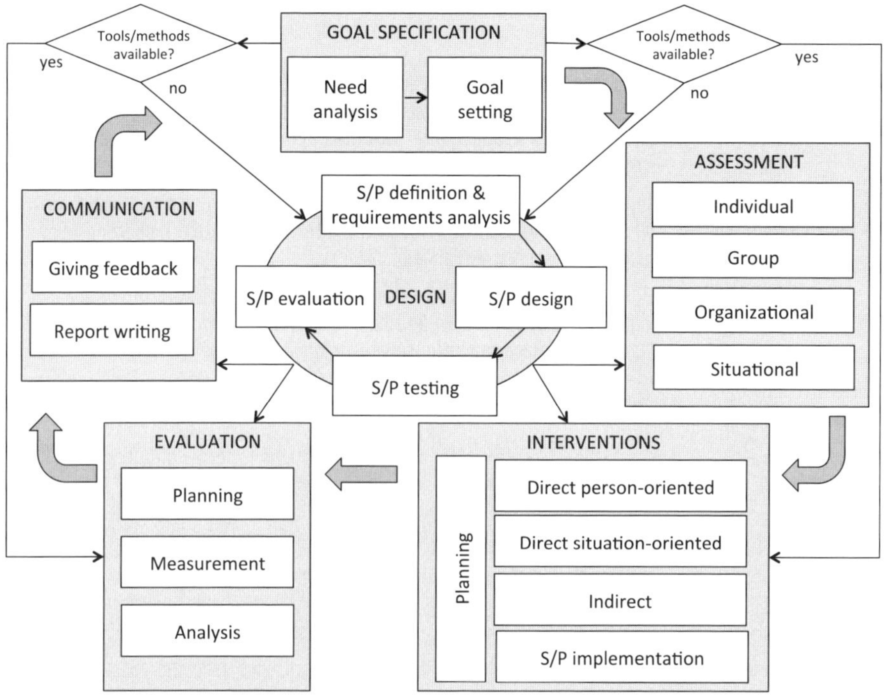

Figure 4. Process model of psychologists' professional competences.

the differences. It is particularly important to emphasise the fact that psychologists cannot be expected to be competent in all these settings, and that being competent in one setting does not imply competence in other settings. Thus, for example, work and organisational psychologists cannot be expected to be competent in clinical psychology, or vice versa, unless they receive additional education and training, including supervised practice.

EuroPsy addresses this issue by distinguishing between so-called "areas of practice." It explicitly states that psychologists' competences should generally be considered as limited to one area or field of practice, unless there is evidence that shows competence in another area. This limitation is important in order to raise the awareness of psychologists, as well as their clients, of the limits of their competence and to prevent them practicing beyond those limits. While this points to the relationship of professional competences with ethics and accountability, there is also an implication for the enabling competences. Effectively managing a psychological practice in school psychology or military psychology, requires similar yet distinct competences in example professional relations, or practice management.

At the launch of *EuroPsy* it was decided to limit the number of areas of practice for which certificates could be obtained to three, namely Clinical and Health, Work and

Table 10. The nine enabling competences of EuroPsy (from EuroPsy Regulations, 2013)

Competences	Definition
1. Professional strategy	Choosing an appropriate strategy for dealing with the problem(s) posed, based on a reflection on the professional situation and one's own primary competences.
2. Continuing professional development	Updating and developing one's primary and enabling competences, knowledge and skills in accordance with changes in the field and the standards and requirements of the psychological profession, national and European EFPA Regulations on *EuroPsy*.
3. Professional relations	Establishing and maintaining relationships with other professionals, as well as relevant organisations.
4. Research and development	Developing new interventions, services and products that have the potential of fulfilling current or future clients' needs and generating new forms of professional activity or business.
5. Marketing & sales	Bringing current and new products and services to the attention of actual or potential clients, contacting clients, making business offers, selling services, providing after-sales services.
6. Account management	Establishing and maintaining relationships with (potential) clients, monitoring clients' needs and satisfactions, identifying opportunities for expanding professional activity or business.
7. Practice management	Designing and managing the practice from which services are rendered, whether as a small business or as part of a larger private or public organisation, including financial, personnel and operational aspects, providing leadership to employees.
8. Quality assurance	Establishing and maintaining a system for quality assurance for the practice as a whole.
9. Self reflection	Critical self-reflection on own practice and competence is a key feature of professional competence.

Organisation, and Education. Areas of practice such as Forensic, Traffic or Sports, were provisionally grouped into one broad category, designated as "Other," with the idea of subdividing it later, depending on the number of psychologists applying for a certificate in each area. New categories may emerge, which reflect specific developments in terms of professional practice, in different European countries or in the whole of Europe. Important aspects of this development would be demand from clients, and the public visibility and recognition of this area of psychological practice. In any case, specialisms are not meant to be included in this "Other" category that aims to classify the contexts of practice at the initial level of independent practice. Table 11 gives a cursory characterisation of these three areas, whereas Table 12 shows some of the similarities and differences at the level of competences.

It will be clear from the descriptions given in Tables 9, 10 and 12, that being competent requires a substantial repertoire of detailed knowledge and a variety of skills and

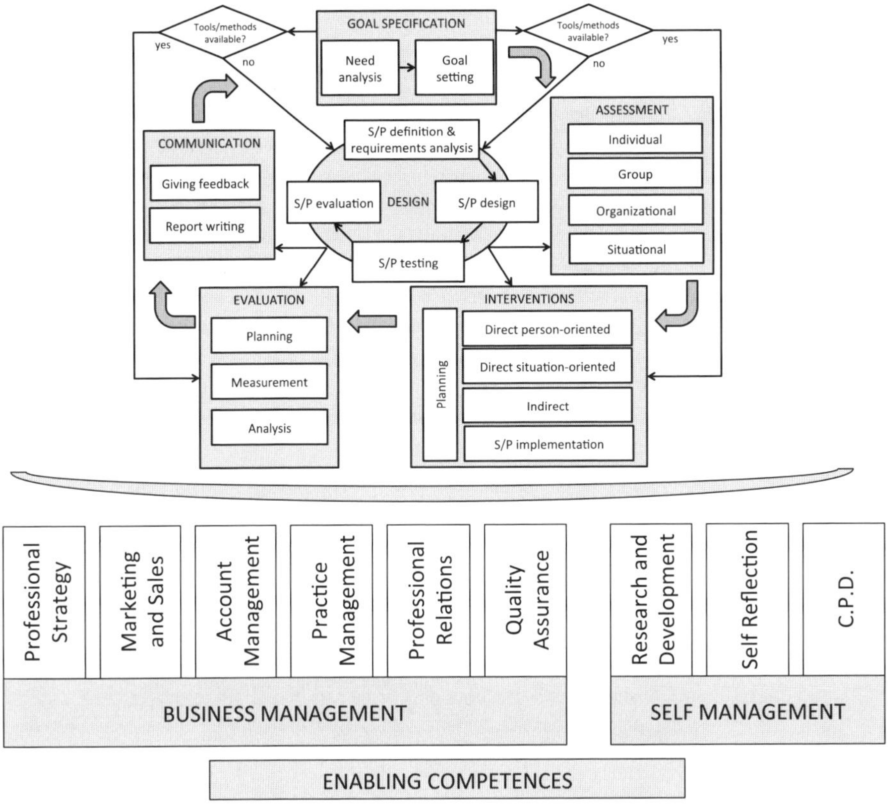

Figure 5. Enabling competences supporting psychologists' professional competences.

attitudes, as well as several basic competences. Ideally, most of these elements would have been acquired during academic education and training, implying that the process of acquiring competences would mainly focus at their integration – as is described below (and in Chapter 6). However, not all academic curricula are the same and it is possible that not all necessary elements will have been covered when the process of competence development should start. This indicates that the list of competences required by *EuroPsy* should have implications for the content of the preceding education and training. As was explained in Chapter 4, the curriculum should not only meet the requirements of content, structure and volume, but also provide the basis for subsequent competence learning. It will often be necessary to refresh and complement what was learned during the academic studies when entering into practice-based learning. Particularly important at this stage is learning the proper attitudes, since in basic education they are often not treated explicitly and are given less attention than knowledge and skills. Yet, they are crucially important in developing the appropriate behaviours vis-à-vis clients and colleagues. Examples of important attitudes are: accuracy, integrity, self-criticism, commitment, responsibility, respect and tolerance for others, ethical awareness, service orientation, etc. (Roe, 2002).

Table 11. Job content in three areas of practice (after Bartram & Roe, 2005)

	Area of practice		
	Health	**W&O**	**Education**
Work setting	Private practice or clinic, public health care institution	Consultancy, business firm, public service, government agency	School, educational institution, public service, government agency
Coworkers	Support staff, medical doctors, social workers	Support staff, economists, engineers, HRM-specialists. managers.	Support staff, pedagogues, didactical experts
Client	Individuals, families or other small groups	Individual employees and managers. Groups, organisations, trade unions, public agencies	Individual students, parents and teachers. Schools, public agencies
Purpose	Promotion of mental and physical health of individuals and families	Optimisation of productivity, social relations and well-being of individuals in organisations	Optimisation of learning and adaptation of individuals in educational settings
Object	Individuals. Household and family arrangements	Individuals, groups, larger entities. Social and physical work environment. Work tools and equipment. Policies and procedures	Pupils, teachers. Educational tools and equipment. Courses and curricula. Policies & procedures
Tools	Tests, observation schemes, interviews; models of disorders and abnormal behavior; therapy protocols	Tests, observation schemes, interviews, surveys, group and organisational assessment techniques; models of behavior in work settings; design and change methods	Tests, observation schemes, interviews, surveys; models of behavior in educational settings; design and change methods
Methods	Individual and family assessment. Counseling, behavior modification, hypnosis, psychotherapy	Job and organisational analysis. Selection, appraisal, training, career development. Job, team, organisation and workplace design. Organisational change	Methods for needs analysis. Methods for curriculum design. Methods for learning and performance assessment
Timing	According to individual needs	According to business needs and cycles	According to educational needs and cycles

Competence Acquisition

The acquisition of competences requires learning processes at three levels. The first level is that of KSAs. The second is that of basic competences, such as planning, documenting or interviewing, which integrate certain elements of KSAs in ways that allow the fulfilment of task demands in the context of various broader tasks. The third level is that of

Table 12. Competences in three areas of practice (after Bartram & Roe, 2005)

	Area of practice		
	Health	W&O	Education
Goal definition			
1. Needs analysis competence	Gathering information by intake interview and anamnesis in clinical setting. Clarification and analysis of client needs.	Gathering information by intake interview and document analysis in industrial setting. Clarification and analysis of client needs.	Gathering information by intake interview and document analysis in educational setting. Clarification and analysis of client needs.
2. Goal setting competence	Proposing and negotiating goals with client. Establishing goals and specifying criteria.	Proposing and negotiating goals with client. Establishing goals and specifying criteria.	Proposing and negotiating goals with client. Establishing goals and specifying criteria.
Assessment			
3. Individual assessment competence	Interviewing, testing, observation in clinical setting.	Interviewing, testing, observation in industrial setting.	Interviewing, testing, observation in educational setting.
4. Group assessment competence	Group interviewing, group observation.	Group interviewing, group observation, role analysis.	Group interviewing, classroom observation, role analysis.
5. Organisational assessment competence	*Does not apply.*	Employee surveys; communication analysis; culture, assessment; structural analysis; performance analysis.	Student surveys; teacher surveys; communication analysis; performance analysis.
6. Situational assessment competence	Analysis of family, school, occupational setting.	Job analysis, work place analysis, employee surveys.	Course analysis, curriculum analysis, analysis of learning environment.
Development			
7. Service or product definition and requirement analysis competence	Therapy and counseling programs and aids; therapeutic training courses; education and prevention schemes.	Tests, AC's, itw's, surveys; HRM procedures, systems and policies; work tools and methods; time schedules; jobs; organisational structures; communication schemes; organisational change schemes.	Achievement tests; assessment techniques; didactical tools and methods; educational procedures, policies; courses, curricula, study aids and methods; educational change schemes.
8. Service or product design competence	Design or adaptation of aforementioned products.	Design or adaptation of aforementioned products	Design or adaptation of aforementioned products.
9. Service or product testing competence	Examination of feasibility, reliability. validity, etc.	Examination of feasibility, reliability, validity, etc.	Examination of feasibility, reliability, validity, etc.

(continued on next page)

Table 12. (continued)

	Area of practice		
	Health	**W&O**	**Education**
10. Service or product evaluation competence	Examination of utility, client satisfaction, user friendliness, costs in clinical use.	Examination of utility, client satisfaction, user friendliness, costs in industrial use.	Examination of utility, client satisfaction, user friendliness, costs in educational use.
Intervention			
11. Intervention planning competence	Developing treatment plan in clinical setting.	Developing plan for personal and situational intervention in industrial setting.	Developing plan for personal and situational intervention in educational setting.
12. Direct person-oriented intervention competence	Individual advice, counseling, behavior modification, hypnosis, psychotherapy, play therapy, psychodrama.	Selection, training, career development; group interventions; organisation development	Individual advice, counseling, remedial teaching; counseling and training of teachers.
13. Direct situation-oriented intervention competence	Implementation of new tools, methods, procedures, schemes. Introducing changes in clinical environment.	Implementation of new tools, methods, procedures, schemes. Introducing changes in work environment	Implementation of new tools, methods, procedures, schemes. Introducing changes in educational environment.
14. Indirect intervention competence	Guidance, counseling, training of partner, parent, staff, community agencies.	Guidance or training of managers or staff in industrial setting.	Guidance or training of managers or staff in educational setting.
15. Service or product implementation competence	Implementation of therapeutic schemes, etc.	Implementation of work took, methods, schemes, etc.	Implementation of educational tools, methods, schemes, etc.
Evaluation			
16. Evaluation planning competence	Plan for evaluation of advice, counseling, therapy, etc.	Plan for evaluation of selection, training, career development, etc.	Plan for evaluation of advice, teaching, counseling, remedial teaching, etc.
17. Evaluation measurement competence	Assessment of criteria for health and well-being.	Assessment of criteria for productivity, effectiveness, efficiency and well-being.	Assessment of criteria for learning, adaptation and well-being.
18. Evaluation analysis competence	Analysis of intervention effectiveness.	Analysis of intervention effectiveness.	Analysis of intervention effectiveness.
Communication			
19. Feedback-giving competence	Providing oral feedback to individual clients.	Providing oral feedback to individual clients; giving group presentations.	Providing oral feedback to individual clients; giving group presentations.
20. Report writing competence	Reports on assessment, products designed, interventions and evaluations.	Reports on assessment, products designed, interventions and evaluations.	Reports on assessment products designed, interventions and evaluations.

job-specific competences (e.g. selection interviewing), which integrate KSAs as well as basic competences (Bartram & Roe, 2008). Typical for the development of competences is that they emerge from learning-by-doing, that is, from the performance of task-related activities in a realistic and representative environment (Bereiter, 2002; Onstenk, 2002). This can either be the actual work setting or a simulated work setting, which allows for better controlled and more effective learning processes. The learning of competences has been described as informal and implicit (Garrick, 1998; Marsick & Watkins, 1990) to indicate that it can take place in the absence of explicit learning goals, formal methods of instruction, learning materials, etc. It can involve a range of different learning processes, such as problem solving, analogous reasoning and exploration, but also following examples from colleagues, leaders or other role models (e.g. Nadler, Thompson & van Boven, 2003). As people start performing new tasks they will start doing so at a knowledge-based level (Rasmussen, 1986), explicitly analysing the problem, demands to meet, circumstances to consider, risks or dangers to be prevented, etc. They will call upon existing knowledge and skills, and follow existing attitudes in designing and trialling suitable actions, and learn from the success and failure in the outcomes of their work. As they build mental models and routines, they will move to a rule-based level and perform the task more swiftly and smoothly. The decreasing mental capacity needed while automating the actions and moving to a skill-based level of execution, opens room for further exploration of additional task demands and conditions, that is, adding complexity.

Competence acquisition can be promoted in several ways (e.g. Bartram & Roe, 2008). A first and obvious way is by creating the opportunity to perform the actual tasks in a realistic or simulated setting. Thus, psychologists should be interacting with real clients and be involved in diagnosing and helping to solve their problems. The situation should be such that it allows for control of the variety and complexity of the tasks, to make sure that all relevant tasks and conditions can be practised. Ideally, there should be opportunity to perform rare tasks and practise exceptional situations, which would not happen frequently enough to allow for learning. Moreover, it is desirable to have room to make mistakes, in order to learn from them. Simulated work settings, equipped with audio-visual aids and gaming tools, and the use of role-playing and exercises may make these requirements easier to meet than the actual work situation, where the psychologist interacts with real clients. The learning process can be enhanced by using particular instructional techniques, such as scaffolding (e.g. James, Milne & Morse, 2008) or deliberate practice (e.g. Sonnentag & Kleine, 2000), which enable the learner to build up competences in a more systematic manner. Secondly, to guide competence development, it is desirable to have, in addition, a plan that lays out which competences need to be developed and which basic competences and KSAs ought to be present (refreshed, or additionally learned). Considering that each psychologist will have been placed in a unique work setting and will have to develop by a personal learning trajectory, such a plan should provide for sufficient degrees of freedom as well as flexibility. Third, competence acquisition will profit from an environment with a positive learning climate (Clarke, 2005) which provides sufficient and appropriate feedback and stimulates critical reflection. Fourth, competence acquisition can profit greatly from the presence of a supervisor who can help to choose learning tasks, monitor the execution of tasks and the learning process, provide guidance and feedback, etc. As will be shown in Chapter 6, this is a major reason for supervised practice in the context of *EuroPsy*.

Describing, Documenting and Assessing Competences

To make the process of competence acquisition more explicit and open to guidance and assessment, some degree of description and documentation is necessary. As for assessments they should make it possible to (1) direct and support the process of competence development, giving information on the learner's latest achievements and signalling possible next steps; and (2) evaluate the degree of competence attained by the end of a training trajectory. This distinction is known as formative versus summative assessment. A minimum requirement is that it is clear – to the learner and the supervisor – which competences are to be attained within the relevant area of practice, and which level of mastery has been obtained for each competence at certain points in time.

Since the descriptions of the professional and enabling competences given by *EuroPsy* are generic, they cannot serve to guide or evaluate learning without some degree of specification. One might say that they have to be operationalised in a way that matches the typical features of the work situation in a particular area of practice. This can be done by writing "task statements" that specify what the psychologist should be able to do in terms of activities, methods, facts and circumstances to consider, and outcomes that should be obtained. Such task statements will allow for differentiation between areas of practice, as well as between more specific settings within these areas (e.g. in the clinical and health area: hospital, community or family settings).

We distinguish between two general ways of documenting and assessing competence development. The first and most common type is *retrospective*; it looks back at what a candidate has been doing during a certain time-period in the past, and compares this to what would be expected based on the aimed-for competence profile. This approach is appropriate when a psychologist applies for *EuroPsy* after having gained substantial work experience, and competences need to be assessed post hoc. The second type is *prospective*; it spells out competences at the start of practical work and uses them as targets that can guide the psychologist's activities, thereby giving a projected individual learning-path. The actual activities and achievements can then be compared with this trajectory, as the learning process unfolds. This second approach is more suitable when psychologists pass through a phase of supervised practice.

There are three main tools that can be used to *document* a person's track record, a structured curriculum vitae, a portfolio and a competence development record (Lunt & Peiro, 2012; Roe, 2007). The structured curriculum vitae should be used in all cases. It is similar to the resumé that people prepare at various moments in their career. The difference is that it has a standardised format and that it contains evidence on the competences that have been acquired at the time that the person files an application for *EuroPsy* certification. It gives a chronological description of the positions fulfilled and professional activities performed, in such a way that it reveals relevant practice learning experiences for each of the required competences. The use of a Portfolio is optional but recommended. It is a folder that contains all sorts of evidence about previous jobs, showing which activities

Competence	What	For whom	When	How	Result
Goal setting	Doing intakes with new clients	Own firm	2001–2002	Interviews with managers and follow-ups	Description of aims in project plans
	Intakes with employees in career planning	Phillips Ltd.	2004	Individual sessions	Aims for development plans
Individual assessment	Testing applicants	AABER Consulting	2002–2003	Administration of test battery	Selection advice for 78 candidates
	Conducting employee interviews	CB bank	2006–2007	Design of interview, 2 hour sessions, writing protocols and giving ratings	Recommendations on improvement in working conditions and employee development
Product design	Knowledge test development	AABER Consulting	2002–2003	Exploring technical knowledge domain, generating questions, field testing, item analysis, making scoring rules and norms	Technical Knowledge Test (on-line, 30 items, for technical sales people)
	Employee attitude questionnaire	CB bank	2007	Generating questions for 4 domains based on exploratory interviews; data gathering, scale analysis	Annual Satisfaction Survey (40 items, 5-point Likert)

Figure 6. Example of a competence development record (fragment).

were performed, for whom, when, how, what was produced, how it was evaluated etc. It serves to back up the Structured CV and to provide proof of positions, activities, outcomes, etc. The use of a competence development record is also recommended. It is a tabular sheet that lists the various activities that have been performed mapping them on the competences to be learned; an outline is given in Figure 6. Moreover, during the supervised practiced either during the "stage" (internship) or during the year of supervised practice we recommend to the student or intern to describe a few professional actions carried out to exemplify how he has practised the different competences of the model (see e.g. in Lunt & Peiró, 2012). The following points may be considered in order to produce the description (Figure 6):

1. The context in which the activities were performed and why they were performed.
2. The client and users (target of the activities) and other relevant parties.

3. The activities performed to show the competence under analysis in operation.
4. Tools Used for Needs Analysis/Identification.
5. Any special actions taken to protect against inadequate judgments, decisions or interventions that might harm the client.
6. The outputs that have been produced during the process and their effectiveness.
7. The kind of evidence that may be presented to demonstrate competent performance of the performed activities.
8. The rationale pointing out to what extent what has been described reflects the implementation of the professional competence under consideration.

Another documentation tool, which is recommended for use in connection with the prospective approach to competence development, is the competence development scheme (Roe, 2007). This represents a plan and a progress chart at the same time. It sets out the competences the person should develop over time, and at which moment a particular level of competence shall be reached. However, it also permits a record of the various levels of competence that actually have been reached, which gives good insight into the overall progress. Its logic is illustrated in Figure 7, which shows the competences that a person intends to work on during the next period, along with target dates at which these competences should be mastered. This scheme is useful as a planning tool during the supervision process. Both supervisor and supervisee may plan using this tool for the activities to carry out during the supervision period, taking into account the sequencing intended during the training and also the contextual factors, such as the demands that the supervisee's clients have during the period under consideration. The scheme also allows for recording progress over time with regard to each competence, which may reach the aimed for level at the target time, or at an earlier or later moment. The scale used for determining the level of mastery is one that is used for assessing competences throughout the whole *EuroPsy* system, and is described below.

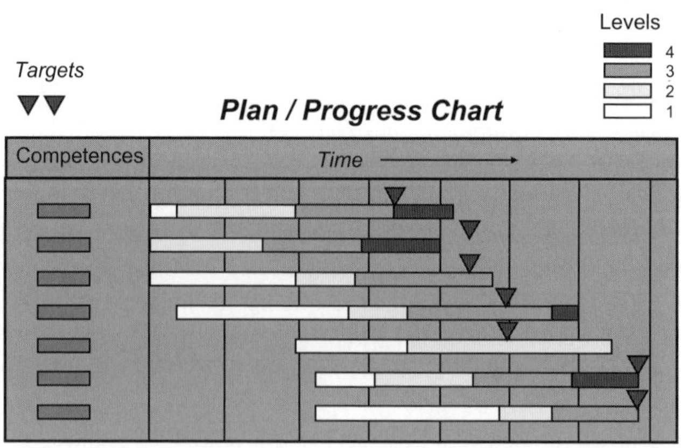

Figure 7. Logic of the competence development scheme (Roe, 2007).

1	2	3	4
Basic knowledge and skill present, but competence insufficiently developed	Competence for performing basic tasks but requiring guidance and supervision	Competence for performing basic tasks without guidance or supervision	Competence for performing complex tasks without guidance or supervision

Figure 8. Scale for competence assessment.

Ideally, both the retrospective and prospective assessment of competences should start with a list of the competences that the psychologist working in a particular area of practice should acquire. However, the actual procedure followed for these two types of assessment differs. In the first case the assessment is normally made by members of a National Awarding Committee who review the psychologist's application, taking into account the Structured CV and – if available – other documents. They may ask for additional information, written or by means of an oral interview. Since the period of supervised work has already passed there is no formative assessment, but only a more general summative assessment that may be accompanied by recommendations for additional training or supervised practice. In the second case there will be a supervisor who regularly meets with the psychologist, making formative assessments and giving guidance on every occasion. These assessments can extend to new KSAs, acquired after the basic education was completed. The summative assessment will follow at the end of the period of supervised practice, and afterwards be reviewed by the National Awarding Committee as part of the overall application.

The rating scale used for the assessment is the same for all competences. It is shown in Figure 8.

Until now, summative assessments have been limited to the six groups of professional competences and to the group of enabling competences as a whole. This implies that not each of the separate competences has to be fully developed, and that there is room for a certain degree of compensation (Bartram & Roe, 2005). The current requirement is that the competences have reached level 3 or 4, which implies that the psychologist can practice independently. This requirement must be met for all groups of competences with regard to a particular area of practice – without the possibility of compensation across areas of practice. For example, a psychologist who is competent in goal specification, assessment, and communication in one area, and in development, intervention and evaluation in another area of practice would not be qualified for independent practice in either of those areas. In order for a psychologist to qualify for independent practice in two or more areas she would need to meet all (group level) competence requirements for each of the areas separately. Figure 9 gives an example of a profile for a psychologist with competence in two areas of practice.

The assessment of competences is a facet of *EuroPsy* that is likely to be revised in future years (see Chapter 10). As the professional training advances and more experience is gained with supervised competence development, we may see a move to a system in

Areas of Practice	*W&O*	*Education*
Functions		
A. Goal definition	✓	
B. Assessment	✓	✓
C. Development	✓	
D. Intervention	✓	
E. Evaluation	✓	✓
F. Communication	✓	✓
Enabling competences	✓	✓

Figure 9. Example of competences across two areas of practice.

which competences are evaluated one-by-one. The summative, overall assessment would then be based on the separate competences in each of the categories.

Experience with developing and assessing competences according to the methods outlined here are still very limited. Lunt and Peiró (2012; See also Martinez-Tur, Peiró & Rodriguez, 2014) describe an application in the context of a curriculum where students have to do practical work with the purpose of developing competences. They give an example of how students employed as "interns," prepare a report for their supervisor in which they describe the context where their work activities were performed, the clients and users, the activities performed, the tools used, special actions to "prevent endangering" the client or users, the outputs produced, the kind of evidence obtained to demonstrate competence, and a rationale for linking all this to particular competences. They also show how such detailed reports enable supervisors to respond and provide guidance. Further experiences with these and other tools will accrue as *EuroPsy* is being implemented in more professional settings and countries.

Conclusion

In order to qualify for professional practice, psychologists should complement their academic education, which provides them with the essential KSAs, as well as basic competences, with a range of competences that are related to interacting with clients and fulfilling the role of professional. *EuroPsy* therefore uses a model that specifies which competences should be acquired and specifies the degree of mastery that is required for entry into practice. In fact, it spells out twenty professional competences and nine enabling competences that should be developed during a period of supervised practice. The competences are described in generic terms, which are applicable to all forms of psychological practice, but they should be specified for the particular area in which the psychologist is going to practice.

6 Supervised Practice and Professional Education

As was noted in the previous chapter, competence development can be greatly enhanced through supervision and supervised practice. For this purpose *EuroPsy* poses the requirement that psychologists have at least 1 year of supervised practice. In this chapter we first provide an introduction to the rationale and general concept of supervised practice. This is followed by a brief discussion of definitions and approaches to supervision and supervised practice. We then present the framework for supervised practice provided by *EuroPsy*. A description of the broad differences in the development of supervised practice in different countries of Europe leads to a discussion of how the implementation of *EuroPsy* represents an opportunity to implement across Europe one of the most powerful tools and procedures of psychologists' education and training as professionals. In this context we will present two case studies on how supervised practice has been undertaken to inform and develop education and training for psychologists in two European countries: Spain and Slovenia. In the final sections we discuss the importance of supervisor training and the use of a Register of accredited or recognised supervisors.

Rationale for Supervised Practice and the Main Functions

The major purpose of supervised practice is to provide the psychologist-in-training (sometimes referred to as the supervisee) with opportunities for learning, that is, to deepen and extend his knowledge, skills and attitudes, and to integrate these in ways that match the demands of professional practice. More specifically, the acquisition of competence requires practice, and feedback on practice. It is not sufficient for psychologists-in-training to rely on the knowledge and understanding acquired through university education, lectures, seminars, reading and coursework, sometimes called "declarative" or "propositional" knowledge. What is also needed is "procedural, or process, knowledge" or what Schön (1987) has referred to as "knowing-in-action," gained through applying knowledge in practice and learning-by-doing. Schön uses the term "professional artistry" to refer to "the kinds of competence practitioners sometimes display in unique, uncertain and conflicted situations of practice" (p. 22), and this, he considers, involves "knowing-in-action," a form of knowledge that is gained through practice, reflection on practice and feedback on practice. Thus Eraut (1994) describes "process" knowledge as

> partly a matter of knowing all the things one has to do and making sensible plans for doing them; and partly a matter of using practical, routinized skills. The former can be grasped intellectually, through reading and discussion, though plans always have to be fitted to each individual context, so it is not just a matter of following simple checklists and algorithms. The latter, however, cannot be learned in this way: practical skills can only be acquired through practice with feedback – a learning opportunity that is often in short supply (p. 81).

Essential for competence acquisition is that existing knowledge and skills are connected to the dynamically unfolding situation, and that rules of professional ethics and relevant social, legal and economic conditions are taken into account, in interaction with the client. Supervised practice helps the newly qualified psychologist to deal with the complexities of this multifaceted learning process. It also enables her to develop reflection, self-awareness and the personal integrity required for competent practice, and forms an important element of socialisation and the development of ethical and accountable practice.

Supervised practice has increasingly become an essential part of the professional training of all the so-called helping or welfare professions (psychologists, social workers, psychotherapists, and indeed nurses and medical doctors) (Hawkins & Shohet, 2006; Scaife, 2001). It is widely regarded both as a means for the trainee to develop competence, and as a form of induction and socialisation into the profession, replicating professional canons and helping to maintain the norms and standards of the profession and of society. From the viewpoint of the profession it serves a "gate-keeping" function, ensuring that only those who are appropriately qualified and competent are admitted, and that the safety and well-being of clients is warranted. In this way, the supervisor fulfils both an educational and an evaluative function, supporting the practitioners-in-training through their learning and development, and then evaluating their competence in order to ensure that they are ready to act as qualified members of the particular profession.

Supervised practice requires arrangements that specify the roles of the psychologist and the supervisor, the setting in which they meet, the ways in which they interact, the documentation of the process and the learning outcomes, and the assessment of the latter. Examples of these are given later in this chapter. It should be noted that the term supervision carries different meanings in different languages and areas of psychology, and that sometimes other terms are preferred. Some examples are: "mentoring," "coaching," "support," "consultation." While mental health professionals tend to use the term "supervision," the terms "coaching" or "mentoring" are frequently used by work and organisational psychologists, while the term "consultation" is increasingly used by school psychologists. In this text these terms will be used interchangeably when referring to psychologists-in-training.

Critical elements of supervision include:

- Helping to identify the learning goals, the tasks to practise and the context where they will be practised and the intended outputs.
- Guidance and modelling in professional actions for practice.
- Transfer of professional expertise.
- Helping to develop the ethical awareness and competence needed to deal with complex cases and tasks.
- Managing increasing complexity in learning.
- Reflection and feedback on learning, including learning from errors, providing assessment of the progress and inputs about next learning steps.
- Monitoring interaction with clients, (including ethical aspects).
- Protecting against inadequate judgments, decisions or interventions that might harm the client.

Finally, an important function of supervised practice is the evaluation of the level achieved by the trainee in the competences of the *EuroPsy* model through performance assessment. The results of these summative or final evaluations are required as an annexe which is presented with the application for *EuroPsy* to the National Awarding Committees (NACs).

These functions of supervision involve competences which can be learned (by those undertaking supervision), and indeed it is possible to identify and describe the essential features of effective supervision. Education and training of psychologists in the practice of supervision is increasingly being provided by various organisations, for example, universities, professional associations and other organisations and will be discussed later in this chapter.

A Closer Look at Supervision and Supervised Practice

There are many different definitions of supervision. Here we select three for illustrative purposes:

> supervision is an intervention provided by a more senior member of a profession to a more junior member of that same profession. This relationship is evaluative, extends over time, and has the simultaneous purposes of enhancing the professional functioning of the more junior person, monitoring the quality of professional services offered to the clients seen, and serving as a gatekeeper for those who are to enter a particular profession (Bernard & Goodyear, 2004, p. 8).

The second definition includes more specific aspects, and defines supervision as:

> the formal provision, by approved supervisors, of a relationship-based education and training that is work-focused and which manages, supports, develops and evaluates the work of colleague/s. The main methods that supervisors use are corrective feedback on the supervisee's performance, teaching, and collaborative goal-setting. It therefore differs from related activities such as mentoring and coaching, by incorporating an evaluative component. Supervision's objectives are "normative," "restorative" and "formative." (Milne, 2007, p. 437)

Finally a third definition is provided by Falender and Shafranske (2004):

> Supervision is a distinct professional activity in which education and training aimed at developing science-informed practice are facilitated through a collaborative interpersonal process. It involves observation, evaluation, feedback, the facilitation of supervisee self-assessment, and the acquisition of knowledge and skills by instruction, modelling and mutual problem-solving. In addition, by building on the recognition of the strengths and talents of the supervisee, supervision encourages self-efficacy. Supervision ensures that clinical consultation is conducted in a competence manner in which ethical standards, legal prescriptions, and professional practices are used to promote and protect the welfare of the client, the profession, and society at large (p. 3).

Important to note from these definitions are the focus on the relationship, the educative function, the evaluative aspect, the use of feedback, and the gate-keeping function. We restrict our discussion here mainly to supervision provided by a more senior member of a profession to a more junior member, in particular to psychologists-in-training, and in the context of the year of supervised practice. However, we emphasise, with Roth (2010), that "supervision is not restricted to individuals in training . . . senior practitioners continue to seek out and receive supervision, making it ubiquitous across the professional lifespan" (p. xiii) and in Chapter 7 we extend the discussion to include other forms of professional support, and professional supervision, as part of Continuing Professional Development, including Peer Supervision or Inter-vision.

There are a number of approaches to supervision in different professional domains, and most welfare professions now require an element of supervised practice as part of the qualification for independent practice. Beinart (2012) has provided a useful overview of different approaches to supervision, which she divides into two main types, those derived from psychotherapy theories, and those developed to explain supervision itself. Within the approaches derived from psychotherapy theories, there are psychodynamic, cognitive and cognitive-behavioural, client-centred and existential-humanistic, and systemic models, as well as models deriving from other psychotherapeutic approaches. The second type of approach has been broadly divided into developmental models, social role models, and integrative models (for a useful discussion see Beinart, 2012; Beinart & Clohessy, 2009; and see Falender & Shafranske, 2004). Falender and Shafranske (2004) add a third approach, the so-called "process-based approaches" (though these are sometimes referred to as "social role supervision models") which aim to provide reliable and valid procedures for analysing and evaluating the supervision process itself, and assessing its outcomes. It is important to be reminded here that supervision is an educative process, and is not a form of psychotherapy. This means that theories of adult learning such as Kolb's Experiential Learning Model (1984), which stresses the importance of the learning cycle, of: do, review, learn, apply or: experience, experimentation, reflection and observation, and the reflective practice model of Schön (1987) have been useful in providing models for supervised practice and for developing training in supervision.

There are different ways in which supervised practice may be arranged. It is normally considered to be a period of full-time work under supervision within a professional setting, either as part of the university education of the psychologist, or, more often, immediately following the university education. At this "stage," the psychologist-in-training is not working as an independent practitioner, but working under the supervision and guidance of a more experienced psychologist who provides regular meetings and feedback, and who takes some responsibility for the work of the trainee.

Supervised Practice as a Central Element of Professional Education in *EuroPsy*

As mentioned at the beginning of the chapter, supervised practice is central to the development of competent performance and the acquisition of competences required for professional practice as a psychologist. Thus it is a key component of the *EuroPsy* Certificate, and provides the opportunity for the psychologist practitioner-in-training to put into practice the knowledge, skills and understanding gained from the university education and other professional experiences ... (and) to develop attributes of self-awareness, reflectivity, personal integrity, ethical competence and robustness which are required to practise competently and responsibly (EFPA, 2013a).

In the previous chapter we described the use of competences to ensure professional competence; this provides the framework for the development and evaluation of supervised practice. *EuroPsy* has established a number of essential features of the supervision required as a part of the process of awarding the Certificate. The main features are as follows:

- It must be based on the *EuroPsy* competence model, which is used as a reference framework for the whole process of competence acquisition and mastery (goal setting, professional practice, feedback and evaluation).
- It establishes the minimal level of competences to be acquired in order to receive the Certificate that entitles the psychologist to act as a *EuroPsy* certified psychologist at the entry level in independent practice.
- This implies that the level of learning of the competences of the model needs to be assessed during the process and at the end of the period of supervised practice and standards have to be met at initial entry level as an independent practitioner.
- *EuroPsy* establishes the minimum duration of the period of supervised practice: 1-year full time professional practice (60 ECTS) (or its equivalent part-time).
- It establishes that most of the period of the supervised practice has to occur in one of the contexts of practice specified in the competence model
- The supervisor has to be a psychologist who fulfils minimal requirements of experience in the relevant field of practice; it is currently accepted that these requirements may differ from country to country based on the level of development and experience in professional supervision of psychologists in the different countries.
- *EuroPsy* requires the collection of some evidence on the activities carried out during the practice to be recorded in a document (portfolio) that is delivered to the NAC with the application form.

It is important to realise that these essential features can only be properly undertaken when the supervisor and the supervisee are familiar with the *EuroPsy* competence model and how to implement this in professional practice. In fact, this is one of the most challenging issues of the implementation of *EuroPsy*. At the same time it has the important function of contributing to the harmonisation of the quality professional standards for psychology in Europe and to the identity of the psychological profession in Europe. In addition, as the competence model becomes more widely known as a central feature of *EuroPsy*, the criteria used for the service quality are made transparent to clients and employers of psychologists in Europe. This does not imply that the model for supervision has no flexibility in its implementation. There is currently a wide variety of practice and substantial differences in the development and implementation of professional supervision of psychologists across European countries, and thus a broad array of arrangements are possible concerning the period, settings and other relevant matters.

As a general model, *EuroPsy* is based on a 3 + 2 + 1 (6 year) system of education and training for psychologists, consisting of 3 year Bachelor degree, 2 year Master degree, 1 year supervised practice. However, the way in which the 6 years are organised is flexible and this varies across European countries. While some countries organise the education and training as 3 + 2 + 1, with a year of supervised practice following 5 years of university education, other countries integrate the supervised practice within and throughout the university education period (e.g. Norway, clinical psychology in UK). In one country (the Netherlands) university programs have a duration of 4 years (3 years Bachelor and 1 year Master degree), with a 2-year period of post university education and training that has a strong emphasis on acquiring competences.

Another difference is found between countries which organise the supervised practice within the framework and duration of the university education, and those countries where the supervised practice is undertaken outside the university framework. In these latter countries individual psychologists may be required to arrange their own year of supervised practice in order to gain a license to practise. *EuroPsy* is neutral as to the organisation of the supervised practice, but requires that the individual psychologist practitioner-in-training undertakes the equivalent of 1 year of supervised practice (generally considered to be about 1,500 hours) to put into practice the knowledge, skills and understanding gained from the university education and other professional experiences in order to be eligible for the *EuroPsy* Certificate.

The supervised practice may be arranged in a clinic setting, in a private agency or other appropriate workplace setting. What is essential is the mentoring relationship between an experienced psychologist and a psychologist-in-training; this involves regular interaction and feedback, the opportunity for observation of tasks (both by the supervisor and by the psychologist-in-training), a form for reporting and reflection, and a protected time where the supervisor and psychologist learner may process the learning and the tasks undertaken, and exchange feedback, reflection, review and goal setting in a constructive environment. This mentoring relationship also involves evaluation; feedback enables formative evaluation, while at the end of the period of supervised practice, the supervisor undertakes summative evaluation to ensure that competences have been developed. Given the intrinsic power imbalance between supervisor and supervisee, it is increasingly common practice to draw up an agreement or contract which specifies the purposes, aims, methods, duration, frequency of meetings, location, expectations, etc of the arrangements. This agreement will vary in terms of formality, but it serves a useful purpose in clarifying expectations on both sides and maximising transparency and accountability.

Diversity in Supervised Practice Across European Countries

The development in *EuroPsy* of an output model for psychologists' education in Europe occurred at a time when the Bologna process was also emphasising the importance of employability for Higher Education Institutions (HEIs). The Bologna process required HEIs to promote the employability of graduates in particular by the use of level descriptors according to the Qualifications Framework of the EHEA (see Chapter 4), and the inclusion of statements of learning outcomes or professional competences. These developments occurred at a time when the tradition in psychology across most European countries, at least for the university basic education or first cycle, was clearly biased towards an "input" model focussing mainly on theoretical and empirical knowledge, with some related skills. At that time, the focus on learning outcomes or an "output" model of education was beginning to be used in a few countries, though more for training in specialisms such as clinical and psychotherapy practice.

During the last two decades there has been an increasing focus in psychology programmes on practical education and placements, with the result that universities in a number of European countries have developed the practical "stage" or "practicum" during the period of the first or second cycle of studies. As described in Chapter 3, the *EuroPsy* education requirements include a minimum of 15 ECTS to be devoted to the "stage." This is generally considered to be a short period of practical activity or placement. It should be noted that this practical placement should not be counted as part of the requirement of 1-year full time supervised practice before entering independent practice at the entry level as a professional. In most countries of Europe this year of supervised practice is an innovation introduced by *EuroPsy*.

We should note here the diversity of practice existing among countries of Europe. In some countries (e.g. Nordic countries and UK), similar or even more demanding requirements for supervised practice prior to qualification as a psychologist were already in existence. In other countries, the 1 year of supervised practice was established during the last decade as a prerequisite for professional practice (e.g. Italy). In most European countries, however, there has previously been no clear well established and regulated system.

An overview can be gained from the applications submitted by the national Member Associations (MAs) to the European Awarding Committee of EFPA. An application by a MA for recognition of the NAC and thus the right to award the *EuroPsy* requires a description of the current arrangements for supervised practice as part of the education and training of psychologists and the planned provision for implementing, developing or adapting supervision arrangements to meet the requirements of *EuroPsy*. Information is also required about the requirements and training for psychologists who undertake or may undertake the role of supervisor. An analysis of 20 applications received up to the end of 2013 shows that although supervision exists, especially at more specialist levels (mostly in clinical psychology and psychotherapy), in most countries of Europe, at this time supervision is rather unusual as a requirement at the level of entry to independent practice. There are only a few countries which make it a general requirement (e.g. Italy 1 year in two different settings; some Nordic countries with supervised practice integrated in university studies, and UK as part of the requirements for Chartered Psychologist status and now for registration with the Health and Care Professions Council). In some other countries, supervised practice may be provided, during a certain period, by some institutions, though it is not required.

Moreover, it is clear from the applications that most countries have not yet made arrangements for evaluating learning outcomes through supervision, and are unfamiliar with the model and the standards that should guide the supervised practice. It is interesting to note, that as part of the preparation for the implementation of the *EuroPsy* awarding process an analysis of the situation of supervised practice for psychologists in the country concerned and a planning process to put in place competences for supervision has been carried out in almost every country seeking to award *EuroPsy*. Furthermore, the profile, requirements and processes of training and professional development for supervisors are also being implemented in order to meet the requirements to award the *EuroPsy* certificate. *EuroPsy* has already had an impact on quality of training in a number of countries (e.g. Latvia, Italy, France, Slovenia, Spain) where projects have been initiated to implement a programme of supervision training and certification based on the *EuroPsy* model of competences.

Two Case Studies: Spain and Slovenia

Spain

As a first example, we discuss the work undertaken in Spain initiated as part of the pilot process of introducing *EuroPsy*. At the time when the *EuroPsy* "Experimental Garden" (see Chapter 2) was being implemented there was no tradition of systematic supervised practice being required prior to psychologists' independent practice. However, this situation has gradually started to change since the early 1990s when faculties of psychology began to offer a "stage" or practicum in an organisation for students to undertake under supervision. The "stage" is undertaken during the 4th year of psychology study and typically lasts between 300 and 450 hr; it is now a compulsory component of the psychology programme in all Spanish universities.

However, at the time of the introduction of *EuroPsy* what was lacking across the Spanish universities was a shared model of supervision, with common goals and criteria for evaluation of supervised experience. During the pilot (or "experimental garden") period the *EuroPsy* competence model was disseminated among the supervisors of the 5,500 or so students who undertake the "stage" each year in the 32 universities in Spain that offer psychology programmes. The aim was to promote its use, to provide clear goals and a framework for the process of the "stage" both for the supervisor and the supervisee involved, and to promote a shared vision of what makes a competent psychologist. In order to achieve this, a supervision process based on the competence model was developed. The prototype was tested in the Erasmus Mundus Master's Course on Work, Organisation and Personnel Psychology (see Martínez-Tur, Peiró & Rodriguez, 2014). From the start, the competence model was embedded in the curriculum and in the "orientation unit" of the Masters programme, and the competences were presented as a relevant goal of the Masters programme. In order to become familiarised with the model the students had to interview a professional psychologist and ask her to describe some professional activities that could serve as an example of one of the competences of the *EuroPsy* model.

The following questions were provided for this exercise:

1. Describe the context in which the activities were performed and for what purpose.
2. Identify the client, users and other relevant parties involved.

3. Describe the activities performed to show the competence in operation.
4. Identify the main tools used.
5. Explore if any action or caution had to be taken to protect against inadequate judgments, decisions or interventions that might harm the client.
6. Describe the main outputs that have been produced during the process and their effectiveness.
7. Mention the kind of evidence that could be presented to demonstrate competent performance.
8. Provide the rationale pointing out how this professional activity reflects the implementation of the professional competence under consideration.

Care was taken to ensure that all the competences of the *EuroPsy* model were covered through the students' interviews. Analysis of the information obtained was helpful for the students to better understand the competences of the model through examples, and to begin to visualise the intended outputs of their studies. During the 2nd year of the Masters program, before the students went into the "stage," a session was held to inform them about its two main aims: to practise activities for professional services in a real context under the supervision of a psychologist; and to document, with evidence, how the performance of these activities has contributed to the acquisition of one or more competences included in the *EuroPsy* model. During the session, the materials relevant for the "stage" were delivered and presented:

1. The portfolio template that was to be completed during the "stage" with the same sections described above (an example of the activities described for the competence of needs analysis and the feedback from the supervisor can be found in Lunt & Peiró, 2012).
2. Guidance for the "stage" was given with relevant information about the meetings with the supervisor. The specific goals and activity plan for a given period of the "stage" (recommended every 2 weeks) had to be described as well as the feedback and appraisal received from the supervisor, and the instructions about how to report on these meetings.
3. A document with the competence model and the assessment sheet that the supervisor had to use. The teaching staff from the Masters programme held an interview with the supervisors to discuss the following topics: aims, main type of activities, and supervision process of the "stage." In that interview a copy of the documents given to the students was also given to the professional psychologists who were acting as supervisors.

After the pilot programme a systematic evaluation was undertaken through questionnaires and meetings with the students and supervisors. Several suggestions were made on the following topics: the *competence model* (useful to set the specific goals of the "stage"), *the portfolio* (not always easy to complete the section with evidence related to the competence acquisition), the *supervision interview* (perceived as useful by the students but often seen by supervisors as time-consuming) and the *competence assessment* (the scale should be improved and some supervisors preferred the alternative competence models they were used to). The experience proved useful for designing and testing in detail a "supervision scheme" for the "stage" based on the *EuroPsy* competences model. This scheme helped to ensure that supervisors and supervisees shared the same understanding about what makes a competent psychologist. Interesting to note is that the students, having received training on the *EuroPsy* competence model, were useful informants about it for their supervisors.

The next step was to extend this experience and adapt it both for the compulsory "stage" included in the psychology curriculum taught in Spanish universities and for the different fields of practice. If the *EuroPsy* model could be introduced to the students before the start of their "stage" and the model could be disseminated among the professionals who supervise these stages, it would provide an opportunity to develop a common language among the faculty teaching staff, the professionals in charge of supervision and the students. Moreover, it would be an opportunity for the students to practise how to prepare for their year of supervised practice and how to assemble the evidence that has to be submitted when applying for the *EuroPsy* Certificate. In order to promote the model among the deans of the faculties of psychology a presentation was made at the national deans' conference where it was agreed that a workshop on *EuroPsy* would be organised by the "Colegio de Psicólogos" (the Spanish psychologists association) for the vice-deans in charge of the "stage." The workshop was well attended and the model and the tools developed during the pilot were presented and discussed. After the workshop, a task force was created to carry out small-scale additional pilots and to generate additional materials, documents, etc. The task force worked over several sessions to discuss the process of implementation with the support of the Spanish NAC. After that, a number of faculties put in place "stage" schemes based on the *EuroPsy* competence model and supervision. It is expected that these developments will provide a positive breeding ground for the generalisation of the 1 year of supervised practice required before entry to independent practice. Moreover, and importantly, the *EuroPsy* model was being disseminated as a way to build the quality of services and identity of psychology in Europe.

Slovenia

A second example is provided by colleagues from Slovenia where the reorganisation of the curricula and structures of university education brought about by the Bologna Process, and the concomitant emphasis on students' active participation in their study were used to support an innovative pilot project to establish a network of mentors using the competence approach to supervised practice (Zabukovec & Podlesek, 2010; Podlesek & Zabukovec, 2012). This approach was also supported by the Bologna-associated *Tuning* project (see Chapter 4) which provides a framework for expressing the standards for degrees in terms of learning outcomes and competences. Given the orientation of both Bologna and *Tuning*, it was seen as an ideal opportunity to use the competence model both to develop the curriculum and the approach to supervised practice.

According to Podlesek and Zabukovec, there is currently no system of or requirement for supervised practice in Slovenia. Although in many areas of psychology, graduates are required to undertake a year's traineeship during their first period of employment, this is not necessarily supervised and there is no framework for the development of competences. This poses an important challenge and an opportunity to develop a system of high quality professional supervision.

In order to promote this, in 2009 the Slovenian Psychologists Association set up a Working Group and applied for funds from the European Social Fund to set up a research and development project. Its main goals were: to establish a mentoring network for supervised practice, to develop a training programme for mentors, to educate them in planning activities and assessing competencies of supervisees, to develop documents that could be used in training and to develop guidelines for internship (Podlesek & Zabukovec, 2012). This educational programme for mentors of supervised practice was developed in the University of Ljubljana and University of Maribor and involved the creation of a network of mentors who undertook training to develop their competences for mentoring supervised practice. The programme consisted of five major components (100 hr of theoretical courses and 160 hr of practical training in supervised practice):

- introductory course to introduce the competences model,
- work in groups from different professional contexts to plan supervised practice,
- a week of supervised practice,
- analysis and reflection of supervised practice,
- evaluation of the programme and development of guidelines for supervised practice.

The course was approved by the Slovenian Psychologists Association which committed itself to the "norms" of *EuroPsy*:

> The European norms emphasise that upon the conclusion of five years of study, candidates have to undergo one year of supervised practice in order to be able to independently practice ... As a member of EFPA, Slovenia has committed itself to following these norms' (Zabukovec & Podlesek, 2010, p. 146).

The pilot project involved 20 mentors (from different fields of practice) and 20 students (also from different fields of practice) who undertook training in the *EuroPsy* competence-based model for implementing internship and supervised practice. Mentors and students worked together in pairs throughout the pilot project, with reflection and evaluation at the end of the period. Amongst the impressive features of the project is the fact that it was set up in a context with no tradition of supervised practice, and enabled the project group to trial a programme of mentor training, actual supervised practice, and the reflections of the mentor-supervisee pairs who had worked together throughout the programme.

It is clear from these two examples that the *EuroPsy* framework coinciding with programme restructuring along Bologna lines has already provided the opportunity for universities and psychological associations to collaborate and develop a robust system of supervised practice and training of supervisors or mentors. *EuroPsy* also provides the opportunity for different countries to share practice and to learn from each other, developing capacity building and shared protocols in this important area of practice. These examples highlight the importance of supervisor training and support.

Supervisor Qualities and Qualification

EuroPsy Requirements

Over recent years, requirements for supervisors have gradually increased and many countries now provide, and some require, supervisor training. Supervision is a competence that can (and should) be learned. In its early days, supervision of psychologists in training tended to be carried out by more experienced and qualified psychologists, who relied only on their experience, without any form of training. It was assumed that experience in the field was sufficient to be able to supervise or mentor less experienced colleagues, and that any competent psychologist could become a competent supervisor simply through "learning by doing." This was clearly an unsatisfactory situation. A psychologist who had undertaken supervised practice would have only one model or experience on which to build their own approach; a psychologist who had not undertaken any supervised practice would have no model at all on which to develop as a supervisor. Given the range of practices and requirements across European countries, and the need to develop training in supervision in order to support the requirement of supervised practice, *EuroPsy* has taken a "hierarchical" approach to requirements for supervisors.

For *EuroPsy* at the most basic level, a supervisor is a psychologist who, within the past 3 years, has had at least 2 years of full-time work or equivalent experience as a qualified practitioner. This means that the psychologist has some experience of practice and actual situations facing the psychologist-in-training, even though she may have limited understanding of the process of supervision itself. At the present time, given the range of practice in European countries, this psychologist may not have had any experience of supervised practice. In this role, the supervisor psychologist is responsible for supporting the learning and assessing the competence of the psychologist practitioner-in-training on a day-to-day basis and encouraging the development of competence and confidence. This experience is a minimum requirement.

The *EuroPsy* framework specifies different quality levels of supervised practice according to the experience and training of the psychologist supervisor. A distinction is drawn between experience as part of training, and the training programme itself (these may be coterminous, depending on the mode and length of the training programme). For example, in some countries where supervisor training is provided, the qualified psychologist may first register the intention to become a supervisor, thus "registering" their professional experience (e.g. 3 years of supervision experience as part of requirement of training in a particular country). Thereafter the required professional training programme (e.g. programme of 1 year) will be followed. The supervisor's experience should be in the same professional context (clinical, educational, work & organisational or other field) as the practitioner-in-training, since some of the competences to be developed will be context-specific.

The following description of levels is adapted from the appendix on Supervised Practice in the *EuroPsy* regulations (EFPA, 2013a).

- *Level 1 (the highest level)*
  The supervisor meets the criteria for the *EuroPsy* Certificate (i.e. has achieved the educational and professional standards required by *EuroPsy* including supervised practice, or its equivalent). In addition the supervisor has had *at least 5 years* full-time (or its equivalent) independent practice as a psychologist, four of which have been obtained within one specific context of practice (clinical, educational, work and organisational psychology). The practice should be within the context within which the psychologist practitioner-in-training is working. The supervisor has at least 2 years supervised practice and has undertaken an authorised or accredited specialist training programme in supervision. The training programme is recognised (accredited) by the relevant governmental body, professional association or HEI.
- *Level 2*
  The supervisor meets the criteria for *EuroPsy* Certificate. Other criteria are the same as for Level 1 (at least 5 years of full-time independent practice as a psychologist including 2 years of supervised practice), but the supervisor has no formal training in supervised practice.
- *Level 3*
  The supervisor meets the criteria for *EuroPsy* Certificate, and has had at least 2 years of full-time independent practice (or its equivalent) within one specific context. In addition the supervisor is required to have had at least 2 years of supervised practice, and to have had at least 1 year of formal training in supervision.
- *Level 4*
  The supervisor meets the criteria for *EuroPsy* Certificate. Other criteria are the same as for Level 3 (2 years of full-time independent practice plus or including 2 years of supervised practice), but the supervisor has had no formal training in supervision or the field of supervised practice.
- *Level 5*
  The supervisor meets the criteria for the *EuroPsy* Certificate, and has had at least 2 years of independent practice in one specific context.
- *Level GP (Grandparenting)*
  The supervisor holds the *EuroPsy* Certificate through grandparenting (transitional arrangements).
- *Level D*
  The supervisor does not meet the *EuroPsy* criteria, and does not qualify for receiving the *EuroPsy* Certificate through grandparenting. However, the supervisor has at least 2 years of full-time work experience as an independent practitioner psychologist within the type of professional context where the supervised practice will take place.

As mentioned above, it is useful for the supervisor and supervisee (psychologist-in-training) to have some form of agreement or contract which clarifies expectations and arrangements. At this early "stage," with different countries at different stages of development of supervised practice arrangements, at least a Level D supervisor is required for the supervised practice to be recognised as part of the *EuroPsy* standard. What is important is (a) that the supervisor has had at least 2 years professional experience within the same context as that of the practitioner-in-training and (b) that the supervisor has access to some form of training or support in their task as supervisor. In countries where there is a very limited tradition of supervised practice, and indeed of supervision for psychologists, it is important to find ways to develop a system of supervision, and an expectation that this should become an essential element of psychologist training and practice. The development of training programs for supervisors may be undertaken by professional associations, by universities or other HEIs, or by other recognised organisations of training providers.

Accreditation and Training of Supervisors

Although supervisor training is still a relatively young activity, there is substantial agreement on what is required. In their review of the research literature on "best" supervision, Falender and Shafranske (2004) identified a number of competences of "best" supervision, mainly focussing on the importance of interpersonal qualities to support a productive relationship between supervisor and supervisee. These include: capacity to enhance trainee self-confidence, ability to dispense feedback, give constructive criticism, knowledge of multiple forms of supervision, excellent communication and openness to self-evaluation. For *EuroPsy*, there are three major components of supervisor training:

- training in supervision as a process, that is, development of supervision competences and development of the ability and interpersonal skills to interact productively with the psychologist-in-training in order to enhance competence, confidence and effectiveness, and to provide feedback in a constructive and effective manner;
- training in the competence model of professional training and supervised practice;
- training in evaluation and assessment of competences.

As demonstrated above, activities are already underway which support these aspects of training. There are a number of countries with established requirements for supervised practice which have developed systems of training and accreditation for supervisors. In Norway, for example, the Norwegian Psychological Association (NPF) arranges supervisor training as part of a specialism. The programme is a 2-year part-time programme in supervision accredited by the NPF. It includes four two-day seminars, 9 days of "supervision on supervision" groups, workshops, readings and a thesis. The requirements for this programme are:

- 5 years' experience as a psychologist,
- 256 hr of courses,

- 240 hr of supervision,
- a written thesis.

In the UK (where psychologists are required by BPS to engage in their own supervision in order to continue to practise) the British Psychological Society (BPS) has arranged accreditation of supervisors since 2009 and provides training courses and (since 2010) maintains a Register of Applied Psychologist Practice Supervisors (RAPPS), using a competence framework for supervisor training. This Register is designed to recognise psychologists with special expertise in supervision, and requires that they have undertaken a BPS approved training course (normally provided by universities within the scope of their professional psychology training programme). Indeed it is a requirement for accreditation of such programmes that training for supervisors is provided. The RAPPS learning outcomes include:

Understanding and application

- Have knowledge of the context (including professional, ethical and legal) within which supervision is provided and an understanding of the inherent responsibility.
- Have an understanding of the importance of modelling the professional role (e.g. managing boundaries, confidentiality, accountability).
- Have knowledge of developmental models of learning that may have an impact on supervision.
- Have knowledge of a number of supervision frameworks.
- Have skills and experience in developing and maintaining a supervisory alliance.
- Have an understanding of the process of assessment and failure, and skills and experience in evaluating trainees.
- Have skills and experience in the art of constructive criticism, ongoing positive feedback, and negative feedback where necessary.
- Have knowledge of the various methods to gain information and give feedback (e.g. self-report, audio and video tapes, colleague and client reports).
- Have knowledge of ethical issues in supervision, and an understanding of how this may affect the supervisory process, including power differentials.
- Have skills and experience of using a range of supervisory approaches and methods.
- Have an awareness of the ongoing development of supervisory skills and the need for further reflection/supervision training.
- Have knowledge of techniques and processes to evaluate supervision, including eliciting feedback.

Attitudes (value base)

- respects trainees,
- values the ethical base guiding practice,
- believes in balancing support and challenge,
- committed to a psychological knowledge-based approach to supervision,
- recognises the need to know own limitations,
- supports the principle of life-long learning.

Capabilities

- the capability to generalise and synthesise supervisory knowledge, skills and values in order to apply them in different settings and novel situations (Fleming, 2012, p. 90).

Each university in the UK which offers the training programme in clinical psychology (a 3 year doctorate, usually titled DClinPsy, which includes the equivalent of a year of supervised practice within the university programme) is required by the BPS and by the Regulatory Body, the Health and Social Care Professions Council to provide training for supervisors. The introductory training module for supervisors will typically involve five full days of workshops over 20 months. This may be followed by further more advanced training.

Falender and Shafranske (2004) emphasise: "becoming a supervisor requires a significant transition from being a clinician ... the technical competency required for being a supervisor ... include(s) general experience in supervision ... competence in a while domain of supervision skills, including trainee assessment, educational planning and intervention, laws and ethics, and evaluation ... and facility in establishing the supervisory relationship" (p. 73). What is clear is that supervision involves skills and expertise, and that supervisors themselves require both training and supervision.

Conclusion

The *EuroPsy* requirement for supervised practice provides both a challenge and an opportunity. The diversity of education and training requirements across European countries creates a major challenge: in many countries there is still no formal requirement for supervised practice prior to independent practice as a psychologist. The requirement of 1 year, or equivalent, of supervised practice thus raises organisational, potentially financial, structural and pedagogical challenges for countries embarking on *EuroPsy* recognition. This also provides opportunities, as already demonstrated by colleagues in Spain and Slovenia amongst others, to develop a system of competence-based supervised practice and to initiate training for supervisors in this model. It also provides opportunities for greater collaboration and sharing of practices across different countries. As an umbrella organisation, EFPA encourages and supports training activities in this area, and is committed to the use of supervised practice to enhance education and training and improve the quality of psychologists' practice across Europe.

7 Continuing Professional Development

Continuing professional development (CPD)[14] is the process through which professionals keep up to date and competent to practise. It has been defined as "any process or activity that provides added value through the increase in knowledge, skills and personal qualities necessary for the appropriate execution of professional and technical duties, often termed competence" (UK Professional Associations Research Network [PARN] www.parn.org.uk). More specifically, as an example, the UK regulatory body for psychologists, the Health and Care Professions Council (www.hcpc-uk.org/cpd) defines it as "a range of learning activities through which health professionals maintain and develop throughout their career to ensure that they retain their capacity to practise safely, effectively and legally within their evolving scope of practice." Both of these definitions imply an element, firstly, of "keeping up to date" and, secondly, of "competent practice" and therefore protection of the client. Continuing professional development may be voluntary, obligatory, or mandatory, depending on the professional context and the regulatory arrangements for the profession in the particular country. It is increasingly seen as an essential element of the ethical principle Competence, and the related concept of revalidation or renewal of license (and see Chapter 8). Many professions regulate their members through registration (entry on a Register) and a requirement of CPD in order to remain on the Register.

In this chapter we will consider the concept of CPD as it applies to psychologists. There is a substantial literature on CPD in relation to a range of professional groups which helps to inform our understanding of the concept and the process. We will then look at the question of the rationale and goals of CPD, distinguishing between voluntary and mandatory CPD (or what might be referred to as the "carrot" or the "stick" approach) and consider this question in the light of changes in understandings of professional accountability. In the third section we describe the CPD framework provided by *EuroPsy*. CPD is a requirement of *EuroPsy*, even though at the present time evidence is required at the individual level only at the point of application for renewal of the *EuroPsy* after the 7-year period of validity. Nevertheless this is related to the *EuroPsy* commitment to adherence to the Code of Ethics, and the implications of this commitment. The final section considers moves for professional revalidation, and their implications for CPD.

Although, on the face of it, we might think that CPD could be considered an uncontroversial concept, in reality it has a number of different aspects, and has been considered to be an "ambiguous concept." From one perspective, it may be considered to foster personal development and to produce professionals who are able to take control of their own

[14] Continuing professional development (CPD) is also referred to as "continuing education," "continuing professional education," "continued professional development," "lifelong learning," "continuing learning," and "education permanent." A related concept "lifelong learning" is also relevant to this discussion, and constitutes a clear goal within the EU.

learning and professional development, while from another perspective it may be seen as a means of ensuring that professionals have the skills for specific work roles and as a guarantee of individual, professional competence, that is a tension between individual and organisational needs (Friedman & Phillips, 2004). There are many different kinds and modes of CPD, various purposes for undertaking CPD, and differing ways in which it has been used by individual professionals, by employing organisations and by professional associations. It is also increasingly used by regulatory bodies and governments as one element of accountability, and thus protection of the public. In the first section of the chapter we consider the complexity and multi-faceted nature of CPD.

The Concept of Continuing Professional Development

CPD for psychologists has a relatively short history, although professionals such as medical practitioners have engaged in CPD as a means of maintaining professional competence in a significant number of countries for around the last 50 years or so: the concept of "continuing professional education" evolved, and the term itself came into general usage late in the 1960s' (Houle, 1980, p. 7). On the one hand, CPD may be considered as a form of personal development or fulfilment undertaken by an individual of their own volition. In this situation, the individual professional engages voluntarily in CPD as a form of intrinsic professional development, for the purpose of pursuing personal interests and/or gaining new knowledge or expertise. Many professionals begin to develop specialist techniques through an initial personal interest which is fostered by CPD. By contrast, CPD may be required by an external body as a form of professional accountability and as a means to demonstrate continued competence, through a form of obligatory or mandatory CPD. In its most formal manifestation, evidence of continued competence provided through CPD is linked to the licence to practise, frequently through a register, and to a system of revalidation. A third aspect of CPD is that it is an individual's personal responsibility to the profession and to her professional integrity, through undertaking professional development and adopting a "learning" and reflective stance to professional life.

Over time, CPD has tended to develop from a voluntary form of personal development to a more mandatory aspect of professional competence, and from a form of personal enhancement to a mode of professional accountability. This reflects changes in the way in which professionals work, and how they relate to clients and the wider public. It also reflects changes in the relationship of professionals and the state, and the ways in which professions themselves approach regulation and professional accountability. This shift has coincided with developments within professional associations and the growing pressures on professions to protect the public by demonstrating competence. The existence of different stakeholders and different perspectives is shown by Madden and Mitchell's definition of CPD as "the maintenance and enhancement of the knowledge, expertise and competence of professionals throughout their careers according to a plan formulated with regard to the need of *the professional, the employer, the profession and the society*"

(Madden & Mitchell, 1993, p. 12, italics added). Lindley (1997, p. 12) differentiates three perspectives:

1. that of individual professionals who are seeking to satisfy their individual, professional and career goals and aspirations at a level commensurate with their area and level of practice;
2. that of the professional body which has the duty to safeguard the standards of the profession and to demonstrate to the public that the body of professionals is up to date and competent;
3. that of the organisation or employer for which the individual is working.

To this must be added a fourth perspective, that of the clients or users, who need to have evidence of a professional's current competence, and her entitlement to practise in that domain.

There are many different ways of maintaining professional competence and of ensuring that professionals' knowledge is current and up to date. One broad distinction is that between approaches which are predominantly "*input*" approaches from those which focus on "*output*" or outcomes. This distinction has already been discussed earlier in a number of chapters in this volume. We also discuss more "process oriented" approaches. Historically earlier schemes of CPD have tended to involve more of an input approach, involving attendance for a certain number of hours on courses, or other formal learning events. More recent systems of CPD have included a consideration of output (or outcomes of learning meeting "standards" of competence) and of the process of learning and development. The different approaches may involve voluntary or mandatory CPD, frequently reflecting a focus on the individual or the profession respectively.

Lindley (1997) draws the distinction between voluntary, obligatory and mandatory CPD. In voluntary CPD "the individual decides whether and how to update and extend his or her competence" and there is no requirement by an external body. Obligatory CPD "means that the professional body requires professionals to maintain competence, but does not or cannot enforce compliance. It may or may not monitor CPD." In mandatory CPD "the professional body requires and enforces compliance .... This has a legal aspect. Members can be refused a license or certificate to practise if they do not carry out the required amount of CPD" (Lindley, 1997, p. 13). Although CPD practices have increasingly moved from voluntary towards mandatory CPD, there are a number of different purposes served by different approaches to CPD.

As an example of a mandatory input approach, some professions, for example lawyers, increasingly require their members to undertake a certain number of hours of courses which update knowledge and enable lawyers to gain further specialist knowledge. For example, all practising solicitors and registered European lawyers who are in legal practice or employment in England and Wales and working 32 hr or more per week are required to complete a minimum of 16 hours of CPD per year. Although the content of these hours is fairly flexible, at least 25% of the 16 hours must involve participation in *accredited* training courses. This means that the profession encourages legal practitioners to assume responsibility for their own development, and to analyse their own training and development needs. However, the CPD scheme is compulsory and noncompliance could lead to possible disciplinary procedures or delays in the issue of a practising certificate by the

Solicitors Regulation Authority. Increasingly within larger companies, training may be arranged, mandated and monitored by the company. Thus, professional lawyers in many European countries are required to provide certificated evidence of course attendance, with a certain number of accredited courses (accredited by a state or professional body). There has been a growing trend for courses to be accredited by an educational or professional body, as a form of quality control, and indeed for "credit" to be acknowledged through forms of certification or credit units.

An example of what might be considered an output approach is that of medical doctors, who are increasingly required to provide certified evidence that they continue to meet certain standards of knowledge, skill and performance (defined by the profession), and are developing the wide range of competences needed to practise high quality medicine in a rapidly changing environment. Competences are identified by the profession (through regulatory and professional bodies) and medical practitioners are required to provide evidence of particular competences, generic and specialist, in order to renew their licence to practise. Again, this is a mandatory approach and is linked to the process of revalidation of the license to practise.

In addition to so-called input or output approaches, we identify process approaches. These approaches recognise the importance of the learning process itself as a form of professional development, rather than the number of hours spent on courses (see Kolb, 1984; Schön, 1987). These can be related to an important approach to CPD that of "work-place learning" and the professional development that takes place at the work place itself, often as incidental learning through collaboration, discussion and mentoring (Eraut & Hirsch, 2007). An important feature of this approach is the question: what and how do professionals learn in the work place, and how is this related to the development of "reflective practice?" Another form of these so-called process approaches, adopted by some professional groups, for example psychotherapists, requires all members to undergo regular supervision, including reflective logbooks, which provides a very different way of maintaining competence. Of course, it is common, in addition, for psychotherapists to undertake courses to further their knowledge, for example through workshops on specific techniques or approaches, Reading Groups on particular scholars or practitioners, or clinical discussion groups.

Psychologists across European countries vary substantially in their approaches to CPD (Hughes, 1994). Analysis of the 20 applications from EFPA Member Associations to award the *EuroPsy* confirms this variation even at the present time (2013). This variation may be linked to the question of professional regulation, though it is also linked to wider questions of professionalisation and the professional status of psychologists in the particular country. In the UK, for example, the long struggle to achieve legal recognition and regulation of psychologists led the British Psychological Society to adopt a policy of obligatory CPD as part of the concept of Chartered Psychologist, the voluntary registration system which pertained prior to the legal registration under the Health and Care Professions Council of the UK. This meant that psychologists were required to undertake CPD and maintain competence as part of retaining an annual practising certificate, but there were no sanctions against noncompliance, since at the time the profession was not legally regulated. When legal regulation was achieved through the Health Professions Council of the UK, CPD became mandatory; the British Psychological Society now recommends that psychologists allocate between half a day and one day a month to CPD. Other countries do not yet have any recommendation or requirement for CPD, and the decision is left to the individual psychologist.

As mentioned, the distinction between input and output approaches reflects a fundamental distinction between approaches to professional education and training, and to learning itself. For CPD, the input approach frequently requires a certain number of hours of courses or "CPD points" of instruction, often relies on structured formal training and has been criticised for leading to a "tick box" mentality. On the other hand, the output approach is based on learning outcomes and competences, increasingly related to specification by a profession of the competences required for particular tasks, or for "high quality" practice. This distinction does not map onto the contrast between voluntary and mandatory CPD, since both input and output approaches may be voluntary or mandatory. In the ideal world we aim for a CPD framework which combines input, output and process approaches and one which encourages the professional's active involvement in identifying their own CPD needs, as well as the professional accountability implied in mandatory CPD.

The literature on CPD is linked to that on adult learning, and a range of models of learning have been discussed (and see Butterworth et al., 2008; Cowan et al., 2005). Here we follow Gear, McIntosh and Squires (1994) in drawing the distinction between three kinds of learning in relation to CPD: specific, general and developmental learning. Specific learning arises from needs relating to particular problems or cases; for example, a psychologist encounters particular cases in their work which lead to a need for mastery of specific interventions. This is contrasted with general learning which involves the need to keep up to date with current developments. The third kind of learning described by Gear et al. is developmental learning which implies the more personal and dynamic learning which arises from the pursuit of particular interests and specialisms.

A wide range of activities may be undertaken as part of CPD. These include a range of forms of work-based learning, professional activity, formal education/courses, reading groups and journal clubs, or self-directed learning. Examples of work-based learning include: reflective practice, case studies, coaching from others, peer review, work shadowing, journal club, supervision of staff or students, project work. Professional activity may involve: involvement in a professional body, mentoring, being an examiner or tutor, giving presentations at courses or conferences, supervising research. Formal education or courses includes attending specialist courses, research, attending conferences, writing articles, or papers. Finally self-directed learning includes reading books or articles, reviewing books or articles, updating knowledge through Internet. A range of different activities is usually encouraged (see below).

Rationale for Continuing Professional Development

The rationale for CPD schemes is usually provided by the profession and its professional bodies, and focusses most strongly on updating and the maintenance of competence (Golding & Gray, 2006). Thus, according to Gear et al. (1994),

> the inadequacy of initial professional education as a preparation for one's entire working life is now well recognized by professional bodies. It is not just that knowledge dates, but that the very conception and interpretation of professional tasks and roles changes over time (p. 77).

This means, for example, that the psychologist who qualified in the 1990s needs to undertake regular CPD in order to update and maintain competence to practise in 2014 and the future. Not only will there be new techniques and approaches, possible new legislation, and new evidence of effectiveness or otherwise, but there is also a need for professionals to engage in their own self-evaluation and reflection, developing the self-awareness required for responsible practice. But this is not the only rationale for CPD. In a rapidly changing world, with changing societal and individual needs and demands, there is a major challenge for psychologists to avoid personal and professional obsolescence. As Green (2006) suggests,

> Ours is a fast-moving and oddly fashion-conscious profession. Ideas and methods that may have been "state of the art" during a psychologist's initial training can fall out of favour remarkably quickly ... new therapeutic approaches are developed and practised enthusiastically. CPD offers the experienced practitioner an opportunity both to appraise carefully the evidence supporting different therapeutic approaches and to undertake some disciplined preparation for the novel tack he intends to take. (p. 18).

This is linked to professional bodies' codes of ethics, all of which contain an article on maintenance of competence (and see Chapter 8). Thus the pressures of increased competitiveness, increased client expectations, concerns about litigation for incompetent practice, a commitment to client welfare and protection, and a general need to maintain and enhance competence all provide a clear rationale for requirement of CPD. Related to this is the danger of professional isolation. Thus, Green (2006) suggests that professionals working in isolation do not have access to the feedback and moderation available to those working in an organisation, and CPD may help to provide the "self-righting social influences" that are part of any learning organisation.

It may be useful here to consider the list of purposes provided by Friedman, Durkin, Phillips and Davis (2000) who surveyed promotional CPD literature produced by professional associations in the UK. According to them, CPD is (and often concurrently):

- lifelong learning for professionals;
- a means of personal development;
- a means for individual professionals to ensure a measure of control and security in the often precarious modern workplace;
- a means of assuring a wary public that professionals are indeed up-to-date, given the rapid pace of technological advancement;
- a means whereby professional associations can verify that the standards of their professionals are being upheld;
- a means for employers to gain a competent, adaptable workforce.

From the perspective of a professional body, CPD is seen as a way by which the profession may be seen to maintain its standards, and is thus part of a wider aspect of professionalisation, and a means of assuring clients and the public that the profession is trustworthy and competent.

Continuing Professional Development (CPD) for *EuroPsy*

The development of *EuroPsy* was motivated in large measure by a concern for quality, and an aspiration to provide a benchmark to ensure and enhance the quality of services provided by psychologists across Europe. Part of this commitment to quality entailed an acknowledgement that certification gained at one point in time should have a fixed duration, and that a qualification should not be valid for life without some updating and renewal. For a number of countries in Europe this was both unfamiliar and controversial.

As discussed in Chapter 2, a number of guiding principles underpin the development of the *EuroPsy* Certificate in Psychology in which the European standard is embedded. Amongst other goals these principles aim to:

> endorse a commitment to the active maintenance of competence. For this reason the *EuroPsy* is awarded for a limited time period, and shall be renewed, again for a limited period of time, on the basis of evidence of continuing professional practice and professional development (*EuroPsy* Regulations, Preamble).

This means that, according to the *EuroPsy* Regulations, "the holders of the *EuroPsy* are expected to maintain and further develop their level of professional competence. This should be achieved by means of work experience and personal professional development, and by meeting local CPD requirements if such exist ..." (*EuroPsy* regulations, EFPA, 2013a, Appendix V). The fact that holders of the *EuroPsy* Certificate are expected to find ways to maintain and further develop their level of professional competence may prove a challenge in countries where provision for CPD is limited. Once more we refer to the distinction drawn above between the accountability function and the developmental function of CPD, and we argue that both are desirable.

The *EuroPsy* appendix on CPD provides a range of different types of professional development activities (see Table 13). The list is useful in indicating the range of activities which may contribute to CPD, and which can be used by individual psychologists to provide evidence. We note that this list is not comprehensive, and that there are many forms of CPD which can enhance psychologists' professional competence, safety and responsible functioning. Evidence of the range and amount of CPD activities is required at the point of revalidation or renewal of the *EuroPsy* Certificate, and may also be used by qualified psychologists applying for *EuroPsy* under transitional arrangements. The table also includes the approximate maximum of percentage of time for which each type of activity can be accepted, in order to ensure that psychologists undertake a range of different activities as part of their CPD. For example, if the total is 100 hr of CPD, this might consist of attendance at a scientific conference (10 hr, max 20), editorial work (10 hr, max 20),

Table 13. List of professional development activities with indicative maxima in terms of percentage time (*EuroPsy* Regulations, Appendix VI, EFPA, 2013a)

- Certified attendance and participation in accredited courses and/or workshops aimed at further professional development (60%).
- Development of specific new skills through practice at work (20%).
- Certified attendance in peer supervision meetings (20%).
- Certified participation as a supervisor provided that this is formally recognised (20%).
- Certified attendance at a professional or scientific conference (20%).
- (Co)authorship and/or editing of publications on research and/or professional issues (30%).
- Presentations to professional audiences (20%).
- Editorial work on journals and books in psychology (20%).

For the purpose of revalidation the sum of the final three categories above cannot exceed 60%.

attendance at peer supervision meetings (20 hr, max 20), certified attendance at accredited courses (60 hr, max 60). This ensures a mixture of different CPD activities. The aim is to ensure that the psychologist is proactive in undertaking different types of learning activities which help to ensure that professional development occurs "outside the comfort zone" of the individual. The nature and range of activities may also be determined by service needs and priorities, or by professional guidelines.

It is useful to consider in more detail how CPD might work in practice.

Accredited Courses

Participation in courses, increasingly accredited, is a familiar means of updating knowledge and competence and learning new skills. There is a range of bodies which recognise or accredit courses, that is give some kind of guarantee of quality. These may be university or other national accreditation agencies, professional bodies, private organisations such as test agencies, and, increasingly, commercial organisations. Accredited courses (or workshops) may range from a one-day workshop, a series of weekly lectures and seminars, a week intensive training course, to university accredited courses such as Certificates, Diplomas, Masters degrees which may be of a year or more duration. Over the past 5–10 years, psychological associations in a number of European countries have been arranging a range of courses and workshops to support their members in gaining additional skills and knowledge. Such courses are normally undertaken as part of their professional work by qualified psychologists during the course of the working year. Courses of longer duration will frequently be of a part-time nature (e.g. a certain number of hours a week); increasingly they are offered by distance learning, e-learning, or blended (mixed mode) learning.

As an example, a visit to the website of the British Psychological Society shows the Learning Centre and CPD pages (www.bps.org.uk/findcpd) with a directory of accredited courses, combining input (structured teaching) with output (statements of objectives and learning outcomes). Examples include: a series of four supervision skills workshops (which confer eligibility to be included in the Register of Supervisors for Applied Psychologists), a 2 day workshop on Using trauma focussed CBT (cognitive behavioural therapy) to work with PTSD (posttraumatic stress disorder), a 1 day workshop on Working successfully in private practice. In similar fashion, the website of the Norsk Psykolog Forening offers a menu of courses for qualified psychologists, for example a 3 day course on psychological work with drug and addiction problems. The Spanish Colegio Oficial de Psicólogos provides a menu of blended or distance learning courses with assessment of the learning output and certification of achievement. These and similar examples are likely to be considerably expanded across other European countries over the next few years.

Accredited courses may also include more formal specialisation or advanced training through university courses which confer a diploma, Masters, or even Doctoral qualification. A number of countries have developed extensive systems for specialisation training (e.g. the Nordic countries have created a rigorous specialisation in clinical psychology), and the *EuroPsy* Specialist Certificates (so far offered in psychotherapy and in work and organisational psychology, see Chapter 3) are intended to enhance qualifications and provide opportunities for recognition of specialist expertise. It should be noted also that professional doctoral qualifications became widely available in the UK following the shift to doctoral level qualifications in clinical psychology over 20 years ago (see Donn, Routh & Lunt, 2000), and may become more widespread in other countries across Europe as requirements for specialised practice are enhanced. These courses and many other university courses will provide additional training in research skills, thus supporting practitioner psychologists in undertaking research, and developing the scientist practitioner approach to practice and a greater focus on evidence and evidence-based practice.

Development of New Skills Through Practice at Work

New skills may be developed through practice in the work place. Examples of this might be the use of new forms of assessment (such as a new psychometric test) or new forms of therapeutic technique. Frequently a psychologist may attend a workshop where the new test or technique is introduced and demonstrated. This is followed up by practice on the job, ideally supported by a more experienced colleague, with follow-up discussion to process and consolidate the learning experience. However, developing new skills through practice at work does not necessarily involve attendance at courses and may also be facilitated through mentoring or supervision by a more experienced colleague who shares their own knowledge and expertise. This may be an important aspect of mentoring or supervision, where a more novice colleague may be able to observe a supervisor (more experienced colleague) in action, then discuss this process, and move on to taking on a new practice or procedure in their own practice. The mutual discussion and feedback can provide a powerful mode of learning and professional development.

Eraut and Hirsch (2007) have provided a useful typology of early career learning (see Table 14).

This emphasises the importance of processes of work-place learning, and the key role played by mentors and colleagues in supporting learning.

Table 14. A typology of early career learning (Eraut & Hirsch, 2007, p. 25)

Work processes with learning as a by-product	Learning activities located within work or learning processes	Learning processes at or near the workplace
Participation in group processes; Working alongside others; Consultation; Tackling challenging tasks and roles; Problem solving; Trying things out; Consolidating, extending and refining skills; Working with clients.	Asking questions; Getting information; Locating resource people; Listening and observing; Reflecting; Learning from mistakes; Giving and receiving feedback; Use of mediating artifacts.	Being supervised; Being coached; Being mentored; Shadowing; Visiting other sites; Conferences; Short courses; Working for a qualification; Independent study.

Peer Supervision

Peer supervision has a strong tradition amongst psychologist practitioners, and is a powerful and effective process of CPD, enabling the psychologist to reflect on the work, to process the different aspects of the tasks, and to engage in reflective questioning and explanation with a colleague psychologist. Here we mean one-to-one peer supervision, or what is sometimes termed one-to-one co-supervision. In this form of supervision, two practitioners provide supervision for each other by alternating the roles of supervisor and supervisee. As implied in the term "peer" this kind of supervision implies an equality of status rather than the more traditional hierarchical notion of supervision. According to Steen (2012) "in clinical psychology it is not unusual to find peer supervision as a model used amongst more senior colleagues who wish to have supervision with someone at an appropriate level of seniority with whom they can share confidential information; this is particularly pertinent when supervision is used in its broadest sense to discuss nontherapeutic components of a practitioner's job, such as management" (p. 164). Peer supervision provides a particular mode of CPD in terms of encouraging reflection on practice, problem-solving and mutual feedback.

Another form of peer supervision also exists, in the form of group supervision. This has been defined as taking place when:

> "Three or more people form a fixed membership group and have planned, regular meetings in which each person gets the chance for in-depth reflection on their own practice and on the part they as individuals play in the complexities and quality of that practice, facilitated in that reflection by the other group members" (Bond & Holland, 1998, p. 173).

Again, this kind of peer supervision plays a particular role in CPD, and has been used successfully in a wide range of settings. Both of these forms of supervision are a very helpful mode of CPD and are relatively straightforward to arrange. It is important that this activity is certified that is reported, possibly within a framework provided by the profession or by the agency or work organisation. We note that this form of supervision may be particularly helpful for psychologists working on their own, as a means to counter the effects of professional isolation, ensuring a moderation and socialisation function through regular contact with peers and colleagues.

Certified Participation as a Supervisor

The process of supervision (whether this be of qualified psychologists or psychologists in training) may also provide a form of CPD, and may be regarded as a key CPD activity for all levels of psychologists. Supervision of psychologists in training provides the opportunity to engage with current issues in training, to discuss professional issues, dilemmas and challenges with aspiring members of the psychological profession, and thus to reflect on one's own professional practice. In a general sense, supervision provides an opportunity to meet many knowledge and skill objectives, and to enhance competence and confidence. As discussed in Chapter 6, there is an increasing demand for training for supervisors, and this constitutes a powerful form of CPD. Again, it is important that the activity is certified, and that records are kept. This may be within an agency framework of activity and record-keeping, or may be a record of the supervision meetings, following an agenda and recording processes, outcomes and action points. It is useful that these are organised within a framework of professional development, setting goals and objectives and reflecting on how far these have been met.

Attendance at a Professional or Scientific Conference

Attendance at a professional or scientific conference enables practitioners to learn about new developments, specialist fields and state-of-the-art psychology, as well as having the opportunity to discuss with old and new colleagues, and develop new insights and perspectives. It is often said that the opportunity to network and discuss with colleagues is at least as valuable as the lecture and workshop input itself, and certainly the process of discussion and reflection facilitated by relevant professional or scientific input can be highly rewarding. There is a wide variety of conferences, ranging from major international congresses such as the quadrennial ICP (International Congress of Psychology) and ICAP (International Congress of Applied Psychology), and biennial ECP (the European Congress of Psychology) to smaller and more focussed conferences which may be local, national or international. In recent years there has been a growth of more specialist and smaller conferences and meetings which encourage a more focussed form of professional developed and scientific exchange.

(Co)authorship and/or Editing of Publications on Research and/or Professional Issues

Psychologists are encouraged to engage in research and/or scholarly reflection on practice. This may take the form of publications in scientific or professional journals, book chapters, or research reports. As mentioned earlier, the model of professional psychology espoused by *EuroPsy* is that of the scientist practitioner, and research-based practice. In some countries and some settings, practitioner psychologists are encouraged to collaborate with research psychologists, developing research projects which draw on theoretical and practical knowledge, either as part of formal collaborations and funded research, or as part of collegial arrangements developed locally. This is to be welcomed, and helps to strengthen the links between researchers and practitioners, and the mutual contributions of research and practice. Given the significant moves across European countries for evidence-based practice over the past decade, professional psychologists are encouraged develop research skills, to engage in research, and to disseminate their findings. Coauthorship is an excellent mode of this form of CPD.

Presentations to Professional Audiences

Making presentations at professional meetings and conferences is an excellent means of reflection, research and professional development. Increasingly psychologists in training are encouraged to make presentations initially to a peer group, and subsequently at wider conferences. The preparation required to make a presentation and the feedback received on the presentation constitute valuable forms of CPD. Both are powerful forms of learning and development.

Editorial Work on Journals and Books in Psychology

Many psychologists engage in editorial work, for example as members of journal editorial boards or as reviewers of manuscripts or book proposals, or editing collections of papers or chapters. This constitutes a valuable form of CPD as well as a contribution to the profession.

We should note here that for the purpose of revalidation of the *EuroPsy* Certificate the sum of the final three categories (coauthorship, conference presentations, editorial work) cannot exceed 60%. There are clear professional reasons for this restriction since it is desirable that psychologists undertake a range of activities to maintain their competence.

Training Needs Analysis and Record Keeping

Recent developments in CPD have involved a more systematic identification of training, either within individuals or across a service. In the UK, training needs are identified as part of a systematic appraisal process, involving the individual psychologist in reviewing her own competences and experience, setting learning objectives for the forthcoming year and building these into a programme of CPD activities (e.g. Golding & Gray, 2006). It is considered good practice to engage in regular training needs analysis and review which is part of planning a CPD programme. Needs may be determined by the organisation (the organisation has the need for psychologists with different sets of skills), or through the individual appraisal identifying areas for further development, or through an individual personal preference and expression of need.

Registered *EuroPsy* Psychologists are required to maintain a record of their CPD. In addition to recording the acquisition of experience of practice in the context of new functions, client groups and settings, this should cover training and development from continuing education. Although the learning process may be considered of equal or even greater significance than the record, the record serves an important purpose in providing evidence and is part of a wider accountability function. This record, with supporting evidence, will provide the basis for the Registered *EuroPsy* Psychologist's Profile as included in the Register, when the *EuroPsy* is renewed after 7 years. Since *EuroPsy* is not a license to practise, this may be regarded as a form of obligatory CPD, required by all psychologists who wish to remain on the Register and retain the *EuroPsy* Certificate.

Revalidation and License to Practise

The concept of revalidation is linked to the license to practise, and applies to professions and countries which require a license to practise and where the profession is legally regulated. Although *EuroPsy* is not a license to practise, the *EuroPsy* system involves the concept of "renewal," linked to a commitment to ethical codes and protection of the public, which means that psychologists are required to renew their certificate after 7 years. The requirements for renewal are: engagement in professional practice (of at least a specified amount), a record of participation in CPD (of at least a specified amount), and a renewed commitment to abide by ethical codes.

Licence to Practise

Increasingly, professions across European countries are moving towards the concept of a license or a certificate to practise. For psychologists in Europe, the license to practise, if required, is a national matter that is issued by the national government or equivalent body. The US and Canada have longer histories of licensing (see Hall & Altmaier, 2008). However, in these countries each state, province, or territory has individual licensing requirements which may differ from each other. Typically, licensing requirements in North America involve:

- graduation from an accredited school/university with an appropriate degree (a doctoral degree is required for most North American jurisdictions);
- completion of required supervised internship;
- examination or test (state or national, such as the Examination for Professional Practice in Psychology or EPPP).

The situation in Europe is somewhat different and differs significantly across individual countries. For example, in Norway, students wishing to become a clinical psychologist follow a recognised 6-year psychology course of study and internship, after which they are authorised by the government as Health Personnel and licensed to practise as psychologists. Similar requirements apply across the other Nordic countries. This is similar to the situation in UK where clinical psychologists undertake a 6-year university education, which includes both academic study and supervised internship, after which they are entitled to register with the Health and Care Professions Council and receive the license to practise. While the licensing and regulation requirements vary considerably across European countries, increasingly the license to practise is awarded for a fixed period after which there is a requirement to renew or to revalidate.

Revalidation

Revalidation is a process by which professionals, in this case psychologists, demonstrate that they are up to date and fit to practise and that they are meeting relevant professional standards and have the current competence to practise. It is usually associated with entry on a Register, and involves renewing status as a registered professional, and thus reassuring the public that the individual psychologist takes their responsibilities to clients seriously, meets certain standards of competence and provides safe and legal care and services. Revalidation has a further purpose which is about maintaining public trust and respect in the profession. It can thus protect the reputation of the profession by ensuring that practitioners maintain professional standards, and that those who are not competent are not able to continue to remain on the Register.

Even outside formal requirements for revalidation, psychologists need to be able to demonstrate that they are practising in accordance with generic standards of practice that is meeting current benchmark standards of practice. At the present time, at the legal level these standards will be set by national registration bodies, although at the professional and ethical level *EuroPsy* provides a European benchmark of competences. There are various ways in which psychologists may provide evidence of current competence; these vary across different countries and include work experience, continuing professional development, the process of supervision, and there are increasingly local CPD requirements developed in different countries.

Under the *EuroPsy* system, psychologists are required to renew the certificate every 7 years and to show relevant evidence of CPD over the past 7-year period of professional practice. The *EuroPsy* provides a standard of quality and is intended to be used to guarantee a level of quality and some degree of protection for clients. This means that a *EuroPsy* psychologist is expected to maintain her/his competence up to date and to undertake activities designed to foster CPD. As indicated above, there is no "one size fits all" approach, and there will be different kinds of activities which are appropriate for different psychologists, different working contexts, stages of the career, and different countries.

Requirements for Renewal of the *EuroPsy* Certificate

Work Experience

The psychologist should show evidence of professional work as a psychologist amounting to not less than 400 hr per year averaged over a period of not less than 4 years over the period of the last 7 years (revalidation period) before the application for renewal. Acceptable evidence includes employment contracts accompanied by a job description, project contracts, or statements of income for tax authorities (in the case of psychologists in independent practice). It is important for renewal that the psychologist has been undertaking work as a psychologist, even if this may be part-time or interrupted, for example through sickness or parental leave.

Continuing Professional Development

The Registered *EuroPsy* Psychologist has a responsibility to keep informed about recent professional developments in psychology, including but not limited to the field of practice. The *EuroPsy* system recommends a minimum of 80 hr per year and psychologists should be able to show explicit evidence of 40 hr CPD per year. Evidence of a variety of activities is required (see above).

These requirements constitute a section of the *Tuning-EuroPsy* Reference points for the design and delivery of degree programmes in psychology.

Conclusion

Continuing professional development is a fundamental aspect of professional practice in psychology. According to Golding and Gray (2006) "there are clear moral obligations, and emerging regulatory requirements that make CPD an integral and everyday part of daily activity for professionals in health and social care" (p. vii). *EuroPsy* aims to enhance the quality of psychologists' education and practice in European countries, and requires psychologists to ensure the active maintenance of their competence. This has a developmental and an ethical aspect, and has a clear link to ethical codes, and in particular the principle of competence. At the present time, *EuroPsy* psychologists commit to abide by the code of the country of practice and the EFPA Meta-Code of Ethics. This means that entry in the Register of *EuroPsy* psychologists implies both an ethical commitment and a commitment to CPD, thus strengthening the goal to protect the public.

8 The Ethical Base of Professional Practice

The ethical basis of professional practice is a fundamental and intrinsic component of the *EuroPsy* system. Psychologists can only be awarded the European Certificate in Psychology if they have committed themselves to abide by the European Meta-code of Ethics (EFPA, 2005) and to the code of ethics of the national association of psychology in their country of practice. As mentioned in Chapter 1, having an ethical code is a defining characteristic of all professions, and codes of ethics specify professional ideals and responsibilities. A major goal is the protection of clients and the public and the justification of public trust. This is achieved by providing guidance to the individual professional and by administering sanctions. By maintaining and enforcing an ethical code the professions justify their high status and freedom from regulatory interference.

In the first section of the chapter we consider briefly the nature of ethical codes. Ethics is defined as "the science of morals or rules of behaviour" (EFPA, 2013a), and codes are underpinned by ethical principles. In the second section we describe the ethical principles used by international, European and national organisations as a basis for the scientific and professional practice of psychologists. We note a considerable degree of commonality and universality in the formulation of ethical principles. The third section considers the functions of codes. Given the imbalance of power between the "expert" (psychologist) and the client or recipient of the service, codes are meant to protect clients against poor professional practices. They also serve to protect the reputation of psychologists who render competent services from less qualified and less scrupulous service providers, and hence maintain the public image and integrity of the profession. In the fourth section we consider the relationship between ethics, expertise and professional behaviour, and examine three features which are advanced to justify the expertise of psychologists in their field of practice: university education in the science of psychology, mastery of competences and work experience in the profession. We next review the way in which *EuroPsy* aims to strengthen systems of professional ethics at the national level, establishing a link between national monitoring of ethical conduct and the issuing of certificates. We develop this by describing the commitment to education, supervised practice and continuing professional development in *EuroPsy* as a means to develop ethical awareness and ethical competence in individuals and the profession. In the final section we look at ethics in a broader professional and European perspective.

What Are Ethical Codes?

Traditionally codes of ethics have been developed by professional associations, as part of a wider process of professionalisation. This applies also to psychologists; national psychological associations in European countries have developed codes which reflect their own diverse professional, historical and legislative contexts. According to Lindsay (2008), "ethical codes ... are a means of translating beliefs regarding necessary behaviour into statements which specify how the professional may act appropriately" (p. 8). What constitutes positive, acceptable, or necessary behaviour is reflected in principles which are often operationalised through standards or rules of behaviour. Ethical codes are normally accompanied by a system of complaints available to clients and the public, and a mechanism for investigatory procedures of such complaints, and disciplinary sanctions for psychologists found guilty of misdemeanours and violations of the code of ethics. There is a range of sanctions available to deal with the psychologist who is found to have contravened the ethical code, varying in severity from a warning or a reprimand, to suspension or expulsion from membership of the association concerned, or withdrawal of the licence to practise. Sanctions are usually determined by a committee of peers (normally both psychologist and non-psychologist) reminiscent of a court of justice.

Although codes of ethics in psychology vary in format, most provide a set of ethical principles, followed by guidelines for interpreting the basic principles and some form of standards for appropriate conduct in exercising the profession. As an example, we consider the structure of the Code of Ethics of the British Psychological Society. The code is based on four Ethical Principles; each Ethical Principle is described in a Statement of Values, reflecting beliefs that guide ethical reasoning, decision-making and behaviour; and each Ethical Principle described is further defined by a set of Standards, setting out the ethical conduct that the British Psychological Society (BPS) expects of its members (BPS, 2009). The principles generally present ideals that psychologists should strive for or aspire to, whereas the standards, while retaining a level of generality, provide more prescriptive guidance. An example illustrates this structure:

Ethical Principle: Competence

Statement of values: Psychologists value the continuing development and maintenance of high standards of competence in their professional work, and the importance of preserving their ability to function optimally within the recognised limits of their knowledge, skill, training, education, and experience.

Standard of recognising limits of competence: *Psychologists should*:

(i) Practise within the boundaries of their competence.
(ii) Engage in continuing professional development.
(iii) Remain abreast of scientific, ethical, and legal innovations germane to their professional activities, with further sensitivity to the broader social, political, and organisational contexts in which they work.
(iv) Seek consultation and supervision when indicated, particularly as circumstances begin to challenge their scientific or professional expertise.
(v) Engage in additional areas of professional activity only after obtaining the knowledge, skill, training, education, and experience necessary for competent functioning.
(vi) Remain aware of and acknowledge the limits of their methods....

(vii) Strive to ensure that those working under their direct supervision also comply with each of the requirements of this standard and that they are not required to work beyond the limits of their competence. (BPS 2009, pp. 15–17, Article 2)

A major challenge for EFPA and therefore for countries in Europe lies in the fact that it was possible for a psychologist disciplined in one jurisdiction to travel and practise in another; sanctions applied in one country did not travel with the psychologist, and information concerning ethical violations was not readily available across borders. EFPA aimed to address this challenge early on in its history when it formed a Task Force on Ethics in 1990. Although the original aim was to develop a European code of ethics, the diversity of codes existing at the time in European countries and the sensitivities of national codes and practices meant that the Task Force abandoned the goal of a common code. Instead the Task force developed the EFPA Meta-Code, accepted in 1995 and revised in 2005 (EFPA, 2005), a code expressing principles to which all EFPA Member Associations could commit (see below). More recently, and in part related to the requirements of *EuroPsy* as a European standard, EFPA has begun to develop a Model Code (EFPA, 2013b and see below), resurrecting earlier aspirations for European harmonisation of ethical codes.

Ethical Principles in Codes of Conduct

In recent years we have seen an increase in attempts to formulate over-arching ethical principles that can provide guidance to the work of psychologists, and which can transcend national boundaries. This is exemplified by the *Universal Declaration of Ethical Principles for Psychologists* (www.am.org/iupsys/resources/ethics/univdecl2008) which was accepted in 2008 by the International Union of Psychological Science (IUPsyS), the International Association of Applied Psychology (IAAP) and the International Association for Cross-Cultural Psychology (IACCP) and which articulated aspirational goals that try to rise above national and historical concerns. Although the Declaration does not provide clear standards for appropriate action or for monitoring and sanctioning, and is therefore not an ethical code, this document is important as it expresses the aspirations of psychologists worldwide and "reaffirms the commitment of the psychology community to help build a better world where peace, freedom, responsibility, justice, humanity and morality prevail" (Universal Declaration, 2008).

The Universal Declaration articulates four principles, each of which is embedded in shared human values. These principles are:

- *Respect for the Dignity of Persons and Peoples*, with values such as respect for diversity and culture, free and informed consent, confidentiality and fairness.
- *Competent Caring for the Well-Being of Persons and Peoples*, with values such as concern for the well-being of others, avoiding harm, maintaining competence and self-knowledge.
- *Integrity* (based on honesty, and open communication), with values such as impartiality, not exploiting others for personal, professional or financial gain, and avoiding conflicts of interest.

- *Professional and Scientific Responsibilities to Society*, with values such as the discipline's responsibility to increase scientific and professional knowledge, the competent use of such knowledge and for beneficial purposes, the promotion of the highest ideals in the scientific, professional and educational activities of psychologists and the care for adequate training of ethical responsibilities and required competencies.

EFPA's Meta-code of Ethics (EFPA, 2005) lists very similar principles (see below), but is more operational as it translates these into matters that should be spelled out in the ethics codes of its member associations, providing guidance on content of ethical codes of member associations (see Lindsay, Koene, Øvreeide & Lang, 2008 for a detailed discussion). The Meta-code thus serves as a benchmark for the Ethical Codes of EFPA Member Associations. The same principles have been retained in the Model Code of Ethics which is now being developed by EFPA, and which "provides guidance in how to apply ethical principles to professional practice in such a way that they will advance ethical awareness and reflection" (EFPA, 2013b). The Model Code represents a further step in the direction of a common European code of ethics and provides a model or template for countries (associations) undertaking development or revision of ethical code, and a framework which may be used to achieve greater coherence and compatibility across European countries.

EFPA's Meta-code and Model Code formulate the following four principles:

- *Respect for a Person's Rights and Dignity*
  This includes respect for the individual's fundamental rights, dignity and values and respect for the knowledge, views, experience and expertise of others. It implies confidentiality and professional secrecy, informed consent and freedom of choice and self-determination.
- *Professional Competence*
  This includes the psychologists' endeavour to develop and maintain their competence, and awareness of their professional strengths and weaknesses. It implies ethical awareness, awareness of the limitations of psychological methods, and external limitations, including the conditions under which psychologists work.
- *Responsibility*
  This includes the psychologists' awareness of their professional and scientific responsibilities to their clients, research subjects, the organisation in which they work and the society at large. It implies avoiding misuse of psychological knowledge and interventions, avoiding harm, managing ethical dilemmas, continuing responsibility for care and extended responsibility in supervision, education and research.
- *Integrity*
  This includes the promotion of integrity in research, teaching and psychological practice, honesty and impartiality to others and clarification of their functioning and roles. It implies openness and clarity, and avoiding conflicts of interest and exploitation.

Although the formulations of the Universal Declaration and the EFPA Meta-Code and Model Code may be slightly different, the elaborations make clear that they address very similar issues. Both sets of principles are aspirational, portraying the profession of psychology as striving for high moral standing. This reminds us that psychologists have responsibilities not only towards their clients, but also towards their profession, the science of psychology and the society at large. It is the nature of ethical principles to provide lofty and over-arching general aspirations, goals to which psychologists should aspire; they do not provide rules or prescriptions. As mentioned, most codes of ethics (or as sometimes named, codes of conduct) translate ethical principles into more rule-like formulations, which can be used to guide psychologists' behaviour. The EFPA Model Code also aims to improve the everyday practice of psychologists by giving more specific guidelines and proposing a system of ethical governance including a description of the roles and operation of an ethical committee, a system for enforcing compliance and the use of sanctions.

The Functions of Ethical Codes

According to Bersoff (2003), "a code of ethics should ideally serve as a guide to resolving moral problems that confront the members of the profession that promulgate it with its primary emphasis on protecting the public that the profession serves. It should be a grand statement of overarching principles that earn the respect of the public by reflecting the profession's integrity" (p. 49). It is generally agreed that ethical codes serve a dual function, on the one hand being aspirational and guiding professionals towards optimal conduct, while on the other hand serving a regulatory function in defining standards that clients can expect, investigating and disciplining malpractice.

Protection of the public is a central feature of the self-regulatory nature of professional codes of ethics. Professions have forged what has been called a "special relationship" with society leading to their greater autonomy in return for their high standards of conduct and discipline (Skrtic, 1991). In this way, the "professions 'strike a bargain' with society in which they exchange competence and integrity against the trust of clients and community" (Rueschmeyer, 1983, p. 41), and use codes of ethics as guarantees of their integrity.

As an example, the code of the Belgian Federation of Psychologists (2004) is explicit on this: "[The Code's] main purpose is to protect the public and psychologists against any misuse of psychology," that is, protection against poor professional services. From the individual perspective, there are two main reasons why psychologists, in spite of knowing the facts and theories of their discipline and the methods for conducting diagnoses, interventions or evaluations, might not automatically act appropriately vis-à-vis a client. First, as in all academic professions, there is a structural misfit between the content and form of scientific knowledge on the one hand, and the problems of clients and the settings they are embedded in on the other hand. Science produces knowledge of human attributes, processes and concurrent or causal relationships, through studies that isolate these factors from other factors that might influence human behaviour. Thus, scientific knowledge comes in well-defined parcels that are considered as valid under the *ceteris paribus* assumption, that is, assuming that all other factors are equal. In the case of an individual client, this assumption does not really apply: all factors operate simultaneously in a unique configuration that science has never studied before and for which it does not provide exact guidance. Therefore, psychologists have considerable degrees of freedom in diagnosing the case and choosing a treatment that matches the condition of the client. This state of affairs is not limited to psychology but characterises all learned professions. Physicians, lawyers, architects, social workers are all confronted with unique and complex problems that give them a great freedom to act, but also the responsibility to act in ways that are effective and that can be justified vis-à-vis members of their profession. Ethics aims to provide guidance for dealing with this freedom in a responsible manner, and to help professionals in exercising judgment in individual cases.

Secondly, psychologists are not just professionals but also individuals with their own needs and interests. This can affect their behaviour in many ways. For instance, they may fail to observe the boundaries of their professional role and use the opportunities of the professional situation to act in ways that are not in the best interest of the client. This may not only be a matter of gaining personal benefit from the situation, but also of not spending enough time and effort on analysing the complexities of the client's case, or neglecting the diverging interests of members of a client system (e.g., parents-children, employer-employees). Other potential risks lie in neglecting the duty of continued learning and staying abreast of new developments in science, ignoring the limits of one's competence, or following personal preferences that diverge from commonly accepted practices. Professional codes of ethics are intended to contribute to the minimisation of such risks. According to Freidson, they perform a "translation function, dealing with the use of specialised skills in circumstances not familiar to lay people but involving familiar sins" (2001, p. 215).

Considered from a different angle, codes of ethics also serve to protect the profession, that is to maintain its integrity and autonomy. As mentioned, upholding high standards of conduct is a basis for trust in the profession by the public, diminishing the need for scrutiny by public agencies (see also O'Neill, 2002). Traditionally the codes have protected the profession from undue interference by external bodies and have allowed the profession to regulate itself, to ensure high standards of education and of discipline and to monitor and ensure its own professional development. Indeed this has led to criticisms of professional protectionism and monopolies (e.g. Clegg, 1998; Larson, 1977; Abbott, 1988). Although this tradition of self-regulation varies across different European countries, codes of ethics enable professions to gain a certain status and position which are not accorded to occupational groups that do not share this practice.

From a societal perspective the main purpose of ethical codes is to regulate the behaviour of members of the profession vis-à-vis clients, among each other, and towards societal institutions. Professional organisations use codes of ethics to guide their members towards optimal conduct and to regulate their behaviour by setting standards that shape clients' expectations, and by investigating and disciplining malpractice. Organisations of psychologists bind their members to the principles of respect, competence, responsibility and integrity, and are intended to protect the rights and interests of clients, aiming to ensure that clients receive services that are based on current science and meet standards of quality. Emphasising that psychologists' responsibilities are not limited to their clients, but extend to the profession as a whole, they aspire to the notion that psychology emerges as a caring and responsible profession that upholds high standards of ethical conduct.

Given their different nature, the relationship between ethical principles and specific rules of behaviour is not always direct, and the formulation of principles is time and culture bound, as shown by the regular revision of codes (O'Donohue & Ferguson, 2003). It is also in the nature of ethical principles that ethical judgment is required for their application. The individual psychologist working with the unique case requires considerable education, experience and judgment in the application of lofty ethical principles. These ethical principles therefore come with obligations; psychologists should make their aspirations visible. In later sections of this chapter we describe how the profession of psychology is trying to realise its ideals, of which the *EuroPsy* system is intended to be an integral part.

Ethics, Expertise and Professional Behaviour

One approach to considering the ground for public trust in professional expertise is to look at the ethical requirements concerning the expertise of psychologists, namely education in the science of psychology, professional knowledge and competences and personal experience accumulated over time in the context of previous interventions. We will briefly examine these three features, and relate them to ethical codes.

Education in the Science of Psychology

High level education and expertise is a defining characteristic of all professions, which claim that specialist expertise justifies public trust. As we saw in Chapters 1 and 4, psychology is a science-based profession. The EFPA Model Code defines psychology as "the scientific study of behaviour" thus endorsing the claim of psychology to be a science-based profession, and states that "the practice of psychologists is based on science and reliable experience" (EFPA, 2013b, art, 1.4). A number of national codes are also specific on this point. For example, the code of the Belgian Federation of Psychologists (2004, art, 3.2) states:

> The psychologist carries out his/her activity ... within the framework of theories and methods recognised by the scientific community of psychologists, taking into account their criticisms and evolution.

The code in France (ratified in Feb 2012) demands:

> The techniques used by the psychologist with the purposes of assessment, diagnosis, orientation, or selection must always have been validated scientifically and with the most recently available information.

There is no code that denies the scientific basis of psychology as a profession, although some codes are more circumspect in their wording than the examples mentioned. Psychologists' codes of ethics articulate noble aspirations, seeking to justify public trust in expertise on the basis of scientific "valid and reliable" knowledge. This, however, raises a significant challenge which is addressed in part, though only in part, by psychologists' commitments to ethical codes. This concerns the status of scientific knowledge: psychologists are expected to do their best to ensure that professional practice is based on knowledge that is *valid*, *reliable* and with *proven effectiveness* at the time. For a number of reasons, this is a major challenge (see Fairbairn & Fairbairn, 1987; Smail, 1984). We have already mentioned the structural discrepancy between scientific knowledge that comes in small packages that pertain under limiting conditions, and the natural complexity of practical real-life problems. The difficulty of finding matching knowledge is aggravated by differences and even potential contradictions in theoretical viewpoints, and the rapid changes in understanding and knowledge of psychological science over time. Science may, therefore, not always be able to provide knowledge that meets reasonable levels of predictability, standardisation of procedures and accountability. The challenge is made even greater by the existence of different paradigms, contrasting understandings and interpretations of terms such as "validity" and "effectiveness," and the different methodologies used to justify evidence. While on the one hand, in several areas of psychology there is an increasing demand for randomised controlled experiments or trials (RCTs) to evaluate interventions and to RCTs being seen as the "gold standard" for research (e.g. Slavin, 2002; and see Shadish, Clark & Steiner, 2008) in other areas this paradigm is considered inappropriate for human interventions where the specificity of each individual case has a greater salience (Howard, Maxwell & Fleming, 2000; and see Williams, 2010).

In the last century psychology in Europe has seen the proliferation of phenomenological, psychoanalytic, behaviourist, cognitivist, constructivist, hermeneutical, postmodernist and evolutionary approaches. In so far as these are paradigms or meta-theories rooted in meta-scientific convictions it may be unrealistic to expect convergence between them. The underlying beliefs are not challenged any more than the religious beliefs of any psychologist, whether Christian, Hindu, Muslim, or atheist. Many psychologists simply respect the paradigmatic beliefs of their colleagues when it comes to science. Nevertheless one can at least inspect the truth-value of the outcomes of investigations on whatever methods these may be based, and this is an ethical requirement. The challenges issued by constructionism and postmodernism have rightly admonished the post-positivistic mainstream in psychology for relying too easily and too heavily on (quasi)-experimental findings (e.g. Denzin & Lincoln, 2005), but such helpful criticisms cannot be taken to substantiate these perspectives as a sound alternative to experimental research. Such substantiation has to come from empirical data gathered by methods that seek to rule out alternative interpretation.

Some have questioned whether there is in fact such a close relationship between science and practice on other grounds. Applied psychology as practised in clinics and work organisations is not always or necessarily the outcome of basic research; the various fields of practice have their own history characterised by substantially autonomous developments. It has even been argued that the reason for psychologists to claim the science of behaviour as the basis for their interventions is that science continues to carry an aura of objectivity and independence (Schönpflug, 1993, 1994). In other words, a function of academic psychology for practitioners lies in the scientific respectability it lends to the profession. This may be an extreme point of view, but it does demonstrate the complexity and contested nature of the relationship between psychological science and practice.

From an ethical perspective psychological science provides the ultimate moral justification for the expertise of psychologists. This does not necessarily imply that each and every action of a psychologist can be evaluated against some standard derived from scientific research. However, it does mean that the profession of psychology should strive to ensure an empirical interdependence between psychology as research and psychology as practice. This raises two important and concrete questions, namely how and how soon new scientific evidence should be impacting on professional practice (e.g. in the form of new interventions) and how long the continued use of a practice can be maintained in the face of negative evidence about its validity or effectiveness. We begin to address these questions in Chapter 10.

Professional Knowledge and Competences

Professional knowledge implies that a psychologist can justify a course of action better if she can refer to procedures or practices that fellow professionals endorse. A hierarchy of overlapping communities of practice can be distinguished, with a global community in areas such as health or work and organisational psychology at the top and local circles of psychologists who meet to discuss cases at the bottom. Such circles of professionals exchange information and develop bodies of expertise partly derived from practice (see also Chapter 7 for discussion of Continuing Professional Development). In professional codes and in the literature, professional knowledge tends to be placed next to scientific evidence (e.g. Lindsay, 2008). For example, the APA code (art. 2.04) states: "Psychologists' work is based upon established scientific and professional knowledge of the discipline," while the code of the Scandinavian psychologists claims that: "The psychologist works in accordance with scientific principles and documented experience." Thus, despite its proclaimed higher methodological rigour, scientific evidence does not appear to take precedence over professional knowledge. It should be noted that most codes of ethics do not mention what should be done when scientific evidence emerges that may be in conflict with professional insights and practices. The potential for contradiction between the two sources of knowledge tends to be glossed over, although the EFPA Model Code (2013b) states clearly that:

> The practice of psychologists is based on science and reliable experience. Psychology and the psychological profession are in a continuous process of development, producing new and more complex knowledge and methods. Since social change continuously brings forth new problematic situations, it is important that psychologists pay attention to their own limitations and are able to turn to their colleagues and other professionals for additional knowledge and competence.

In the *EuroPsy* system (see Chapter 3) professional competence is seen as based on but not limited to scientific knowledge. This implies the necessity of a mutual influence and interdependence of scientific and professional research, and of scientific and professional practice.

The following example illustrates the risk of a disconnect between science and practice. About 25 years ago sexual abuse became a major focus of psychological diagnosis and treatment, spurred on by surveys showing that many women had experienced such abuse in their early youth. Numerous psychologists (and psychotherapists) – in Europe and elsewhere – identified such abuse also in some of their clients who had apparently forgotten about it. These "recovered memories" were presented as unassailable facts in court cases where reparative compensation was claimed by the (alleged) victims. A few years later there were cases in various countries in which psychologists were repudiated by the courts for having testified that their clients had suffered abuse (Lipton, 1999). Research and debate on true and false recovered memories continue (Belli, 2012; Milchman, 2012a, 2012b), but that is irrelevant to the question how it could happen that an issue so central to psychology had to be decided by the legal profession. An uncomfortable, but in our opinion likely answer is that psychology as a science and profession did not have its house in order.

This contention is supported by a debate in the APA regarding the 2003 Award for Distinguished Scientific Applications of Psychology to Elisabeth Loftus whose research on implanted memories had been instrumental in challenging the validity of recovered memories as they come about in therapy (e.g. Loftus, 2003; Loftus & Ketcham, 1996). Representatives of some divisions in the APA argued that this research had undermined public trust in psychology, a point that was apparently deemed by some to be more important than the validity of the research findings. We note that ethical codes prescribe that psychologists should be greatly concerned about something as serious as sexual abuse and that assessment and treatment of its negative psychological aftermath is to be seen as a moral obligation of the profession, but this cannot be an excuse for over-stretching the understanding of the issue.

Pertinent for the relationship between science and practice is the notion of evidence-based practice (EBP), which seeks to include both scientific and critically examined professional experience to justify interventions. In an authoritative article (APA Presidential Task Force on Evidence-Based Practice, 2006) EBP is defined to integrate research with clinical expertise "in the context of patient characteristics, culture and preferences" (p. 273). The Task Force emphasises the variety of methods, the need for changes if an intervention does not work, and the role of the client in providing information about the intervention. We note that no doubt is left about the scientific underpinnings of the psychologist's interventions: "The scientific method is a way of thinking and observing systematically, and it is the best tool we have for learning about what works for whom" (p. 278) (see also Roth & Fonagy, 2006). The need for clear evidence and the importance of EBP have been widely accepted within psychology. Yet, as pointed out by Briner and Rousseau (2011), there are a number of obstacles to be overcome. They identify four major obstacles (p. 19): (1) the apparent lack of demand by clients for EBP; "it is readily apparent from looking at the rapid adoption of some new and 'cutting-edge' practices that such decisions are not made in an evidence-based way;" (2) the number of Masters level qualified practitioners with "a limited understanding of research, a limited capacity to access new evidence and lack (of) the skills to conduct their own systematic reviews let alone primary research;" (3) the desire to "market" services leads to a reluctance "to acknowledge the limitations of ... knowledge where evidence is mixed or where there are grounds for uncertainty;" (4) "the politics of evidence in organisations:" "the need to be explicit in evidence-based decision-making means that those with vested interests in a particular course of action may find it more difficult to hide such interests." Although the authors focus here on W&O psychology, the obstacles are relevant to all fields, as is their conclusion that "scepticism is fundamental to scientific enquiry and to any area of practice based on science" and "evidence-based practice is not about perfection. Rather it is about on-going pursuit of mindful improvement in . . . uptake and use of both scholarly research and practice-related facts and assessments" (p. 20).

It remains a core problem that professional psychologists are often confronted with issues for which there is not an unambiguous diagnosis or treatment, even in the light of the best available scientific evidence. In other words, issues tend to be complex, fuzzy and to form an "open problem space." Moreover, interventions are dynamic, as clients and their needs are changing during the course of an intervention. Given these conditions, psychologists cannot be expected to limit themselves to methods for which there is "sufficient" scientific evidence as to their validity and effectiveness (leaving aside the question how sufficient might be defined precisely). Imposing limitations on the choice of interventions and treatment by practitioners may be seen as interfering with their professional responsibility to pursue the best interests of their clients, which is a basic ethical principle underlying these interventions. Respect for professional knowledge implies the need to leave space for practitioners to select and to evaluate their own interventions. A demand for such space appears to underlie the subtle shift in orientation from EBP to a slightly differently worded notion, namely practice-based evidence (PBE) that places more emphasis on clinical practice settings as a source of evidence and on understanding and description as methods (e.g. Barkham, Hardy & Mellor-Clark, 2010; Warner & Spandler, 2012).

Personal Experience and Understanding

Of the three bases of expertise, personal experience and understanding are the least accessible to independent empirical scrutiny. There is no doubt that well-trained psychologists are aware of the subjectivity of their understanding and interpretation, and make use of a variety of checks to find evidence for the validity of their diagnoses and the effectiveness of their interventions. Such assessment remains linked to the psychologist as a person, and this emphasises the crucial importance of supervision or inter-vision, and the opportunity for moderation and checking of insights with peers. Nevertheless, the validity of subjective evidence may be problematic. A psychologist who has established an idea may search for convergent evidence and neglect negative evidence. It is hard, if not impossible, to look for evidence falsifying one's perceptions of the effects of one's interventions. Poortinga and Soudijn (2003, p. 73) have illustrated this point as follows:

> Imagine a clinical psychologist who engages in a series of therapy sessions with a client. Usually at the start of such interventions the client is in evident need of help and more often than not shows signs of improvement over time. These improvements are what the therapist aimed at and worked hard for. It is extremely difficult for the therapist not to perceive a relationship between these interventions and the improvement of the client.

Contrary to the frequent view that experience for psychologists is inevitably an asset, research on the relationship between experience and quality of outcomes has not found much support for this belief. Various studies have reported that there is little correlation between the length of experience of therapists and the effectiveness of their interventions (e.g., Andersson, Carlbring & Furmark, 2012; Beutler et al., 2003; Jacobi, Uhmann & Hoyer, 2011). Furthermore, studies comparing professional judgments of more experienced and less experienced psychologists showed that experience at best has a limited impact on the quality of judgments in diagnosis (e.g. Spengler et al., 2009).

However, although psychologists have reason to be cautious about their personal experience and understanding, they often have to act on that basis and, perhaps, more than other professionals, rely on their own insight into what is happening in the course of an intervention.

Professional Ethics and *EuroPsy*

Although the challenges discussed are not unique for psychology, we should be aware of the potential vulnerability of the psychological profession, and the need for developing systems of accountability and of professional support in order to maximise the power and effectiveness of ethical codes, and to minimise the misdemeanours which are, wittingly and unwittingly, committed by members of the profession and by the profession itself. *EuroPsy* aims to provide such systems.

As mentioned at the start of the chapter, psychologists wishing to obtain a *EuroPsy* Certificate must fulfil two requirements regarding ethics: (1) they must declare that they will abide by the principles as stated in the EFPA Meta-Code; (2) they must commit themselves to the code of ethics of the national association in the country of practice. This is formalised by their signing an ethical declaration in which these two points are laid down. The intended effect of the first requirement is that all psychologists will follow the same ethical principles in their work. The second requirement implies that all psychologists submit themselves to a monitoring and disciplinary mechanism that is operating in the country where they work. As a result, any holder of a *EuroPsy* certificate exposes him/herself to the possibility that a complaint will be filed, and that his/her conduct will be investigated and sanctioned according to rules applying in the country of practice.

The more serious sanctions have consequences for the psychologist's *EuroPsy* Certificate and her status in the *EuroPsy* Register. The psychologist's name is removed from the *EuroPsy* Register when a court of law or a national committee has imposed a sentence or measure against the holder that prohibits her from exercising the profession of psychologist (such as removal from a national register or withdrawal of a national licence). The record of a psychologist in the Register is marked as "suspended" when a court of law or a national committee has imposed a sentence or measure that suspends the holder's right to exercise the profession of psychologist. This mark will be removed when the suspension in the respective country ends (*EuroPsy* regulations, 2013a; art. 11). This mechanism helps to address the challenge of cross-border mobility articulated at the start of this chapter.

The enforcement of ethical rules in relation to *EuroPsy* takes place at the national level, according to the procedures laid down in the national code, and set out in the application for approval of the National Awarding Committee. Complaints or allegations of professional misconduct can be brought to the attention of an Ethical Committee (or Disciplinary Committee) that investigates eligible complaints or accusations by hearing the complainant and the psychologist. After all the information has been received and evaluated the Committee rules whether the code of ethics has been violated and if so, which sanction should be applied. It notifies the parties of its verdict and publishes it to inform the public and other members of the profession. The verdict of the Ethical Committee is normally open to appeal with an Ethical Appeal Committee, which can conduct a further investigation and give a final verdict. The *EuroPsy* Regulations do not provide any additional procedure for examining complaints at the European level. However, the national Ethical Committee and Appeal Committee are obliged to bring their verdicts to the attention of the European Awarding Committee of *EuroPsy*, and the sanction issued may have consequences for the status of the psychologists in the *EuroPsy* Register. As mentioned above, the psychologist may be removed from the register or suspended (*EuroPsy* regulations, EFPA, 2013a, art. 11). Hereby, the wider public and all European psychologists will be informed about the ethical transgression and the sanction applied, in a way that bears similarity to the alert system for health professionals that has been built into the revised EU Directive on the Recognition of Professional Qualifications.

EuroPsy and the Importance of Education, Supervised Practice and Continuing Professional Development

In discussions of professional ethics the focus is usually directed towards ethical principles, and the prescriptions and standards derived from these with links to the apparatus of enforcement. There is a third aspect that is of equal importance and helps to support the notion of ethical awareness and ethical competence. This is the way in which psychologists are taught what professional ethics is and how it should be incorporated into their everyday professional activity, and – even more important – how psychologists can remain aware of the ethical aspects of their work. Studying the ethical code and developing a capacity for ethical judgment using cases and dilemmas from other psychologists' practice is probably the easier part of this. Much more difficult is developing and retaining awareness of the ethical dimensions of one's own condition while working, that is, while applying various competences in an unfolding trajectory of assessment and intervention, interacting with clients and other people. This awareness is not only threatened by the complexity of the case the psychologist is working on (as the limit of processing capacity is reached), but also by the routinisation that occurs when similar cases are handled (because processing capacity declines). It is something that requires explicit on the-job training, which aims to integrate the ethical aspects of work into the psychologist's personal behaviour repertoire. The learning process is not just a matter of learning "how to" recognise ethical aspects or handle ethical imperatives, but extends to seeing the "why" of this as part of the socialisation into the profession. This type of learning requires a realistic, complex work situation, with ample opportunity for feedback. For unqualified and junior members of the profession gaining such experience is an important function of supervised practice, while for more experienced and senior psychologists this is part of the function of continuing professional development, and forms of peer support such as inter-vision.

The development of ethical awareness and ethical competence is a central aspect of the processes of supervised practice and of continuing professional development. The EFPA Model Code provides a guide to ethical decision-making. In our view supervised practice, peer supervision and inter-vision, and engagement in ethical discourse are essential features contributing to the ethical competence of psychologists. Protection is required both for clients and for practitioners given the complexity, the unpredictability and the uniqueness of psychologists' cases.

A specific aspect that is hard to learn but nonetheless critical for ethical conduct is related to the rule "when in doubt, ask." Just like other professionals, psychologists must learn to ask for the views and advice of colleagues, when they are confronted with difficult ethical choices and dilemmas. The basis for this may be laid in the supervision setting, or through continuing professional development, but psychologists need also to learn to contact colleagues or an ethical advisory committee, if available.

However, the promotion of ethical conduct should not be seen as limited to teaching and training individual psychologists with respect to professional ethics. On the contrary, it is a matter of developing and maintaining collective awareness and understanding of what the current state is of scientific knowledge and what represents appropriate practice. There is, in other words, a need for a discourse on ethical issues that includes both presentation and discussion of experiences and dilemmas on a case-by-case basis, and extends to broader analyses and debates about shared practices that may be questionable as part of a wider ethical discourse.

A more general function of ethical discourse is to ensure that the profession remains anchored in science, and that advances in theory and methods are reflected in the profession's standards of good practice. This has two sides, first the propagation of new theories and methods of assessment and intervention, and second the rejection of theories and methods that are no longer considered adequate. An example of the former is neuropsychological assessment with MRI (magnetic resonance imaging), and an example of the latter is handwriting analysis in personnel selection. New developments tend to find their way to the profession through the education of new generations of students and continued training of professionals. They may therefore need less debate than the discarding of theories and methods that older generations of psychologists grew up with, but which can no longer be considered valid and useful. This chapter is not the place to draw the borders between the new and the old, or the acceptable and the unacceptable, but we would like to emphasise the importance of debating theories and methods that ought to be discarded because they are no longer upheld by scientific evidence.

As we have already suggested above, it would be naïve to expect that there is a single, universally shared view of what represents the "body of scientific knowledge" in psychology. Science itself is an open and democratic endeavour, which implies debate between opposing views. Thus, there are diverging views across countries and generations of psychologists, and the borders of consensus and disagreement vary with the areas of research and practice. We cannot expect that the evolution of science over time and its reflection in accepted standards is a smooth and homogeneous process in which all members of the profession have the same understanding of progress and the current "state of the art." This makes an on-going ethical discourse among individuals, groups and communities even more needed. It is indispensible to make psychologists aware of where psychological science is moving and how the standards of practice should change.

Ethical debates often take place at the national level, with reference to the practices that prevail in the particular country, and among psychologists speaking the same language. Given the diversity in the psychological profession that results from socio-economic and political conditions across Europe, as well as scientific and educational traditions, this is understandable and makes sense. However, it is desirable to transcend the national level and extend the discourse to the European level, as many issues have fundamental aspects and are of relevance to a broader circle of professionals and clients. This is something that EFPA might stimulate in the years to come.

A Broader Perspective

As we have argued above, national codes of ethics for psychologists are of obvious importance in protecting psychologists' clients, etc. and in maintaining the integrity of the profession. *EuroPsy* aims to strengthen the power of national codes, through its requirements for supervised practice, continuing professional development and revalidation. The European standard implicit in the European Certificate provides a common understanding of ethical behaviour and implies greater transparency and information across European countries in relation to psychologists who have violated an ethical code. EFPA, too, aims to consolidate ethical codes at European level with the Meta-Code and the Model Code. However, a number of questions can be raised when looking at the function of these codes in a broader perspective and with an eye on the future.

As most existing codes are maintained by associations with jurisdictions limited to their members, the first question that arises is whether they could be expanded into national codes that cover all psychologists in the country. As *EuroPsy* is being implemented on a growing scale this would seem to make sense, since it provides for greater transparency and uniform protection of clients within European countries. By the same token it would seem meaningful to promote the adoption of a single ethical code – comprising a single set of principles and the same mechanism of enforcement at the European level. Although this may take considerable time to achieve, it would be something that would fit into the logic of *EuroPsy*, namely to provide uniform quality standards and equal protection to psychologists' clients throughout Europe. The development of the EFPA Meta-Code of Ethics (EFPA, 2005) followed by the EFPA Model Code of Ethics (EFPA, 2013b) fosters this development. One might, of course, carry this line of reasoning further and ponder the desirability and feasibility of a universal code of ethics that applies to all countries in the world. The acceptance of the Universal Declaration of Ethical Principles for Psychologists by IUPsyS, IAAP and IACCP in 2008, mentioned earlier in this chapter, shows widespread acceptance of the principles that should guide psychologists' professional conduct. However, the translation of these principles into rules and standards is a much more cumbersome process that may take a long time and is likely to be frustrated by divergences in professional practice, definitions of human rights and the relationship with national legislation. From a European perspective it would seem worth exploring, provided that a bottom-up procedure would be followed with input from national associations (Lindsay, 2008).

A second question is how ethical codes for *psychologists* relate to codes for other professions and whether a separate code will be needed in the long run. It is interesting to note that there are tendencies to adopt a broader approach to the regulation of professional conduct that looks beyond the limits of a single profession. Of immediate relevance for European psychologists is the EU Services Directive (2006/123/EC), intended to promote the free movement of services in the Single Market, which encourages the development of codes of conduct at European level to promote high quality services and the establishment of a relationship of confidence between consumers (clients) and professionals. These codes should preferably be established at a European level, avoiding national borders where the different perceptions of quality might lead to market segmentation. The directive covers services provided by a wide range of professions, including architects, lawyers, tax advisers, real estate agents, tourist operators, financial advisors and builders, but also psychologists. It shows that the availability of a wide array of codes and the promotion of awareness of these codes is seen as being in the interest of European citizens. The EFPA Model Code could provide the basis for a European code of conduct for psychological services. It is also worth noting the interest of national legislators in harmonising the many systems of disciplinary law that have emerged in the course of time, and to provide a more transparent and consistent framework for legal control of professionals.

Following another line of reasoning, namely starting from the fact that ethical codes of all professions should respect international declarations and conventions on human rights, one would wonder how much need there is for specific rules concerning psychology. Relevant are: the Universal Declaration of Human Rights (UDHR) adopted by the United Nations General Assembly on December 10, 1948; the Convention for the protection of human rights and fundamental freedoms of November 4, 1950, now the European convention on human rights; the Convention for the protection of human rights and dignity of the human being with regard to the application of biology and medicine of April 4, 1997 (Convention on human rights and biomedicine); and the Convention on the rights of the child of November 20, 1989 (UN Convention on the rights of the child). Current codes of ethics for psychologists are not limited to the principles formulated in these legal documents, and they make useful additions by translating the principles into enforceable standards, but it would be conceivable that at some point in the future the control over actions by professionals – psychologists and others – would move towards public, civil and penal laws at the national level, in accordance with European legislation.

Conclusion

EuroPsy requires ethical commitment at national and individual level. At national level, the country applying for recognition of the National Accreditation Committee (NAC) is required to demonstrate robust ethical procedures in the country and to provide the text of its code of ethics. At individual level the applicant for *EuroPsy* is required to sign a commitment to abide by the national code of ethics in the country of practice and the EFPA Meta-Code of Ethics. The third level of ethical commitment is for the profession itself. For qualifying psychologists, *EuroPsy* requires supervised practice, an important element of which is development of ethical awareness, and for experienced psychologists continuing professional development and revalidation of the Certificate which provide the opportunity for psychologists to maintain their ethical integrity, and use their experience to develop a more nuanced and sophisticated ethical intelligence.

We emphasise here that a further requirement of the profession is to make the best endeavours to ensure that psychological practice is rooted in sound evidence, and that ways are found to incorporate new insights and findings into psychologists' professional work, and to interrogate procedures for which evidence of effectiveness begins to weaken. While the complexity and uniqueness of psychologists' case work often imply idiographic approaches and the exercise of spontaneous subjective judgement, this has to take place within a robust framework of ethical awareness and integrity which ensures that practice is characterised by "wise judgement under conditions of considerable uncertainty" (Eraut, 1994). This requires effort and commitment on the part of the individual psychologist, the national psychological association administering the ethical code and the psychological profession itself.

9 *EuroPsy* in Context

This chapter describes *EuroPsy* in the context of the psychology profession, as it is being practised and developing in Europe today. We begin by providing a framework for understanding the implementation of *EuroPsy* by describing the current state of the profession in Europe, in terms of numbers of professionals and the areas of practice in which they operate. Next, we describe where *EuroPsy* is today, that is, in which countries and on what scale it has been implemented to date. We subsequently turn to the impact of *EuroPsy*, beginning with a discussion of how it is becoming a new institution within the world of psychology that is changing and consolidating relationships between various parties involved in psychological education, research and professional work, including psychological associations. Looking beyond *EuroPsy* as a mere certification system, we give a preliminary assessment of the impact that *EuroPsy* seems to be exerting on legislation and executive functions at the national as well as the European level. We pay special attention to the way in which *EuroPsy* can be linked to European legislation to promote the mobility of professionals and the protection of consumers. Finally, we discuss the significance of *EuroPsy* in a global perspective, relating it to initiatives to develop common standards for the education and professional work of psychologists throughout the word.

State of the Profession

As discussed in Chapter 1, European psychology displays a continuously moving and changing picture. Psychology continues to develop along different paths and with different profiles in each of the European countries. We begin by presenting some basic figures regarding psychology in Europe, that is the approximate numbers of psychologists that are members of national psychologist associations and the numbers of inhabitants in the 36 countries represented in EFPA (see Table 15). It should be noted that it is difficult to provide exact numbers since membership criteria of national psychologist organisations (EFPA Member Associations) vary considerably. In one country membership of a psychologist organisation is restricted to fully qualified psychologists, in other countries membership may include students of psychology and in yet other countries membership may be available to those with lower than full qualifications in psychology for example at Bachelor level. These criteria are to an extent related to the function served by the national association, for example trade union, learned society, professional association, etc. The actual numbers of psychologists in the countries may also be higher than those belonging to the EFPA Member Association, since some countries have more than one national psychology association, while in other countries it may not be mandatory to belong to an association in order to practise as a psychologist. The degree to which numbers vary is not exactly known and varies per country; the difference is small for countries with

Table 15. European countries by numbers of psychologists in EFPA Member Associations and overall, and size of population (2013)

Country	Number of members in EFPA Members Associations	Estimated total number of psychologists	Population
Austria	4,200	10,000	8,477,000
Belgium	1,950	8,000	11,162,000
Bulgaria	500	500	7,261,000
Croatia	600	2,400	4,258,000
Cyprus	200	350	1,117,000
Czech Republic	850	2,000	10,519,000
Denmark	7,200	7,200	5,612,000
Estonia	100	500	1,283,000
Finland	4,100	4,500	5,436,000
France	1,750	35,000	63,820,000
Germany	13,600	61,000	80,640,000
Greece	500	2,000	1,075,8000
Hungary	900	6,000	9,894,000
Iceland	400	450	324,000
Ireland	2,200	5,000	4,662,000
Italy	80,000	80,000	59,789,000
Latvia	200	450	2,011,000
Liechtenstein	50	50	37,000
Lithuania	450	900	2,956,000
Luxembourg	200	200	542,000
Malta	100	100	419,000
Netherlands	13,100	14,400	16,795,000
Norway	6,300	6,750	5,077,000
Poland	1,600	1,600	38,548,000
Portugal	15,000	15,000	10,609,000
Romania	13,800	13,800	19,858,000
Russia	5,000	5,000	143,455,000
San Marino	50	50	32,000
Serbia	450	450	7,203,000
Slovakia	350	2,000	5,413,000

(continued on next page)

Table 15. (continued)

Country	Number of members in EFPA Members Associations	Estimated total number of psychologists	Population
Slovenia	150	1,150	2,062,000
Spain	56,050	56,050	46,958,000
Sweden	8,450	12,500	9,595,000
Switzerland	6,800	6,800	8,075,000
Turkey	1,300	1300	75,549,000
United Kingdom	42,150	42,150	6,4231,000
Total	290,600	405,600	744,437,000

obligatory membership of a single national association based on law; for other countries the number of psychologists may be more than 100% higher than the number in the EFPA member association. What is evident from the table is that psychology is quite unevenly developed across Europe, ranging from countries with about 1 psychologist for fewer than 1,000 inhabitants (including Italy, Spain, Portugal, Netherlands, Denmark, Sweden and Norway) to countries with 1 psychologist for more than 3,000 inhabitants (as, e.g., in countries like Malta, Cyprus, Greece, Turkey, Czech Republic, Lithuania, Latvia and Poland). The table provides a useful illustration of the spread of psychologists, even though this may not have exact significance in terms of service provision.

There are also differences in the areas in which psychologists work, and the kind of work in which they are engaged. We have no robust figures, but data from a recent EFPA survey (2013) suggest that some 50% are clinical and health psychologists, 18% work and organisational psychologists, 16% school psychologists and 5% transport or traffic psychologists. In terms of sectors it appears that about half of all psychologists work in the health sector, 14% in education, 12% in business and public administration, 7% in communities. There are some remarkable differences between countries. For instance, we find substantial numbers of traffic psychologists working in transportation in countries such as Germany, Czech Republic, Hungary, Ireland and Spain. The number of psychologists in law enforcement (including forensic work) is significant in Italy, Germany, the Netherlands, Croatia and Estonia. Community psychology is particularly strong in Italy, Croatia, Ireland and Norway. Counselling psychology is more prominent in the United Kingdom and Cyprus. These differences show that psychology has developed under unique circumstances and that every country has its own profile. This is also apparent from data on the academic education of psychologists in Europe presented in Table 16. This table lists the numbers of psychology programs (Bachelor, Master or Doctoral level) offered by European Higher Education Institutions (HEIs), as documented by the German Leibniz Centre for Psychological Information and Documentation (ZPID; http://www.zpid.de). The number of universities where psychology is taught ranges from 1 in small countries, like Luxembourg, Malta and San Marino, to 80 in Russia, 113 in the United Kingdom and 120 in Germany. As was mentioned in Chapter 1, psychology has a history of more than

Table 16. Numbers of psychology programs at European universities (based on http://www.zpid.de, 2013)

Country	# Programs
Albania	2
Austria	10
Belarus	8
Belgium	10
Bosnia and Herzegovina	4
Bulgaria	11
Croatia	5
Cyprus	5
Czech Republic	19
Denmark	7
Estonia	3
Finland	11
France	43
Georgia	3
Germany	120
Greece	10
Hungary	11
Iceland	5
Ireland	10
Italy	34
Latvia	5
Lithuania	10
Luxembourg	1
Macedonia	3
Malta	1
Moldova	7
Netherlands	16
Norway	6
Poland	27
Portugal	28
Romania	8

(continued on next page)

Table 16. (continued)

Country	# Programs
Russia	80
San Marino	1
Serbia	5
Slovakia	12
Slovenia	3
Spain	48
Sweden	17
Switzerland	19
Turkey	24
Ukraine	12
United Kingdom	113
Total	777

a century in countries like Germany, Italy and the United Kingdom, while in other countries it began much later or its development was interrupted for a significant amount of time.

There are several indicators of growth in the number of psychologists in Europe. For instance, a report of the EU Skills Panorama from November 2012 mentions that amongst the professionals in Europe, psychologists were amongst the top three growth occupations over the past few years. The number of psychologists that found a job in 2010 amounted to 25,300, a growth of 108% since 2007 (http://euskillspanorama.ec.europa.eu). Interest in psychology amongst university students is high. According to the same Skills Panorama the number of tertiary education graduates in the area "social and behavioural sciences," which includes psychologists, grew from 200,000 in 2000 to over 350,000 in 2010 (EU-27). A survey by the European Federation of Psychology Students Associations (EFPSA) estimated the number of psychology students in Europe in 2003 to be around 200,000.

EuroPsy Today

The figures presented in the previous section are helpful in beginning to understand why countries entered the *EuroPsy* system at different times. Amongst the countries participating in the pilot project (see Chapter 2) were some that had considerable experience in certification, like the United Kingdom and Finland, but also some that were eager to participate because this coincided with new developments, like Hungary. Something similar was seen when *EuroPsy* was launched. France, Norway, Italy and Spain were quick to join, while some other associations with well-established certification systems, like the

United Kingdom and Germany, needed more time to prepare for the formal launch of *EuroPsy* in their country. At the time of writing (autumn 2013) associations from the following 20 countries, over half of the EFPA members, had an approved National Awarding Committee (NAC). This means that they are allowed to issue the *EuroPsy* Basic Certificate: Austria, Cyprus, Czech Republic, Denmark, Estonia, Finland, France, Germany, Greece, Hungary, Italy, Latvia, Lithuania, Netherlands, Norway, Russia, Slovenia, Spain, Turkey and the United Kingdom. A number of other countries were in the process of preparing for the implementation of *EuroPsy*, namely Cyprus, Ireland, Malta, Poland, Slovakia, Sweden and Switzerland. The remaining 10 countries are likely to follow in the near future.

During the start-up phase, for some countries the number of certificates issued was rather modest. Since in most countries the application and assessment process began only recently the number of certificates issued by the Summer of 2013 was only some 7,000, of which more than half were *EuroPsy* Basic Certificates and the remainder were *EuroPsy* Specialist Certificates in Psychotherapy. It is expected that these numbers will soon rise and may well double by 2014. Since the *EuroPsy* Specialist Certificate in Work & Organisational Psychology was only established in the summer of 2013, the issuing of this certificate will only start in 2014. As expected, most basic certificates were issued for the area of practice Clinical and Health; Work and Organisation takes the second place and Education the third one. The number of certificates in the area of practice designated as "Other," which comprises, traffic psychology, forensic psychology, sport psychology, etc., is gradually growing. In the future decisions will need to be taken in relation to designated areas of practice; as psychologists' practice (and education) extends to sports psychology, traffic psychology and other areas, these may need to be included in the areas recognised and specified on the Certificate. For example, the UK Register includes seven areas of practice: clinical, counselling, educational, forensic, health, occupational, sports and exercise psychologists. These areas have grown as they develop formal education and training routes.

Impact of *EuroPsy*

As a certification system for psychologists in Europe, *EuroPsy* may be supposed to promote the visibility of qualified psychologists, their accessibility for clients, and at the same time raise the prestige and transparency of psychologists' certification, as *EuroPsy* is endorsed by the European Federation of Psychology Associations. In this section we will argue that the potential impact of *EuroPsy* reaches far beyond this. We will first consider some effects within the "inner" world of psychology, and next discuss the impact of *EuroPsy* in the public realm at the European as well as the national level.

The Inner World of Psychology

In the previous chapters we have pointed out that as a certification system *EuroPsy* is making a distinction that did not previously exist, namely between psychologists who have provided evidence that they meet certain standards of education and professional training, professional ethics and continuing education, and those who have not. By doing so, it is improving transparency on the market of psychological services, helping clients to find the way to more qualified and trustworthy professionals, and enhancing client protection. The information presented above on how the implementation of *EuroPsy* is proceeding helps to convey an understanding about this dimension of *EuroPsy*.

However, there are other facets of *EuroPsy* that reach beyond its function as a tool for certification. The reality is that *EuroPsy* is on its way to becoming a new institution in the field of psychology in Europe, one that strengthens the links amongst older and younger professional associations across Europe, and that improves, renews and expands relationships between psychologists' associations and universities as well as other research bodies. Universities are interested in educating students for professional careers that may extend across national borders, and are keen to ensure that the curricula they offer match the requirements of *EuroPsy*. Those involved in psychological research, at universities or other research institutions, increasingly realise that their work is an input for the evidence-based practice that *EuroPsy* stands for. It is worth noting that in the preparation phase of *EuroPsy*, during the pilot project as well as the actual implementation, officials from the national psychologists' associations were frequently in touch with deans of faculties and heads of departments in their country about the implications of *EuroPsy* for curricula and educational practices. University officials, being aware that the curricula followed by their graduates would be evaluated when applying for *EuroPsy* certificates, have often made efforts to adjust curricula in order to optimise the career opportunities of their graduates. A similar strengthening of ties, based on common interests, is starting to emerge on the part of those involved in the further education and continuing professional development of psychologists.

It is also worthy of mention that since *EuroPsy* supports a broad and integrated conception of psychology, it has the potential to promote collaboration between representatives of psychology's many specialties. That is, *EuroPsy* covers all areas of practice in which psychologists are professionally active. Using the same standards for education and professional training it emphasises that all psychologists should engage in science-based practice. By putting all areas and specialities – from traffic psychology to gero-psychology, and from school psychology to clinical neuropsychology – on the same footing, it offers a basis for balanced relations and cooperation amongst academics and professionals in the different areas and provides a basis for joint action that can strengthen psychology as a whole. This is particularly valuable in view of the centripetal tendencies that have for long plagued psychology and weakened its position in comparison with other academic professions.

Another important facet of *EuroPsy* that lies beyond the certification function per se, is that it requires a close and continuing collaboration of psychologists from different countries, with their different cultures and languages. The *EuroPsy* project is probably the greatest collaborative experience of psychologists from Europe – from North to South and East to West, including EU and non-EU countries, that has ever taken place. Both the preparatory activities which, as Chapter 2 has pointed out, took more than 10 years and the following implementation and further development, show that psychologists are able to share experiences from different countries in a flexible and productive way, and work on a matter of common interest and develop considerable strength while spanning different cultural and linguistic realities.

Apart from these aspects, *EuroPsy* has had a clear impact on the standards for education and training at the national level. By requiring a minimum of 5 years (300 ECTS) of academic education plus 1 year of supervised practice it has set a standard that national governments and universities cannot ignore. In some countries this has helped to counteract pressures to reduce the resources and time devoted to the education and training of psychologists. The requirement regarding supervised practice has triggered a variety of national initiatives to improve existing supervision practices or to establish supervision in areas where it did not yet exist. The same can be said with respect to continuing professional education, which is required for renewal of *EuroPsy* certificates. In addition, *EuroPsy* has provided a shared model of competences that is increasingly adopted in Europe, and that helps to achieve greater convergence and rigour in the professional training of psychologists.

The European Context

The impact of *EuroPsy* is not limited to the inner world of psychology. *EuroPsy* is already changing the position of psychology amongst the professions at the European and the national level. By launching *EuroPsy*, psychology has joined the ranks of professions with European-level self-regulation, demonstrating very widespread consensus on a standard across European countries. It has created more clarity on how the psychological profession and its specialities differ from other human professions that are based on other scientific disciplines, as well as professions that lack a clear scientific foundation or accept less rigorous standards regarding education, professional training or ethical conduct.

The National Level

Although *EuroPsy* is aimed at the European level and its implementation is still at an early stage, it is worth noting that *EuroPsy* is already having a significant impact at the national level. As *EuroPsy* is becoming more well-known, it is changing relationships with national authorities in matters of credentialing, certification and licensing. This effect is due to that fact that *EuroPsy* complements national systems of credentialing, certification and licensing which have been set up by public agencies and professional associations, and in many ways reaches beyond these in scope and level of requirements. It is increasingly recognised that *EuroPsy* provides a more comprehensive and up-to-date framework, and that it constitutes a sound base for legislation regarding the professional activities and title psychologist. EFPA places a strong emphasis on this and recommends national governments that are considering revision of existing legislation or development of new legislation on the profession and title of psychologist to incorporate the *EuroPsy* standards as far as possible. To this purpose (at the time of writing), EFPA is in the process of developing a Model for a Psychologists Law that provides examples of how legislation can be made compatible with *EuroPsy* and benefit from it. To facilitate the nation-wide application of *EuroPsy*, EFPA is also addressing the desirability of a national Code of Ethics for psychologists. As mentioned earlier, it has recently developed a Model Code of Ethics

(EFPA, 2013b) and an ethical governance structure that can supplement or replace ethical systems established and held by associations that fail to reach psychologists who are not members of such associations. This should help to achieve greater homogeneity in ethical rules and in the systems of monitoring psychologists' professional conduct and sanctioning infringements of the code. The impact of *EuroPsy* extends to the recognition of professional qualifications by national authorities. We will discuss this in the context of EU legislation, in the following section.

Finally it should be emphasised that *EuroPsy* does not limit itself to psychologists working in the health sector as is the case for many existing credentialing, certification and licensing systems at the national level. *EuroPsy* helps to create clarity regarding psychologists working in other sectors, such as education, industry, transportation or public administration, and helps to resist undue pressures from existing health care legislation to define psychology as predominantly a (mental) health profession.

EuroPsy and the Mobility of Psychologists in Europe

As mentioned above, the corner stone of the European Union is the notion of a Single Market, which is characterised by free flow of goods, capital, services and people, sometimes referred to as the "four freedoms." The free flow of people was defined in the 1957 Treaty of Rome and intended to make it possible for citizens to travel to another Member State, to live there, to study, work or conduct a business there, without needing a visa or permit. Part of the EU legislation regarding this right pertains to the mutual recognition of professional qualifications. The current act regulating this is known as the EU Directive on the Recognition of Professional Qualifications 2005/36/EC, also known as the European Qualifications Directive or EQD. As described in Chapter 2, it makes a distinction between professions with automatic recognition of qualifications, which are covered by the so-called "sectoral system," and professions for which recognition must be obtained on a case-by-case basis. The seven professions covered by the sectoral system are: architects, dentists, physicians ("doctors"), midwives, nurses, pharmacists and veterinary surgeons. Psychologists belong to the so-called "general system," along with thousands of other professions and occupations. The 2005 Directive focuses on differences between qualifications required by Member States and the compensation which may be demanded by a Member State for these differences. It states that compensation may only be required in the case of substantial differences – a training that is at least 1 year less or covers substantially different matters than is required in the host country – and that it may take the form of an adaptation period of up to 3 years or an aptitude test.

An evaluation of the directive, its transposition into national law, and the actual process of recognition by "competent authorities"[15] in the EU Member States, carried out by the European Commission in 2010–2011, revealed that the directive did not sufficiently remove barriers to mobility and therefore did not contribute enough to the realisation of the Single Market as aimed for in the Lisbon Treaty (2009). During the evaluation,

[15] The term "competent authority" refers to an administrative entity that is charged by a national government to fulfil certain tasks on its behalf. In the context of the EQD it is an entity charged with determining whether a person's professional qualifications meet the national qualification standards.

the Commission also consulted European organisations representing professions, which gave EFPA an opportunity to inform the Commission about *EuroPsy* and to suggest that it would be the most appropriate basis for (automatic) recognition of psychologists' qualifications in the future. On December 19, 2011 the Commission presented a proposal for modernisation of the Qualifications Directive to the European Parliament and the European Council. This proposal aimed to simplify the rules of the directive and to make recognition of qualifications easier and faster, in order to promote the mobility of professionals in the EU. It also addressed concerns over language skills and alerts in case of malpractice. A critical element in the modernisation proposal from the perspective of psychologists was that the Commission would be able to propose a Common Training Framework as the basis for EU-wide recognition of professional qualifications. EFPA and several other organisations representing professions at European level argued that they should have the opportunity to propose a CTF, and that they should at least be consulted if the Commission were to establish a CTF. This would give EFPA the opportunity to propose a CTF based on *EuroPsy*. During the review of the modernisation proposal by the European Parliament and the European Council in 2012, EFPA filed an amendment with such a proposal. This amendment gained the support of the European Council of Liberal Professions (CEPLIS) of which EFPA and organisations representing other professions are members.

The final text of the proposal for modernisation of the qualifications directive, known as Directive 2013/55/EU, has meanwhile been accepted by the European Parliament in its plenary session of 9 October 2013 and was ultimately adopted by the Council of the European Union on 20 November 2013. Its main elements are:

- Introduction of a *Professional Card* issued by the Competent Authority in the home country.
- Possibility to establish a *Common Training Framework* (*CTF*) replacing the former compensation of differences between national qualification requirements by general exemptions.
- Power for the Commission to establish a CTF by *delegated* act when the profession is regulated in at least 1/3 of the Member States.
- Through the CTF, de facto *automatic recognition* of qualifications for non-sectoral professions (including psychologists).
- Testing *language skills*, after the qualifications check.
- A *malpractice alert* mechanism for Competent Authorities (only for professions in the Sectoral System).
- *Partial access* for professionals qualified for activities that are part of a profession with a larger scope of activities in the host country.

Directive 2013/55/EU recognises the role of professional organisations and other stakeholders. It requires that a "common training framework has been prepared following a transparent process, including the relevant stakeholders from Member States where the profession is not regulated." It also states that: "Representative professional organisations at the Union level as well as national professional organisations and competent authorities from at least one third of the Member States may submit to the Commission suggestions for common training frameworks" (CEPLIS Telegram, 2013). This suggests that the role of the European professional associations put forward by EFPA, CEPLIS and other organisations will be taken seriously.

A future Common Training Framework for psychologists will provide the opportunity for *EuroPsy* to become the basis for the recognition of professional qualifications in all 28 countries of the European Union, as well as in countries of the European Economic Area – Iceland, Liechtenstein, Norway – and Switzerland, which tend to follow EU directives. However, it should be acknowledged that it will not be possible to map all *EuroPsy* requirements onto the CTF. It may well be that the requirements for supervised practice and the professional competences will fall beyond the scope of the CTF, as is also likely to be the case for the requirements concerning ethics and continuing professional development. It is likely that recognition based on CTF will be valid for life, while *EuroPsy* requires revalidation after a certain time. How the *EuroPsy* Specialist Certificates would fit into CTFs will also need to be clarified. Nonetheless, there will be an important role to play for *EuroPsy* in connection with mobility in Europe. One of the forms this may take – already while the 2005 Directive is still operational – is that *EuroPsy* Certificates are accepted as a waiver for the recognition of the qualifications of psychologists crossing borders within Europe. This is something for EFPA to discuss with the competent authorities of the EU Member States in the recently formed network European Network of Psychological Competent Authorities (ENPCA).

A few words should be added about *EuroPsy* in relation to the free movement of services. In 2006 the EU established its Services Directive (2006/123/EC), which requires the Member States to simplify procedures and formalities that service providers need to comply with when establishing services in other Member States or providing services across national borders. It appears that the transposition of the directive is an administratively hugely complex operation that is taking more time than expected. An important issue that is contributing to the slow implementation of the directive is concern over the protection of clients when services become very mobile. Although psychological services are currently not attracting much attention, it is worth noting that *EuroPsy* offers an effective protection for consumers. The development by EFPA of a Model Code of Ethics to be used in conjunction with *EuroPsy* is in line with the idea that professions should design a quality charter to protect consumers. What remains to be considered is how the National Awarding Committees of *EuroPsy* could be of help to the "points of single contact" – for the Qualifications Directive as well as the Services Directive.[16]

Mobility in a Wider Perspective

It is important to bear in mind that mobility is not just an issue for psychologists who want to practise in another country. As has been pointed out earlier, there is also increasing mobility of clients and employers. Although this issue is beyond the boundaries of the

[16] A "point of single contact" is an administrative entity at the national level from which citizens can obtain all relevant information regarding a topic regulated by European law.

European Qualifications Directive, it is important in connection with the right of free movement as laid down in the European Treaties. Here we can consider the role of *EuroPsy* from another angle. When clients or employers move to another country they are able to consult the *EuroPsy* Register as a way to distinguish between holders of the *EuroPsy* Certificate and other service providers in the country. It will also make it easier for them to find qualified psychologists speaking the required language.

Mobility is of increasing importance for students and graduates of psychology. As discussed earlier in relation to the Erasmus programme (see Chapters 2, 4), the promotion of mobility for students has long been an important policy objective for the European Union; a range of instruments have been developed to encourage students to study and live abroad, and to ensure that their credits are transferred and their degrees recognised. For students of psychology *EuroPsy* is likely to provide an added value, as its curriculum framework and minimum standards give students greater confidence that they can continue studying psychology in another country without running the risk that the content of their studies will not be recognised, or that credits will not count when applying for a *EuroPsy* Certificate. The same applies for graduates who decide to work abroad and engage in supervised practice, after having completed a curriculum that matches the *EuroPsy* requirements. The latter group will profit from a new article in the EQD stating that graduates have the right to do remunerated supervised practice in another Member State.

Higher Education in Europe: *EuroPsy* as a European Standard

As higher education becomes more globalised, and the significance of the European Higher Education Area is strengthened, *EuroPsy* is making a contribution to the standard and quality of psychology education at a European level. The Bologna Process has created a momentum for the further integration of higher education across European countries (see Curaj, Scott, Vlasceanu & Wilson, 2012; Gaston, 2010). As part of this process, the *Tuning* project[17] has enabled subjects and disciplines to collaborate at European level and provide subject reference points for common curricula. During 2010–2011 the opportunity arose to build the *Tuning* standards onto the *EuroPsy* framework given the compatibility of the goals of the two initiatives. This means that *EuroPsy* has contributed to the creation of a standard not only across Europe but also more widely across the world. As noted by Knight (2013) and Wagenaar (2012) there has been a chronological expansion of *Tuning* across the globe to include Latin America, North America, the African continent and beyond. The *Tuning* approach of learner-centred programmes, a focus on employability and relevant skills for the world of work, providing a robust methodology for designing, implementing and enhancing degree programmes, and a commitment to the use of competences as part of learning outcomes has extended worldwide. This means that the *EuroPsy* standards are also likely to have an impact worldwide.

[17] We note: "the name *Tuning* is chosen for the Process to reflect the idea that universities do not and should not look for uniformity in their degree programmes or any sort of unified, prescriptive or definitive European curricula but simply look for points of reference, convergence and common understanding" (*Tuning* website).

EuroPsy in a Global Context

With psychology being studied and practised all around the world, it is no wonder that – as was mentioned in Chapter 3 – there are multiple credentialing, certification and licensing systems in place. Although it may seem that the stakeholders involved in these systems understand which requirements psychologists should meet, what evidence they should provide to "prove" their expertise, competence and ethical standing, and how all this should be evaluated, everyday practice suggests something else. All of these systems have their own history and logic, and reveal a remarkable variety in standards, up to a point where psychologists from adjacent states, fulfilling similar roles and speaking the same language may not be allowed to practise across the border. For this reason, there have been a number of efforts to compare systems and to seek common standards that might be applied across the same continent or even across continents. Interest in this matter has also grown because of the more frequent and closer links between psychologists from different countries, produced by the on-going process of globalisation. In recent years we have seen a number of meetings of national and regional licensing organisations, as well as number of joint conferences of stakeholders from different parts of the world. In the latest conference, the 5th International Congress on Licensure, Certification and Credentialing of Psychologists held in Stockholm, Sweden, in July 2013, the question was discussed whether it would be possible and desirable to define a common set of competences to characterise the work of psychologists worldwide. A similar question concerning the education and training of psychologists was addressed in an international conference organised by the International Union for Psychological Science, held in Jena, Germany, in May 2012 and dedicated to questions such as: "How is psychology taught across the world?" and "Is it possible to define commonalities, perhaps a common curriculum?" (Silbereisen, Ritchie & Pandey, 2014).

These initiatives are worth mentioning because they give us the opportunity to clarify the nature and meaning of *EuroPsy* in a global context, not just as a certification system but also as an instrument for the development of psychology and its identity in Europe. As was briefly pointed out in Chapter 3, *EuroPsy* clearly represents a regional project that aims to meet the challenges of psychology in Europe and does not seek to make any claims of applicability of usefulness beyond the borders of this continent. As all chapters of this book testify, there are close links between *EuroPsy* and the politically, culturally and linguistically diverse environment in which it was developed and is being applied. The chapters on this history (Chapter 2) and future (Chapter 10) clearly show that, in spite of the firm standards it poses today, *EuroPsy* is a system-in-change that exhibits the transition of the profession and the European environment in which it is being practised. In this respect it seems more appropriate to point to its adaptive qualities and its merits as a benchmarking tool that is able to bring about a certain degree of convergence and shared identity, rather than compare the standards of education and competence of *EuroPsy* with those of other systems. We might also say that *EuroPsy* represents a negotiated view of psychology that accepts a substantial degree of plurality and makes sense given the state of the profession in Europe by the beginning of the 21st century.

The quest for common definitions of professional psychology that can facilitate credentialing and certification in wider zones of the world is understandable and legitimate. But if the success of developing common standards lies in the legitimacy and effectiveness of the process, that should be reflected in the way in which such standards are sought. It should respect the historically and socially determined variety in psychological concepts and practices, and try to capture the distinctive features of the profession at its actual stage of development. Seeking common standards – via competences or otherwise – may be a worthy cause, provided that it is done in a bottom–up way, with all countries at the table, and that sufficient time is allowed for the process to unfold and produce solutions that are recognised as being in the interests of psychologists and their clients worldwide. The *EuroPsy* experience might well be helpful in this respect.

10 *EuroPsy* and the Future of Psychology in Europe

In the previous chapters of this book we have introduced *EuroPsy* and described its development and related it to the history of the psychological profession. We have given an overview of *EuroPsy* and described each of its components, that is education, supervised practice, competences, continuing professional development (CPD) and ethics. We have also placed *EuroPsy* in a European and global context. In this final chapter we will present some thoughts about the ways in which *EuroPsy* may develop further, addressing current ambitions and plans, and some challenges and opportunities that the profession and science of psychology are likely to encounter. In the first section we look briefly at what has been achieved so far through *EuroPsy*. We then move to discuss the way in which *EuroPsy* is expected to develop further according to EFPA's perspective for the next few years. However, we also consider broader issues connected with possible developments in society and psychological science, as well as the links between them, and the implications they could have for the psychological profession in Europe, taking into account changes in the professions in general. We finish with some reflections on *EuroPsy* in relation to similar initiatives in other parts of the world, and the prospect of a global definition of the psychological profession.

The Achievements of *EuroPsy*

Although it took more than a decade to develop *EuroPsy,* the unanimous acceptance in 2005 by the psychologists associations of EFPA's 36 national Member Associations is a remarkable fact, demonstrating an unprecedented consensus at the European level. The European Register of *EuroPsy* psychologists opened in January 2010 and since that time National Awarding Committees (NACs) in 20 countries – a number that is still growing – offer psychologists from these countries the possibility to apply for the *EuroPsy* Certificate and entry into the European Register. Information about *EuroPsy* and application materials for psychologists are available in 18 languages via national websites, which are all related to the website of the EFPA Head Office in Brussels. The number of basic *EuroPsy* certificates by the beginning of 2014 is almost 5,000.

The fact that European psychology has a common qualification standard for all 36 countries involved and for all areas of practice is of great significance, since it allows for guarantee of the same level of expertise and competence to clients and employers, regardless of the place where the psychologists are providing their services. This adds to the transparency of the market for psychological services and the protection of clients. For psychologists *EuroPsy* is above all a means to demonstrate their commitment to developing and maintaining a high level of professional expertise. It certifies that they have not just had a comprehensive education in psychology, but also possess practice-based competences, operate under a common set of ethical rules, and engage in CPD – something which clearly reaches beyond the former standard which was limited to having an academic diploma. This is not only likely to enhance psychologists' professional status in their own country, but also in other European countries. Moreover, holders of *EuroPsy* demonstrate that they meet a European standard, which enables them to identify themselves as European psychologists who can be considered qualified to work in any European country.

An important step forward with regard to mobility of psychologists (and clients) in Europe, is that *EuroPsy* requires the same qualification level for psychologists from all countries involved. It supports the recognition of qualifications of psychologists working in other countries of the EU as laid down in the European Directive 2005/36/EC (Qualifications Directive) by facilitating evaluations of their qualifications by Competent Authorities of the respective countries. However, it should be kept in mind that Member States have their own systems for regulating professions and for issuing the license to practice, which means that psychologists wishing to practise in certain areas (e.g. in the health sector) still need to meet national requirements. *EuroPsy* may facilitate psychologists in obtaining a license to practise within their own country or another European country, since it indicates a high level of competence, even though it does not automatically provide such a license.

EuroPsy's Further Development

Since the implementation of *EuroPsy* has begun only recently and several further steps are already envisaged, it makes sense to structure our discussion along the lines laid down in the strategy of EFPA as defined in 2013. In this strategy EFPA makes a clear distinction between the status of *EuroPsy* as a certification and quality assurance system on the one hand, and its role as an instrument for developing the psychological profession in Europe on the other hand. In the following paragraphs we consider both topics.

Certification and Quality Assurance

As mentioned above, the number of countries issuing *EuroPsy* certificates and the number of certificate holders have grown quickly during the first 3 years. Given the substantial effort involved in establishing a NAC and putting the administrative systems in place, and the fact that these countries have joined on the basis of their individual application at different stages over the 3 years, this is quite remarkable. However, to attain the impact that *EuroPsy* is envisaged to have it will need to reach a critical mass, and the number of certificates issued has to grow considerably. EFPA sees this as a major target for the next few years, and it aims to reach this through more applications from the participating countries as well as through new countries joining. In EFPA's 2013 strategy document the top priority is assigned to promotion of *EuroPsy* through targeted actions aimed at older and younger generations of psychologists as well as graduates and students, and by enhanced publicity.

As a system for certification and quality assurance *EuroPsy* has a series of features that require further development, most of which have been evident since the *EuroPsy* pilot project (see Chapter 2). Here we address nine aspects: academic education, competences, supervised practice, CPD, areas of practice, specialisation, the value for individuals and organisations, accreditation and the standard itself. It is important to review these aspects in order to identify where further developments are needed.

Education

A major achievement of *EuroPsy* has been the adoption of a common Curriculum Framework and Minimum Standards that is rather comprehensive and exhibits a careful balance between several components. It requires that curricula, in order to be recognised, cover certain educational objectives and types of content. Thus, curricula should contain explanatory and technological theories, cover theory and application, include a research project and an internship, and the content should relate to individuals, groups and society. The framework provides guidance for the different areas of theoretical and applied psychology that should be covered. There are at least three kinds of changes that are likely to be addressed in the future. First, new content may be added in order to reflect the growth of scientific knowledge. Second, requirements on content may be revised in order to include important topics that all future psychologists should gain knowledge and understanding of. For instance, it has been proposed that the curriculum should include knowledge of crisis and disaster intervention, which is currently not included. Third, the standards might be revised to include the core knowledge and skills that are minimally required for the three areas of practice. This has been identified as an important gap in the current standards, since they only require competence in one of the three areas of practice. Such revisions will inevitably trigger discussions about the relative importance of various types of content, as well as general and specialist forms of education.

Competences

Another remarkable feature of *EuroPsy* is the incorporation of competences as a fundamental and defining feature of the professional training of psychologists. This was an unfamiliar concept to many countries during the development of *EuroPsy*, yet within 10 years has been accepted as an essential part of professional qualification. What is largely lacking to date is a formal structure to support competence development. Although there is some experience with ideas and models that can guide and facilitate the systematic acquisition of competences (see Chapter 5), further work is needed and, as supported by the Bologna Process, competence learning is to be incorporated in the academic education as well as supervised practice.

Supervised Practice

Although the importance of supervised practice has been widely endorsed, the reality is that only a few European countries have a tradition of supervised practice and structures for appointing and training supervisors, delivering supervision, recording activities and progress, formative and summative assessment and so on. This is an area in which – triggered by *EuroPsy* – many new initiatives have been launched and where rapid developments are taking place. Although setting up and managing cost-effective supervision systems, which include the development and assessment of competences, requires a large effort from professional associations, universities and psychologists themselves, we are likely to see advances in the years to come. While the notion of supervision is rather well known in clinical psychology, it is less familiar for psychologists in areas such as work and organisation, or education, and some time will be needed for its acceptance. In such areas, as well as in certain languages, the term supervision itself may be less appropriate and may be replaced by other terms, such as guidance or coaching.

Continuing Professional Development

In the 1990s when discussions started about what ultimately became the *EuroPsy* Certificate, the entitlements that came with the university diploma in psychology lasted a lifetime in most countries, with the UK as the most notable exception. Qualified psychologists retained their qualification without further question, examination (or revalidation) for life. As discussed in Chapter 4, the legal or administrative status of the title of psychologist differed considerably across countries, but whatever rights were attached formally or by custom stayed with the person. There was an understanding that a psychologist should keep abreast of scientific and professional developments and this was even stated in professional codes of ethics. However, it was left to the individual psychologist to decide what this might entail. In less than two decades this has changed dramatically. It is now accepted widely, in psychology as well as in other academic professions, that CPD is a necessary requirement for continuing practice as a professional psychologist.

The situation regarding CPD in the countries participating in *EuroPsy* is somewhat comparable to that of supervision: the need for it is widely recognised, but few countries have well-developed systems and the actual practice is quite diverse. It is therefore understandable that EFPA is aiming for an assessment and evaluation of current practices, knowledge transfer between, and the development of common frameworks and uniform procedures. Since CPD differs not only in content but also in the ways in which it is conceptualised, financed, organised and assessed, which are tightly connected with national institutions, it may take several years before there will be a common system and expectations that can be incorporated into *EuroPsy*. At the same time, it should be seen as an urgent objective to share best practices in CPD and to bring current systems to a higher level. This is not only necessary to narrow the gap between science and the profession, but also to endow psychologists with the necessary self-criticism and to stimulate their readiness to keep learning.

Areas of Practice

The three areas of practice, that is, Clinical & Health, Work & Organisation and Education reflect well-established areas of practice across Europe, which are distinguished by knowledge, skills and competence and clearly identified by clients, users and society in general. As might be expected (and see Chapter 9), the majority of applications and registrants fall into the area of Clinical & Health, with Work & Organisation taking a second place and Education the third. Nevertheless, there are a significant number of psychologists who work in areas such as community psychology, sports psychology, forensic psychology, traffic psychology or aviation psychology, who place themselves in the category of "Other." It seems that at least some of these will wish their expertise to be recognised and their area of practice to be represented in the Register in future years. This will also add to the visibility of their professional area. Such further differentiation will be welcomed in countries where certain areas of practice are rather prominent, such as traffic psychology in Austria and Hungary, or community psychology in Italy or Norway. It will also match the higher level of differentiation in the psychological profession that has emerged in some countries due to its historical and societal development. In the UK, for example, there are now seven "adjectival titles" (i.e. areas of practice) recognised by the regulating body, the Health Professions Council. The criterion for recognition of a "title" is the existence of a recognised training route in that field of practice. Of course, this has implications for the operational definition and assessment of the competences, which should be elaborated for each newly added area of practice.

Specialisation

The issue of areas of practice relates to that of specialisation. Currently, there are two specialisations for which a Specialist *EuroPsy* Certificate has been defined, that is Psychotherapy and Work & Organisational Psychology. In anticipation of other specialisations, *EuroPsy* has established a framework of requirements for the Specialist Certificate which applies across all areas of specialisation. There are signs that psychologists from other areas of practice are interested in developing additional specialist certificates. Among them are educational, sports, aviation and crisis and disaster psychologists. Defining the knowledge and competences that specialisations require, in ways that are congruent with the basic *EuroPsy* and that are acceptable across countries, is no easy task.

A major challenge, and one similar to that existing for CPD, is to create a system at European level that links with national systems for training and recognition of specialists, making sure that new schemes are compatible with existing ones. Since specialist certifications have often been developed by professional bodies and training institutions, either outside of the higher education system or in collaboration with universities, the routes and modes for getting a certificate tend to be diverse. Therefore, there are considerable barriers to overcome when striving to bridge the differences between countries where specialist training is provided through universities and preceded by extended generic education and training, as in Scandinavia, and countries where specialisation starts earlier (as in the United Kingdom) and/or is largely organised outside of the universities (e.g. the Netherlands). There is also an increasing trend in some countries for further specialisation within fields, for example clinical child psychology or adult learning disabilities specialisation, or clinical geropsychology.

It is worth noting that the specialisation of psychologists has, at the present time, not been defined through the European Qualifications Framework (EQF). We recall that the level of qualification for independent practice as a psychologist is defined at EQF level 7 (Masters level). It would be a logical development – and in line with *Tuning-EuroPsy* – if specialisation qualifications were in the future to be linked to EQF level 8. However, this would require a shared system of accreditation and specification of requirements and learning outcomes at European level.

One option for the future is the recognition of specialisation through a professional doctorate title, reflecting the progression from EQF level 7 to 8 in terms of professional competence and understanding. The professional doctorate title (e.g. DClin Psy) has been used in UK to recognise professional experience, additional training and the completion of a research dissertation, thus enhancing both professional and research competence for clinical psychologists (Lunt et al., 2011). This move, combining CPD with additional specialist and research expertise through a professional doctorate has been adopted in UK by an increasing number of professions, and would seem worthy of exploration.[18] If we look at the descriptors for EQF level 8, it becomes apparent that they may fit the high level expertise developed through professional specialisation.

Value for Stakeholders

A key question for *EuroPsy* concerns its value to different stakeholders. A guiding principle for its development was to "contribute to mechanisms to promote the mobility of psychologists by enabling them to practise anywhere in Europe, provided that they have the proper qualifications" (Preamble to *EuroPsy* Regulations, EFPA, 2013a). At the present time, *EuroPsy* has been agreed by all member associations of EFPA, yet decisions on equivalence of qualifications are still taken at national level. With the revision of the EU Qualifications Directive, EFPA has taken the opportunity to propose *EuroPsy* – or at least its educational requirements – as the basis for a Common Training Framework (CTF) for psychologists in Europe. If this proposal is successful *EuroPsy* would directly facilitate mobility. It would provide considerable assistance to competent authorities and might even become a waiver for the assessment that would be needed to obtain a Professional Card. Individual psychologists would value *EuroPsy* as a passport or even as a license enabling them to practise in any country in Europe. However, it should be kept in mind that the EU follows the principle of subsidiarity and that governments of EU Member States are still able to pose national licensing requirements beyond the educational qualifications, at least for certain areas of work such as healthcare, and that automatic licensing for the whole EU will take more time to develop. *EuroPsy* also has a value to employers who are hiring psychologists, and to organisations such as universities and professional associations, which aim to develop high standards of education and training in psychology, and which both have an interest in accreditation.

Accreditation

As mentioned, *EuroPsy* is not an education programme accreditation process. Nevertheless, a NAC is required to provide a list of the psychology programmes which meet the *EuroPsy* standard, and automatic recognition of university education for the Certificate is restricted to graduates from those programmes. At the same time higher education systems in European countries are committed to the Bologna guidelines for quality assurance, which are likely to have an impact on universities and on psychology programmes. Most

[18] We note that initial qualification in clinical psychology has moved to doctoral (level 8) level across the UK, and newly qualified psychologists are all required to obtain a doctoral qualification at initial entry to the profession (see Donn et al., 2000).

European countries now have national accreditation agencies which may find *EuroPsy* to be a useful standard for quality assurance as they accredit their own psychology programmes, As a result we can expect that the quality of psychology education will increase, and the transparency of programme descriptors will be enhanced.

The Standard Itself

With enhancement of quality of psychology programmes and an inevitable convergence in terms of competences and learning outcomes, *EuroPsy* is likely to become more rigorous. During the 3 years in which *EuroPsy* has been in existence, there have been 20 applications from countries wishing to establish a NAC to award *EuroPsy* to suitably qualified psychologists. In applying the standards, EFPA's European Awarding Committee has sought to achieve a balance between inclusivity and exclusivity. Given the existing diversity in education and training programmes, approval was given to NACs with clear plans for the development of e.g. supervised practice or CPD. Approval of a NAC lasts for 4 years. *EuroPsy* has already had a clear impact on systems of education and training in a number of countries (e.g. Spain and Slovenia, see Chapter 6). In order to ensure the validity and the credibility of *EuroPsy* it is likely that in the course of time standards will be applied with greater rigour, for example in relation to scrutiny of curricula, and the arrangements for supervised practice or CPD. This is also what the EFPA strategy explicitly aims for.

Apart from raising the requirements, EFPA may at some time in the future decide to revisit the decision to set a 7-year period for revalidation of the Certificate. The period of 7 years for the validity of the *EuroPsy* Certificate was considered to strike a balance between a too frequent administrative burden for Certificate holders and a too long period without any check on the maintenance of professional competence. Although this period emerged as a fairly easy choice at the time, a period of 5 years was discussed (now the norm for revalidation in a number of countries).

EuroPsy as a Tool for Developing the Profession

EuroPsy is more than a certification system; it is also a process that aims to change the psychological profession in Europe, and to bring it to a higher level. This is, in fact, already happening, as countries aspire to award the *EuroPsy* and thus develop their education and training to meet *EuroPsy* criteria. Further convergence and enhanced quality is likely to be achieved by what was mentioned above, that is further development of the psychology curriculum (e.g. specifying minimum content for areas of practice) and raising the requirements for supervised practice and CPD. The challenge for EFPA will be to take a gradual approach to raising standards, aiming to provide support for countries in their own efforts, and to share expertise across different European countries. This would help the realisation of a greater common understanding of standards and practice, while also respecting the diversity that is a characteristic of European countries and the EU approach to convergence. This continues to require a balance between an inclusive approach, aiming to include as many countries as possible, followed by a gradual tightening of criteria over time, and an increased rigour in the requirements for re-recognition of NACs and revalidation of individuals over time.

However, there are limits to what can be achieved by sharing knowledge and best practices between countries and by working together in setting new standards for education, supervised practise and CPD. The future meaning and impact of *EuroPsy* will also depend on the institutional environment in which the psychological profession is being practised. This has been a reason for EFPA to seek greater convergence in two important domains where substantial divergence between countries has continued to exist, namely professional ethics and legislation. Although EFPA recognises that substantial time may pass before countries will be similar in these respects, it has taken the initiative to create a model for a common ethical code, referred to as the "Model Code" (see Chapter 8), and a model for a legal arrangement that recognises and protects the profession and title of psychologist, referred to as a "Model Law" (see Chapter 1). The idea behind these initiatives is that the continued existence of national differences carries the risk of unequal treatment of clients and psychologists, and hinders them in fully exercising the freedoms defined in the EU Treaty. If the treatment of a client is not permissible in one European country, it should – as a matter of principle – not be permissible in another country. A person permitted to use the title psychologist or to conduct psychological interventions in one country, should not be denied access to the title or to the use of such interventions in another country. Increasing convergence in these two domains, even if it takes years to gradually adjust ethical codes and national legislation, will ultimately create an environment in which *EuroPsy* can function optimally and help to advance the psychological profession.

EuroPsy for Academics?

One aspect of *EuroPsy* which is sometimes mentioned as a limitation is that it does not cover all those who call themselves psychologists. As it stands, *EuroPsy* focusses exclusively on practising psychologists and does not include academic teachers and researchers in psychology – even though they have expertise in psychology and have responsibility for helping students to become psychologists. The designers of *EuroPsy* have chosen an occupational rationale for this, arguing that the primary professional work role of psychologists is to clarify and help to resolve clients' problems, whereas those teaching psychology at educational institutions are in fact teachers and those undertaking research are in fact researchers. Their occupational roles resemble those of teachers in areas such as sociology, geography or pharmacy, and of researchers in such other areas. Although academic teachers and researchers may share a great deal of knowledge with practising psychologists and some of them may practise as psychologists as well, they will often not have the professional competences required for diagnosis and intervention with clients. By the same token, practising psychologists will not have the full range of didactical and research competences required in teaching psychology and doing psychological research. It remains an open issue whether *EuroPsy* should in the future be extended to include a special certification for teachers of psychology – at the academic level and perhaps even the level of secondary education – and for psychological researchers.

This question also has implications for the unity and identity of psychology, and for the relationship between practitioners and researchers in psychology.

The Future of Psychology and *EuroPsy*

Although the further implementation and elaboration of *EuroPsy* is likely to have an influence on the psychological profession in Europe, the reverse also holds. The rate at which *EuroPsy* will be adopted, the standards that will be applied, the forms of specialisation that will emerge are all dependent on how the profession will develop in the years to come. As this is dependent on many factors it is hard to predict what the major trends in European psychology will be. A few factors that we would like to discuss here are: the "demand" for psychological assessment and intervention resulting from demographic, social and economic changes, the "supply" of psychological knowledge arising from on-going scientific research, and the ways in which demand and supply will meet each other through evolving forms of education and newly developed "tools," that is methods and techniques. An additional factor is the change in the nature of the professions and their interrelations.

Societal Developments and the Demand for Psychology

There are a number of changes and developments in society which are highly likely to affect demand for and nature of psychological services. Here we briefly mention five: demographic changes, in particular ageing, changes in the "welfare state," forced migration and refugees, technological advances and globalisation. Like other parts of the world, European society is experiencing a number of *demographic changes* that impinge in various ways on the demands for psychological services. Ageing is without doubt one of the most important demographic phenomena that creates a demand for psychological knowledge and research, assessment and intervention in many different areas: health, work, education, transportation, etc. (Peiró, Tordera & Potocnik, 2012; Fernández-Ballesteros, 2014). This is true not only for the rapidly growing population of older people, but also for younger people. As they become absolutely and proportionately less numerous they are faced with high expectations and demands, which put them under growing pressure while preparing for their adult roles in society and developing their careers.

The *crisis of the Welfare State* amplified by the recent and persistent economic and financial crisis is leading to the adoption of free market and neo-liberal models of public management with emphasis on greater cost-effectiveness, reduced service concepts and more self-reliance of citizens, threatening what had become known as the "European social model" (see Giddens, 2014). A number of services that were previously guaranteed in countries under a Welfare State model are being reviewed (e.g. to reduce the financial burden of mental illness or dementia) and calls for novel and more cost-effective services, which involve other roles for psychologists are often heard. Budget cuts have led to a smaller number of psychologists being employed and a rise in self-employment and in some countries unemployment, and to a greater emphasis on value for money, with inevitably increased competition.

A significant development, already inherent in the Bologna agreement but enhanced by the financial crisis, is the drive of a number of governments to promote employment after 3 years of academic study (i.e. after gaining the Bachelor Degree). Although this may be good to stimulate the labour market in general, it poses difficulties for the field of psychology, since the Bachelor Degree offers very limited possibilities for employment as a psychologist. Three years of study may be enough to prepare for the position of psychological assistant or for a range of other positions in the labour market, but it is certainly not sufficient to qualify as a psychologist. Initiatives towards lowering educational demands and costs may pose risks for clients and are not in the interest of psychologists. By setting clear standards *EuroPsy* may be helpful in raising awareness about the disadvantages of this policy trend and in defining realistic job options for young people with a Bachelor degree in psychology (as already demonstrated in *Tuning-EuroPsy*, Lunt et al., 2011). Somewhat related are the recent initiatives in the face of the ever-growing demand for mental health services within the context of finite or shrinking resources; these aim to provide access to mental health services by psychotherapists with a limited training, even if accredited. An example is the "Improving Access to Psychological Therapies" (IAPT) initiative undertaken by the National Health Service in the United Kingdom. While such initiatives may bring treatment within the reach of many, there are reasons for concern about the competences of those employed as therapists and the protection of clients. There is a need to be clear about ways to demarcate the boundaries between lower qualified occupations and to establish effective collaboration with fully qualified psychologists meeting the standards of *EuroPsy* system.

Migration is a further social factor likely to lead to increased demands for psychological services. The increase in worldwide forced migration and the growth of refugee populations due to man-made and natural disasters such as conflict and war, famine and poverty has already had an impact on demands for psychologists in a number of European countries. Migration is typically associated with increased social tensions in neighbourhoods, work organisations, and schools, and in some places with xenophobia and aggression. It produces an enhanced need for community building and for professional help at the family and individual level, in order to prevent and manage conflicts and cope with the strains of the migration experience. It produces a more diverse demand for psychological services in these areas as well as in healthcare, particularly in mental healthcare. Migration brings greater diversity from which the society may profit in the long run, but – in combination with the effects of ageing – it also offers challenges in the short run that psychologists should help to address, in order to promote positive social relations and guarantee health and well-being for the individuals involved.

Advances in Technology have transformed the ways in which societies and therefore professionals function, with innovative developments fundamentally affecting many facets of society and human life. The relentless growth in digital infrastructure, with ever finer ramifications in physical and social spaces, the continuing introduction of new tools and gadgets, the explosive use of new media with their own modes of communication (Facebook, Twitter, Skype) by people of all ages are changing the way in which people live and various aspects of social and human life. Changes in the meaning of such fundamental notions as "social relationship" and "privacy" are just two examples of how the world in which we live is changing. These examples point to important cultural changes that are occurring at the same time, and that affect life styles and values, and even modify social institutions.

These developments have numerous implications for the work of psychologists. Firstly, they imply a need to participate in and study the new society and the new forms of expression, in order to understand the behaviour of today's population and to effectively diagnose the challenges and problems that people experience. Secondly, they pose a need for innovation to ensure that psychological services effectively address the specific needs arising from demographic, technological and social changes in areas such as work, education, transport, communication, leisure, family and daily life. Thirdly, they call for changes in how psychological services are delivered: at which time, by which means, by whom and to whom. It is no longer sufficient for psychologists to conduct face-to-face interventions at agreed times within office hours. They may be required to use other delivery modes, including Voice-over-IP technology and Apps on mobile phones, and work from distant locations. New delivery modes may also open the way to innovations in the nature of service provision. For example, it is conceivable that psychologists will remotely assess clients' states and experiences in real time and intervene on these – something which has been impossible until now. Finally, the huge increase in information available on the internet is leading to an increased tendency for online self-diagnosis and self-help, which may also affect demand for services of psychologists.

Finally, *globalisation,* that is, the integration of national economies and the development of a global economy through trade, investment, migration and the use of new technologies and perhaps the most significant of societal changes. Although the phenomenon of globalisation is hard to grasp, because of its diffuseness and multidimensionality, its societal impact is tremendous. This is certainly the case in Europe as a continent with a long-standing history of colonisation and foreign trade, strong international presence, deep involvement in global economic and political processes and a substantial level of inward and outward migration. The impact of globalisation is visible in all domains of society, including the economy, where it affects employment, consumption, income levels, and law, politics, culture and religion. European integration itself is a facet of globalisation, and the emergence of the European Union is both a product and a motor of globalising activity.

Globalisation is changing the stage on which psychologists act as well as the nature of their work roles in many respects, by driving changes in demography, economy, public management, migration and technology. Further, it has major impacts on individuals' thoughts and behaviours, their social interactions, their lifestyles and consumption, their contacts and experiences with people from other cultures, religions and languages, their values and norms, their social and self-identities and so on. The pervasive change that is inherent in this poses both challenges for learning and adaptation, and threats from ambiguities, conflicts and loss of previous identities and so on. These factors are likely to have an influence on the psychological profession both as human beings and professionals. Certainly, access to psychological knowledge and contact with colleagues from other continents promotes more collaboration and integration, and offers new bases for specialisation – as is already happening in EFPA and in the many specialist psychologists associations that have been established over the past few decades. It may also lead to new initiatives for collaboration on a global scale, as will be illustrated at the end of this chapter.

Related to globalisation as an outcome of spreading economic activity, is *climate change*. Although this is often regarded as an inevitable change of the natural environment that is of little relevance for psychology, there is a growing recognition that human behaviour – in industrial production, and in transport and consumption – is a key factor in the output of CO_2. Nowadays, the issue is conceived much more broadly and the notion of *sustainability* is used to refer to the potential to maintain resources while using them, thereby creating the conditions for a continued harmony between humans and nature and for sufficient resources for future generations. Invariably, human behaviour is seen as crucial for sustainability, making behaviour change in various life domains an important issue for psychological research and intervention. As psychologists are already involved in sustainability initiatives (Ones & Dilchert, 2012), it is conceivable that this might develop into a new area of professional practice in the future.

Although the nature and possible impact of societal changes are broad and complex, it seems likely that over time they will affect both the nature of psychologists' work, and therefore influence the *EuroPsy* requirements and structure, both in terms of explanatory and technological knowledge and in terms of professional and enabling competences. It is also likely that as additional competences are needed, these will have to be addressed in supervised practice and in competence assessments. What is clear, however, is that *EuroPsy* will need to remain flexible and receptive to changes and developments in order to avoid obsolescence and to maintain its relevance.

Psychological Science

A century ago, when psychology was still in its infancy, a fierce debate took place about the issue of diversification of the discipline. Whether there was a real demand for specialised knowledge or rather psychologists taking the opportunity for marketing such specialised knowledge, the fact is that within a few decades several specialities emerged. Wilhelm Wundt, widely seen as the founder of scientific psychology strongly opposed this trend, as he saw it as a threat to the unity of psychology and its inherent connection with philosophy (Wundt, 1913). Scholars working in applied psychology defended the trend towards differentiation, believing that it would stimulate psychological research and lead to applications that would better match the needs of society. Today we can only conclude that history has been on their side (and see Chapter 1). Diversification is a fact and there is a tendency for ever-increasing specialisations or divisions in psychology; the American Psychological Association now has 54 Divisions, while the British Psychological Society has 10 professional Divisions and 13 scientific Sections reflecting the growth of specialist areas of research and practice. The process has not stopped as new fields of psychology – as a profession and science – are still emerging, partly in response to new demands from society and new research technologies, and partly as cross-overs with other sciences. While on-going diversification is inherent in the growth of knowledge and may help in better addressing human problems, it may also threaten the unity and identity of psychology. However, there are also integrative forces that seek to link the various theories, methods and applications in order to maintain a certain degree of unity, important for the identity of psychology as a science, a field of study and a profession. It is difficult to predict how things will develop further though we may expect a growth in the number of areas of practice in which psychologists work, and therefore increased demand both for differentiation of the basic *EuroPsy* Certificate and further demand for specialist certificates. Important for *EuroPsy* will be to define the core knowledge and competencies which define the psychologist, and to begin to articulate a broader range of knowledge and competencies which map onto recognised fields of practice.

Another issue concerns the relationship between pure or basic research and applied research and, as Spielberger (2004) suggests,

> Meaningful applications of psychology must be based on a sound scientific foundation. Consequently, ethical applications of psychological principles to social problems must await the development of relevant theory which has been tested by empirical research (Spielberger, 1984, p. xi)

Advances in technology, for example imaging and bio-markers, have stimulated an increasing interest in basic research in neuropsychology, biological psychology, psychopharmacology and broader psycho-biological aspects of the discipline. There is an expectation that such research, which implies collaboration with medical and biological sciences, may lead to new insights and change the direction of psychological research in the future. The question arises whether this type of research becomes more attractive to funding bodies (such as the EU) and how that will affect research in other fields that are more related to the social and cultural determinants of human behaviour. A similar question can be raised regarding funding for applied research of which the outcomes are of more immediate relevance and utility for the psychological profession. Limited funding means increased competition for resources which is likely to impact the nature of research which is supported and thus the nature of theory underpinning psychological practice. This is a matter of concern at the European as well as the national level. To raise the quality and effectiveness of the psychological profession, both levels should guarantee a certain level of applied psychological research in order to contribute to development of suitably rigorous psychological models and tools as well as evaluation of their effectiveness in the context of practice.

There are also questions regarding the content of psychological science and the research methods used. A rather fundamental issue is whether the evidence on which psychology has been built and the specific theories that have been advanced, can be trusted to be true for people in general. It has been noted that what is commonly designated as "mainstream psychology" is in fact a Western psychology that has originated from research in North-America, much of Europe, and the English speaking parts of the world. There is currently not sufficient evidence to justify knowledge claims regarding people living in other parts of the world. The argument has been made that mainstream psychology is an "indigenous" Western psychology (e.g. Roe, 2014, Silbereisen & Ritchie, 2014) and that the empirical basis on which it has been built is heavily biased towards people living in affluent Western countries, and the United States in particular. It has not been established how far the evidence and the theories make sense in other parts of the world, because of the predominant use of English language. What does make sense to people locally, and what is needed to understand and resolve the problems they experience, may not be adequately captured in the language and thoughts of English language psychology.

For Europe a somewhat similar argument can be made. Due to the growing internationalisation and strong competitive pressures, psychological scholars are required to publish in English language scholarly journals and to use theories and methods that are internationally accepted. However, in a continent where people speak dozens of different languages, this may have an adverse impact, since it may draw resources and attention away from behaviours and issues that are locally important. In fact, it might add to the growth of mainstream psychology to the detriment of a psychology that is relevant for and applicable to most of the people in Europe. Although *EuroPsy* was based on the recognition of diversity in psychology – as a science and profession – and has room for accommodating differences, this issue is potentially relevant for *EuroPsy* in the future since psychology's scientific development will help to shape the profession. For instance, the more future research is able to establish what is common to all people and what is dependent on economic, geographic and cultural factors, the more it will be possible to define a common "canon" for psychology as well as sets of knowledge and methods with a regional or local reach. The development of appropriate methodologies for regional or local research is also a possible outcome. In so far as they are pertinent to Europe, such outcomes might affect the requirements defined in *EuroPsy*.

The Link Between Science and Professional Practice

As described in Chapter 1, scientific knowledge is one of the pillars of all learned professions and this is no different for psychology. Psychological practice relies heavily on scientific evidence and methods, and throughout the history science has been essential in improving the effectiveness of the interventions and the reputation of the profession. The scientist-practitioner model has been clearly established as the predominant model of psychological practice in Europe since the middle of the last century (Peterson & Park, 2005; Lunt, 2014) with the assumption that professionals should be educated as scientists in order to carry out a rigorous and scientifically mindful practice. Moreover, over the past few decades, it has been increasingly emphasised that practice should be based on research evidence and where possible follow standardised protocols that ensure a certain degree of effectiveness. There is an urgent need to strengthen the reliance of interventions on scientific evidence and closer links between practice and science (e.g. Baker, McFall & Shoham, 2009).

As psychological science develops further we are likely to see a growing body of evidence, as well as methods and protocols that can be used to further improve practice. However, there is a general problem affecting psychology as well as other professions, namely the "lag" between scientific discoveries and the introduction of innovations in practice. There is inevitably a time lapse before new discoveries and insights have reached the professional domain and before professionals have substituted the knowledge and practices that were taught at an earlier stage of their careers. Thus, it cannot be assumed that new results of scientific research automatically and directly translate into professional practice, which poses a major challenge.

As in any other profession, targeted and organised activities are needed to ensure that the practice of psychologists remains in line with, and is aware of, advances in science. First of all, there is a need for "applied" research that investigates phenomena and uses methods in real-life contexts, and for research and development (R&D) with an application focus, that is, designing and optimising actual intervention methods, and evaluating their effectiveness, efficiency, utility and practicality. Secondly, there is a need for scientific findings to be made available to a wider audience which includes professions, for example through presentations at conferences and publications in journals that are attended and read by professionals. This requires translation from researchers' language into the language of professionals and normally from English to local languages. Thirdly, newly developed methods have to be marketed to make professionals and their clients aware of their availability, and the added benefits they offer. Fourth, professionals have to be educated to incorporate the new science results into their repertoire of knowledge, and instructed and trained to develop the proper competences. This is where CPD comes in. Fifth, what is equally needed, but unfortunately often neglected, is to inform professionals with regard to knowledge claims and methods that have meanwhile become obsolete. This may have to do with the fact that psychology – at the present stage – lacks the mechanisms for deciding and proclaiming what is no longer considered valid, effective, harmless, etc. As a result, psychologists who were trained in earlier decades will in some cases continue to use approaches that newer generations of psychologists would not normally use. This phenomenon is to some degree apparent in the continued adherence of psychologists to particular schools, such as the behaviourist, cognitivist, constructivist, evolutionary, hermeneutical, phenomenological and psychoanalytic schools, whereas according to present-day insights they should rather be seen as options that can provide notions or tools that are only relevant or useful with certain clients and under certain circumstances. What would be needed as part of an effective knowledge management system is a mechanism that alerts psychologists when well-disseminated and established knowledge has become obsolete, and should expire and be replaced.

Although all these activities are important for building the bridge required to connect science to practice, it is clear that updating the knowledge and competence of psychologists and eradicating obsolete views and practices are crucial in the context of CPD and ethical practice as envisaged in *EuroPsy*. Drawing upon experiences in other sciences, such as medicine (http://www.cochrane.org) or pharmaceutics (http://www.ohsu.edu/xd/research/centers-institutes/evidence-based-policy-center/derp/index.cfm) and mental healthcare (http://www.nrepp.samhsa.gov/Index.aspx), we would expect that psychologists could benefit from databases that offer information about the current state of the art in various fields of applications. Learning to use such databases and to incorporate the information while taking account of the complex arrangement of factors that may be operating in a specific case – a particular challenge in psychological practice – might become part of supervised practice as well as CPD in the future. Access to up-to-date information in order to replace obsolete knowledge is not the only thing that matters. Equally important is that psychologists learn to be aware of the need to learn and to change their behaviour, as to avoid the risk of professional arrogance that comes with growing experience.

A related issue, which relates to the international dimension of psychological science that was discussed above, is the growing need to clarify the context where evidence has been obtained and the one in which it is being considered for practice. In many areas of basic as well as applied psychology, the cultural, socioeconomic, legal and political context matters and the generalisability of the evidence obtained through research in one context to another context for intervention cannot be taken for granted. This underlines the importance of conducting applied research in the proper contexts of practice and to pay attention to other relevant sources of evidence, such as practitioners' experience and judgment, stakeholders preferences and values and context, actors and circumstances in which the intervention is developed.

We would like to add that the interaction between science and practice should not be seen as a one-way street, it is equally important to have opportunities for feedback from practice to theory – which is one of the basic ideas in the scientist-practitioner model. The current mechanisms for this are underdeveloped and more should be done to take account of information from the field in applied research and application-oriented R&D. In summary, better links between science and practice will be beneficial for both sides, as they can enrich and deepen psychology and make its applications more relevant and useful.

Psychologists Among the Professions

Although the psychological profession is rather young, its development has been impressive. As we explained in Chapter 3, the number of psychologists in Europe is likely to be over half a million, there are hundreds of university-based curricula that prepare students for becoming psychologists, there are one or more associations publishing journals and arranging conferences in every European country and the profession is legally recognised and regulated in most countries. *EuroPsy* serves as a powerful socialisation tool for the profession in Europe and its common aims and ambitions, same processes in education, supervised practice and CPD create the potential for sharing key ideas, values and norms among the psychologists of Europe. A powerful feature is the competence model as a shared mental model about the core competences for professional practice across Europe and as the reference model for carrying out supervised practice; this will help to enhance the identity of psychology, create the shared views about standards, professional quality services and the key elements of good practice. The Register of European psychologists will contribute to the image and the reputation of Psychology as a profession and in this way also enhance the visibility and reasonable shared understanding between the clients and psychologists as service providers. It will take some time to see the results of this, but it is likely that a professional community of European psychologists will emerge whose members identify simultaneously and equally as European psychologists with their own nationality. These developments are important because they may help to balance the centrifugal forces of specialisation and national articulation that have characterised psychology for much of its history.

In Chapter 1 we noted that the context for the professions is changing. Not only is there a change in notions of professional accountability and professional expertise, but the professions themselves are gradually changing in nature with new professions emerging that draw their support from their clients and the nature of a particular type of service, rather than from a single scientific discipline. Although this trend is still relatively new, there are already cases where psychologists are in competition with other professionals supplying a particular type of service based on a multidisciplinary knowledge and competence base, which lacks clear boundaries and well-defined educational preparation. Examples here are psychotherapists, coaches and management consultants. In the mental health area, where the demand for services is much greater than psychologists can meet, there is ample room for other professionals (psychiatrists, educators and social workers) and paraprofessionals.

EuroPsy is and will remain a marker of knowledge and competence above the level of the academic Master Degree, and in the same way the *EuroPsy* Specialist Certificates clearly demarcate a high level of expertise based in a general education and training in psychology. However, the development of other professions – some more and others less psychological – and their emergence on the labour market, may be a reason to consider new and perhaps other forms of specialisation. What is clear here is that, in common with other professions, the psychologists profession cannot rely on its "status" alone, and needs to demonstrate high level competence, robust and reliable integrity, and an adaptability which enables it to meet new challenges in the changing societal and professional context in which it finds itself.

Psychology and *EuroPsy* in Europe

Developments in the EU

Psychology is one of the professions within Europe that are working on the improvement of its qualifications and the protection of the public at the European level. In fact, *EuroPsy* is the prime instrument of the psychological profession, and is similar to professional cards of architects or pharmacists. Given the overall focus of the EU on mobility, freedom to work in different countries, and hence comparability of qualifications, *EuroPsy* is of considerable interest in connection with the recognition of professional qualifications across Europe. It might be able to serve the same purpose as the sectoral directives that were issued by the EU in the 1980s for seven professions, namely achieving Europe-wide harmonisation. That is, *EuroPsy* might enable automatic recognition of the qualifications of psychologists who meet its standards (see Chapter 4).

The philosophy is that *EuroPsy* might become the basis for the CTF mentioned in the modernised Qualifications Directive (2005/36/EC), and be recognised as a waiver for the professional card that competent authorities of the EU states will issue. How that will work in practice, and whether it will promote automatic recognition remains to be seen. *EuroPsy* is different from the new professional card, though, since its meaning and significance are not limited to international mobility of professionals. It can also be expected to help in promoting transparency of the market of psychological services, enhancing the professional accountability of psychologists and providing protection to clients.

In this context, we should point to the changes in the nature of the professions and their role in society that was mentioned above. The classical professions have lost much of their privileged status and autonomy, as many new professions are emerging, increasing emphasis is being placed on the accountability of professionals. There is, for instance, much greater attention to malpractice in national as well as European legislation. With patient and consumer protection high on the EU agenda, we are likely to see stricter demands on self-regulation in the domain of professional ethics and legal mechanisms for applying Europe-wide sanctions. Examples are the malpractice alert in the EU Qualifications Directive (2005/36/EC) and the European codes of conduct recommended by the EU Services Directive (2006/123/EC). The general trend is towards stricter self-regulation of the professions and towards protection of clients via the legal system. This will have implications for all professions, including the psychological profession. It calls for a number of further developments, including the Common Ethical Code for European Psychology mentioned in Chapter 8.

Developments in European Countries

EU pressures towards greater convergence and greater Europeanisation require a balance with forces to retain national solutions and identities. While a fundamental principle of the European Treaty and the Bologna initiatives is to "respect the rich diversity of Europe," this is sometimes threatened by the pressures of globalisation. Such counteracting forces may be seen in all domains, including university education and professional work. For *EuroPsy*, this implies, for example, the use of both English and the different European languages, and perhaps a greater challenge – the integration of different paradigms and practices within professional psychology. While *EuroPsy* has set a European standard, the European principle of subsidiarity and the demands of individual countries mean that decisions concerning education and training, accreditation and quality assurance and equivalence of qualifications continue to be taken at national level. Crucially, the right to practise, in this case as a psychologist, is determined at national level by national laws and regulations.

At the same time it can be noted that the very existence of *EuroPsy* is recognised and used to leverage change at the national level. As pointed out before, the curriculum model and its minimum standards have been welcomed as an aid in the updating of curricula at national universities. Other components of *EuroPsy* have, in a similar way, been used to introduce new types of internships, supervised practice or CPD. The status of *EuroPsy* as a European benchmark and of possibilities to apply that benchmark in different countries with different languages is also a factor that matters for the development of the profession.

An important challenge will remain the balancing of qualification requirements between countries. As in the years when *EuroPsy* was being established there are differences between countries with higher standards and countries with lower standards, and it is only natural that such divergence with its own historic and economic explanations, produces opposing forces. Under the current economic conditions, in which national governments have taken severe austerity measures and push for lowering qualifications, this could potentially turn into conflict. However, this is all a matter of time. In a scenario of economic recovery there will likely be less need for idiosyncratic policies at the national level, and there may even be an interest in seeking greater harmonisation – something which would favour the further development of *EuroPsy*.

EuroPsy in a Global Context

We would like to finish with a note on the development and certification of psychology at the global level. As should be clear from what has been written in the previous chapters, *EuroPsy* is a system that was developed for Europe with its unique and historically determined pattern of diversity, similarity and collaboration. All components of *EuroPsy* are tailored to this specific context and represent viable compromises between many national stakeholders. That means it defines common standards at a level that is seen as desirable but also as achievable for the national psychologists associations organised in EFPA. The parties involved in developing *EuroPsy* never had the intention to tailor this system to other parts of the world, nor envisaged the possibility of export. Yet, it is clear that development and certification of the psychological profession is a matter of interest for psychologists in other parts of the world, and that the question arises how *EuroPsy* compares to other systems. Since *EuroPsy* seems to be one of the first systems that spans multiple countries, it is understandable that psychologists associations from other continents show an interest (and even that individual psychologists are eager to obtain a *EuroPsy* certificate).

Both the individual persons involved in designing *EuroPsy* and EFPA as the organisation responsible for *EuroPsy* seem ready to share the experiences they have gathered thus far. Certain lessons may well be drawn from the process by which *EuroPsy* was created as well as from the values that guided the project and the principles of mutual respect and flexibility. At the same time, we believe that the best outcomes will be obtained if each region of world develops a system that meets the regional conditions best. Following formative, stepwise and customising approaches, which take into account socioeconomic and institutional realities, and respect historical traditions as well as linguistic and religious diversity, are likely to have the greatest chance of success. It will not only make the development process more viable but also leave room for defining professional standards in a way that best matches the needs of people in society. After standards have been defined and certification systems built up, it is time to look for the possibilities and needs for integration at a global scale.

Conclusion

In this book we have introduced *EuroPsy* and discussed it from several angles to highlight its specific features, and we have pointed at the needs for further development. We are aware that in doing so we have celebrated the achievement of this European standard across the diversity of European countries. At the same time, our commitment to the search for higher standards, integrity of the profession and justification of the public's trust is an ongoing endeavour. It involves a continued willingness for individuals, associations and the profession to learn and to question, a commitment to raising awareness of the need to strengthen psychological interventions, and a willingness to adopt new interventions and discard those no longer effective. We are optimistic that *EuroPsy* will help with these endeavours, and have reasons to be confident. The framework and standards of *EuroPsy* have been agreed by consensus across the 36 countries of EFPA, that is the majority of European countries. The framework was developed through a combination of bottom–up and top–down process, involving widespread consultation with a wide range of stakeholders. The standard of *EuroPsy* is robust and reflects international consensus, both in terms of length of education and training and in terms of the substantive content of curriculum and competences. *EuroPsy* has the implicit support of the EU and fits the wider Bologna process; it can take advantage of the opportunities provided by these two powerful European bodies (e.g. CTF and EQF, QF-EHEA). What is needed is for EFPA to take the lead in using *EuroPsy* to enhance the profession, and to balance confidence with concern in the face of the on-going changes in the contexts in which psychologists work.

References

Abbott, A. (1988). *The system of the professions*. London, UK: University of Chicago Press.

Adair, J. G. (2006). Creating indigenous psychologies: Insights from empirical social studies of the science of psychology. In U. Kim, K.-S. Yang, & K.-K. Hwang (Eds.), *Indigenous and cultural psychology: Understanding people in context* (pp. 467–487). New York, NY: Springer.

Adelman, C. (2009). *The Bologna Process for U.S. eyes: Re-learning higher education in the age of convergence*. Retrieved from www.ihep.org/assets/files/EYESFINAL.pdf. Washington, DC: Institute for Higher Education Policy.

Adelman, C. (2010). The US response to Bologna: Expanding knowledge, the first steps of convergence. *European Journal of Education, 45*(4), 612–623.

Aelterman, G. (2006). Sets of standards for External Quality Assurance Agencies: A comparison. *Quality in Higher Education, 12*(3), 227–233.

Allsop, J., Bourgeault, I. L., Evetts, J., Le Bianic, T., Jones, K., & Wrede, S. (2009). Encountering globalization: Professional groups in an international context. *Current Sociology, 57*(4), 487–510.

Allwood, C. A., & Berry, J. W. (2006). Origins and development of indigenous psychologies: An international analysis. *International Journal of Psychology, 41*(4), 243–268.

Amaral, A. M. J., & Tavares, A. M. (2009). Supra-national accreditation, trust and institutional autonomy: Contrasting developments of accreditation in the United States and Europe. *Higher Education Management and Policy, 21*(3), 1–18.

Andersson, G., Carlbring, P., & Furmark, T. (2012). Therapist experience and knowledge acquisition in internet-delivered CBT for social anxiety disorder: A randomized controlled trial. [On-line]. *PLoS ONE, 7*(5), e37411.

APA Presidential Task Force on Evidence-Based Practice. (2006). Evidence-based practice in psychology. *American Psychologist, 61*, 271–285.

Baker, T. B., McFall, M., & Shoham, V. (2008). Current status and future prospects of clinical psychology: Toward a scientifically principled approach to mental and behavioral health care. *Psychological Science in the Public Interest, 9*(2), 67–103.

Barkham, M., Hardy, G. E., & Mellor-Clark, J. (Eds.). (2010). *Developing and delivering practice-based evidence: A guide for the psychological therapies*. Oxford, UK: Wiley-Blackwell.

Barriball, K. L., While, A., & Norman, I. J. (1992). Continuing professional education for qualified nurses: A review of the literature. *Journal of Advanced Nursing, 17*, 1129–1140.

Bartram, D. (1996). Occupational standards and competence-based qualifications for professional applied psychologists in the UK. *European Psychologist, 1*(1), 157–165.

Bartram, D., & Roe, R. (2005). Definition and assessment of competences in the context of the European diploma in psychology. *European Psychologist, 10*(2), 93–102.

Bartram, D., & Roe, R. (2008). Individual and organisational factors in competence acquisition. In W. J. Nijhoff, R. J. Simons, & A. F. Nieuwenhuis (Eds.), *The learning potential of the workplace* (pp. 71–96). Rotterdam: Sense.

Beinart, H. (2012). Models of supervision and the supervisory relationship. In I. Fleming & L. Steen (Eds.), *Supervision and clinical psychology: Theory, practice and perspectives* (2nd ed.). London, UK: Brunner-Routledge.

Beinart, H., & Clohessy, S. (2009). Supervision. In H. Beinart, P. Kennedy, & S. Llewelyn (Eds.), *Clinical psychology in practice*. Oxford, UK: Wiley-Blackwell.

Belgian Federation of Psychologists. (2004). *Code of Ethics*. Brussels, Belgium: Fédération Belge des Psychologues/Belgische Federatie van Psychologen.

Belli, R. F. (2012). Epilogue: Continuing points of contention in the recovered memory debate. In R. F. Belli (Ed.), *True and false recovered memories: Toward a reconciliation of the debate* (pp. 243–255). New York, NY: Springer.

Ben-David, J., & Collins, R. (1966). Social factors on the origins of a new science: The case of psychology. *American Sociological Review, 4*, 451–465.

Benjafield, J. G. (1996). *A history of psychology*. Boston, MA: Allyn & Bacon.

Benjamin, L. T., & Baker, D. B. (2000). "History of psychology" the Boulder conference. *American Psychologist, 55*, 233–254.

Benjamin, L. T., & Baker, D. B. (2004). *From Seance to Science. A history of the profession of psychology in America*. Belmont, CA: Wadsworth/Thomson Learning.

Bereiter, C. (2002). *Education and the mind in the knowledge age*. Mahwah, NJ: Erlbaum.

Bernard, J. M., & Goodyear, R. K. (2004). *Fundamentals of clinical supervision* (3rd ed.). Boston, MA: Allyn & Bacon.

Bersoff, D. N. (2003). *Ethical conflicts in psychology* (4th ed.). Washington, DC: American Psychological Association.

Beutler, L. E., Malik, M., Alimohamed, S., Harwood, T. M., Talebi, H., Noble, S., et al. (2003). Therapist variables. In M. J. Lambert (Ed.), *Handbook of psychotherapy and behavior change* (5th ed., pp. 227–306). New York, NY: Wiley.

Birtwistle, T., & McKiernan, H. (2008). The changing landscape of higher education: An analysis of how national change might be brought about in American higher education compared with the Bologna signatory states. *Education and the Law, 20*, 317–336.

Bologna Declaration. (1999). *The Joint declaration of the European Ministers of Education convened in Bologna on 19 June 1999.*

Bond, M., & Holland, S. (1998). *Skills of clinical supervision for nurses: A practical guide for supervisees clinical supervisees and managers*. Buckingham, UK: Open University Press.

Brandal, N., Bratberg, Ø., & Thorsen, D. E. (2013). *The Nordic model of social democracy*. Basingstoke: Palgrave Macmillan.

Brante, T. (2011). Professions as science-based occupations. *Professions and Professionalism, 1*(1), 2–20.

Briner, R. B., & Rousseau, D. M. (2011). Evidence-based I-O psychology: Not there yet. *Industrial and Organizational Psychology, 4*, 3–22.

British Psychological Society. (1998). *Consultative Working Group National Occupational Standards in Applied Psychology*. Leicester, UK: British Psychological Society.

British Psychological Society. (2006). *Code*. Leicester, UK: BPS.

British Psychological Society. (2009). *Code of Ethics and Conduct*. Leicester, UK: British Psychological Society.

Butterworth, T., Bell, L., Jackson, C., & Pajnkihar, M. (2008). Wicked spell or magic bullet? A review of the clinical supervision literature 2001–2007. *Nurse Education Today, 28*(3), 264–272.

Capshew, J. H., & Hilgard, E. (1992). The power of service: World War II and professional reform in the American Psychological Association. In R. B. Evans, V. S. Sexton, & T. C. Cadwallader (Eds.), *100 years. The American Psychological Association. A historical perspective*. Washington, DC: American Psychological Association.

Carpintero, H. (1988). Psicología en España, ciencia y profesión [Psychology in Spain, science and profession]. *Aldaba, 6*(11), 83–93.

Carpintero, H. (2002). *From the stimulus to the person. Studies of the History of Psychology*. Valencia, Spain: University of Valencia.

Carpintero, H. (2006). Towards a history of applied psychology in the 20th century. In Q. Jing, H. Zhang, K. Zhang (Ed.), *Progress in psychological science around the world* (pp. 433–442). New York, NY: Psychology Press II.

Carpintero, H., & Herrero, F. (2002). Early applied psychology. The early days of the IAAP. *European Psychologist, 7*(1), 39–52.

Cattell, J. M. (1890). Mental tests and measurements. *Mind, 15*, 373–381.

CEPLIS Telegram. (2013). Brussels, Belgium: European Council of the Liberal Professions.

Cheetham, G., & Chivers, G. (2005). *Professions, competence and informal learning*. Cheltenham, UK: Edward Elgar.

Clarke, N. (2005). Workplace learning environment and its relationship with learning outcomes in healthcare organisations. *Human Resources Development International, 8*(2), 185–205.

Clegg, J. (1998). *Critical issues in clinical practice*. London, UK: Sage.

Cowan, D. T. Norman, I., & Coopamah, V. P. (2005). Competence in nursing practice: A controversial concept – a focused review of literature. *Nurse Education Today, 25*(5), 355–362.

Cumming, G. (2013). The new statistics: Why and how. *Psychological Science*. Published online 12 November 2013. doi: 10.1177/0956797613504966.

Curaj, A., Scott, P., Vlasceanu, L., & Wilson, L. (Eds.). (2012). *European higher education at the cross roads. Between the Bologna process and national reform*. Heidelberg, Germany: Springer.

De Groot, A. D. (1990). Unifying psychology: A European view. In P. J. D. Drenth, J. A. Sergeant, & J. T. Roelf (Eds.), *European perspectives in psychology* (Vol. 1, pp. 3–16). Chichester, UK: Wiley.

Denzin, N. K., & Lincoln, Y. S. (2000). *Handbook of qualitative research* (2nd ed.). Thousand Oaks, CA: Sage.

Donn, J., Routh, D., & Lunt, I. (2000). From Leipzig to Luxembourg (via Boulder and Vail): History of clinical psychology training in Europe and the United States. *Professional Psychology: Research and Practice, 31*, 423–428.

Economic and Social Research Council (ESRC). (2011). *International benchmarking review of UK psychology*. Swindon, UK: ESRC.

Eraut, M. (1994). *Developing professional knowledge and competence*. London, UK: Falmer Press.

Eraut, M., & Hirsch, W. (2007). The significance of workplace learning for individuals, groups and organisations. In *SKOPE Working Paper*. Oxford, UK: SKOPE.

European Association for Quality Assurance in Higher Education (ENQA). (2005). *Standards and guidelines for quality assurance in the European higher education area*. Retrieved from www.bologna-bergen2005.no/Docs/00-Main_doc/050221_ENQA_report. Helsinki, Finland: ENQA.

European Association for Quality Assurance in Higher Education (ENQA). (2009). *Regulations of the Association for Quality Assurance in Higher Education*. Retrieved from www.enqa.eu/becomeamember.lasso. Helsinki, Finland: ENQA.

European Federation of Professional Psychologists Associations (EFPPA). (1990). *Optimal standards for the training of psychologists*. Booklet no. 3. Brussels, Belgium: EFPPA.

European Federation of Psychologists Associations (EFPA). (2005). *Meta-code of ethics* (2nd ed.). Retrieved from www.efpa.eu. Brussels, Belgium: EFPA.

European Federation of Psychologists Associations (EFPA). (2013a). *EuroPsy regulations*. Retrieved from www.efpa.eu. Brussels, Belgium: EFPA.

European Federation of Psychologists Associations (EFPA). (2013b). *Model code of ethics*. Retrieved from www.efpa.eu. Brussels, Belgium: EFPA.

European Network of Work and Organisational Psychologists (ENOP). (1998). *European curriculum in work and organisational psychology. Reference model and minimal standards*. Paris, France: ENOP/Maison des Sciences de l'Homme.

European Parliament. (2008). Recommendation of the European parliament and of the council of 23 April 2008 on the establishment of the European qualifications framework for lifelong learning. *Official Journal of the European Union, C111*(6.5), 1–8.

European Social Survey. (2004). Data are available at http://ess.nsd.uib.no

Evans, R. B., Sexton, V. S., & Cadwallader, T. C. (Eds.). (1992). *The American Psychological Association: A historical perspective*. Washington, DC: American Psychological Association.

Evetts, J. (2011). Sociological analysis of professionalism: Past, present and future. *Comparative Sociology, 10*(1), 1–37.

Eysenck, H. J. (1990). Clinical Psychology in Europe and in the United States: Developments and future. In P. J. D. Drenth, J. A. Sergeant, & R. J. Takens (Eds.), *European perspectives in psychology* (Vol. 2, pp. 3–17). Chichester: Wiley.

Fairbairn, S., & Fairbairn, G. (1987). *Psychology, ethics and change*. London, UK: Routledge.

Falender, C., & Shafranske, E. P. (2004). *Clinical supervision. A competency-based approach*. Washington, DC: APA.

Fernández-Ballesteros, R. (2014). Implications of emerging areas for psychology education and training. The case of geropsychology. In R. Silbereisen, P. Ritchie, & J. Pandey (Eds.), *Psychology education and training: A global perspective*. Hove, UK: Psychology Press.

Fleming, I. (2012). Developments in supervisor training. In I. Fleming & L. Steen (Eds.), *Supervision and clinical psychology. Theory, practice and perspectives* (2nd ed.). Hove, UK: Routledge.

Fowler, R. D. (2006). *Professional Psychology around the world. A fifty-year progress report*. In Q. Jing, H. Zhang, & K. Zhang (Ed.) *Progress in psychological science around the world* (pp. 199–206). New York, NY: Psychology Press II.

Freeman, R., & Steyaert, S. (2011). The History and organisation of the European federation of Psychologists Associations (EFPA): Reflections on the first 30 years of EFPA. *European Psychologist, 16*(2), 90–99.

Freidson, E. (1994). *Professionalism reborn. Theory, prophecy and policy*. Cambridge, UK: Polity Press.

Freidson, E. (2001). *Professionalism. The third logic*. Cambridge, UK: Polity Press.

Friedman, A., Durkin, C., Phillips, M., & Davis, K. (2000). *Continuing professional development in the UK: Policies and practices*. Bristol, UK: PARN.

Friedman, A., & Phillips, M. (2004). Continuing professional development: Developing a vision. *Journal of Education and Work, 17*(3), 361–376.

Froment, E. (2003). The European higher education area: A new framework for the development of higher education. *Higher Education in Europe, 28*, 27–31.

Garrick, J. (1998). *Informal learning in the workplace*. London, UK: Routledge.

Gaston, P. (2010). *The challenge of Bologna. What United States higher education has to learn from Europe and why it matters that we learn it*. Sterling, Virginia: Stylus.

Gear, J., McIntosh, A., & Squires, G. (1994). *Informal learning in the professions*. Department of Adult Education, University of Hull.

Ghiglione, R. (1998). *Les métiers de la psychologie* [The professions of psychology]. Paris, France: Dunod.

Giddens, A. (2014). *Turbulent and mighty continent. What future for Europe*. Cambridge, UK: Polity Press.

Golding, L. & Gray, I. (Eds.). (2006). *Continuing professional development for clinical psychologists. A practical handbook*. Oxford, UK: BPS Blackwell.

González, J., & Wagenaar, R. (2003). *Tuning educational structures in Europe. Final report phase one*. Bilbao, Spain: Universidad de Deusto.
González, J., & Wagenaar, R. (2008). *Tuning educational structures in Europe. Universities' contribution to the Bologna Process*. Bilbao, Spain: Universidad de Deusto.
Green, D. (2006). CPD: Why bother? In L. Golding & I. Gray (Eds.), *Continuing professional development for clinical psychologists*. Oxford, UK: BPS Blackwell.
Haaksman, D. (1990). The European Directive and its implications for psychologists, their associations and EFPPA. *News from EFPPA, 4*(1), 24–27.
Hall, G. S. (1923). *Life and confessions of a psychologist*. New York, NY: Appleton.
Hall, G. S., Baird, J. W., & Geissler, L. R. (1917). Foreword. *Journal of Applied Psychology, 1*(1), 5–7.
Hall, J., & Altmaier, E. (Eds.). (2008). *Global Promise. Quality assurance and accountability in professional psychology*. Oxford, UK: Oxford University Press.
Hall, J., & Lunt, I. (2005). Global mobility for psychologists: The Role of Psychology organisations in the USA, Canada and Europe. *American Psychologist, 60*(7), 712–726.
Hawkins, P., & Shohet, R. (2006). *Supervision in the helping professions* (3rd ed.). Buckingham, UK: Open University Press.
Henrich, J., Heine, S. J., & Norenzayan, A. (2010). The weirdest people in the world? *Behavioral and Brain Sciences, 33,* (2–3), 61–83. doi: 10.1017/s0140525x0999152x
Houle, C. O. (1980). *Continuing learning in the professions*. San Francisco, CA: Jossey Bass.
Howard, G. S., Maxwell, S. E., & Fleming, K. J. (2000). The proof of the pudding: An illustration of the relative strengths of null hypothesis, meta-analysis, and Bayesian analysis. *Psychological Methods, 5*(3), 315–332.
Hughes, A. K. (1994). *Developing European professions: Delivering continuing professional development in Europe*. Bristol, UK: University of Bristol.
Huisman, J., & Westerheijden, D. F. (2010). Bologna and quality assurance: Progress made or pulling the wrong cart? *Quality in Higher Education, 16*(1), 63–66.
Jacobi, F., Uhmann, S., & Hoyer, J. (2011). Wie häufig ist therapeutischer Misserfolg in der ambulanten Psychotherapie? Ergebnisse aus einer verhaltenstherapeutischen Hochschulambulanz [How frequent is negative outcome in outpatient psychotherapy? Results from a CBT outpatient clinic]. *Zeitschrift für Klinische Psychologie und Psychotherapie: Forschung und Praxis, 40*(4), 246–256.
James, I. A., Milne, D., & Morse, R. (2008). Microskills of clinical supervision: Scaffolding skills. *Journal of Cognitive Psychotherapy, 22*(1), 29–36.
Jern, S., Nieminen, P., & Odland, T. (2002). The equivalence framework in relationship to the basic training of psychologists and specialization training: The Nordic scene. *European Psychologist, 7*(3), 213–220.
Judt, T. (2005). *PostWar. A history of Europe since 1945*. London, UK: William Heinemann.
Keeling, R. (2006). The Bologna process and the Lisbon Research Agenda: The European Commission's expanding role in higher education discourse. *European Journal of Education, 41*, 203–223.
Kladis, D. (2003). The social dimension of the Bologna Process. *Higher Education in Europe, 26*, 27–38.
Knight, J. (2013). A model for the regionalization of higher education: The role and contribution of Tuning. *Tuning Journal for Higher Education, 1*, 105–126.
Knight, A. R. (1954). The British Psychological Society: Problems and prospects. *Bulletin of the British Psychological Society, 1*(24), 1–8.
Kolb, D. A. (1984). *Experiential learning: Experience as the source of learning and development*. Englewood Cliffs, NJ: Prentice Hall.

Larson, M. S. (1977). *The rise of professionalism: A sociological analysis*. London, UK: University of California Press.

Le Bianic, T., & Svensson, L. G. (2008). European regulation of professional education. *European Societies, 10*(4), 567–595.

Lévy-Leboyer, C. (1992). Unité ou diversité de la psychologie? [Unity or diversity in psychology?] *International Journal of Psychology, 27*, 275–282.

Lindley, P. (1997). Continuing professional development in the British Psychological Society: The differing needs of the professional and the professional body. *European Psychologist, 2*(1), 11–17.

Lindsay, G. (2008). Professional ethics and psychology. In G. Lindsay, C. Koene, H. Øvreeide, & F. Lang (Eds.), *Ethics for European psychologists*. Cambridge, MA: Hogrefe & Huber Publishers.

Lindsay, G., Koene, C., Øvreeide, H., & Lang, F. (2008). *Ethics for European psychologists*. Cambridge, MA: Hogrefe & Huber Publishers.

Lipton, A. (1999). Recovered memories in the courts. In S. Taub (Ed.), *Recovered memories of child sexual abuse: Psychological, social, and legal perspectives on a contemporary health controversy* (pp. 165–201). Springfield, IL: Charles C. Thomas.

Loftus, E. F. (2003). Make-believe memories. *American Psychologist, 58*, 867–873.

Loftus, E. F., & Ketcham, K. (1996). *The myth of repressed memory: False memories and allegations of sexual abuse* (1st ed.). New York, NY: St. Martin's Griffin.

Lovie, A. D. (2001). Three steps to heaven: How the British Psychological Society attained its place in the sun. In G. C. Bunn, A. D. Lovie, & G. D. Richards (Eds.), *Psychology in Britain: Historical essays and personal reflections*. Leicester, UK: BPS Books in association with the Science Museum.

Lunt, I. (1998). Psychology in Europe: Challenges and opportunities. *European Psychologist, 3*(2), 93–101.

Lunt, I. (1999). The professionalization of psychology in Europe. *The European Psychologist, 4*(4), 240–247.

Lunt, I. (2000). The profession of psychology. In K. Pawlik & M. Rosenzweig (Eds.), *The International handbook of psychology*. London, UK: Sage.

Lunt, I. (2002). A common framework for the training of psychologists in Europe. *European Psychologist, 7*(3), 180–191.

Lunt, I. (2005). The impact of the "Bologna Process" on the development of a European Qualification in Psychology. *European Psychologist, 10*(2), 86–92.

Lunt, I. (2008). Psychologist qualifications in Europe: Common standard for quality and mobility. *Australian Psychologist, 43*(4), 222–230.

Lunt, I. (2011). EuroPsy: The development of standards and competence of psychologists. *European Psychologist, 16*, 2.

Lunt, I. (2014). International frameworks for psychology education and training: A European perspective. In R. Silbereisen, P. Ritchie, & J. Pandey (Eds.), *Psychology education and training*. Hove, UK: Psychology Press.

Lunt, I., Baneke, R., Berdullas, M., Hansson, B., & Nevalainen, V. (Eds.). (2001). *Laws and regulation for psychologists in European countries*. Brussels, Belgium: EFPPA.

Lunt, I., Bartram, D., Döpping, J., Georgas, J., Jern, S., Job, R., . . . Wilpert, B. (2001). *A European framework for psychologists training*. London, UK: Institute of Education.

Lunt, I., Brauner, B., Georgas, D., Holte, A., Jern, S., Job, R., . . . Roe, R. (2005). *EuroPsy. The European diploma in psychology*. Brussels, Belgium: EFPA.

Lunt, I., Job, R., Lecuyer, R., Peiró, J. M., & Gorbeña, S. (2011). *Tuning-EuroPsy: Reference points for the design and delivery of degree programmes in psychology*. Bilbao, Spain: Publicaciones de la Universidad de Deusto.

Lunt, I., & Peiró, J. M. (2012). The Bologna Process, education and assessment in psychology. In D. Dunn, S. C. Baker, C. M. Mehrota, R. E. Landrum, & M. M. McCarthy (Eds.), *Assessing teaching and learning in psychology: Current and future perspectives*. Belmont, CA: Wadsworth.

Lunt, I., & Poortinga, Y. H. (1996). Internationalising psychology: The case of Europe. *American Psychologist, 51*(5), 504–508.

Lunt, I., & Poortinga, Y. (2009). Certification of psychologists in Europe: Implications for teaching psychology. In S. McCarthy, K. Laurie Dickson, J. Cranney, A. Trapp, & V. Karandashev (Eds.), *Teaching psychology around the world, Vol. 2*. Cambridge Scholars.

Madden, C. A., & Mitchell, V. A. (1993). *Professions, standards and competence: A survey of continuing education for the professions*. Bristol, UK: University of Bristol.

Malloch, M., Cairns, L., Evans, K., & O'Connor, B. (Eds.). (2011). *The Sage handbook of workplace learning*. London, UK: Sage.

Marquand, D. (2011). *The end of the west. The once and future Europe*. Princeton, NJ: Princeton University Press.

Marsick, V. J., & Watkins, K. E. (1990). *Informal and incidental learning in the workplace*. London, UK: Routledge.

Martínez-Tur, V., Peiró, J. M., & Rodriguez, I. (2014). Teaching and learning work, organization and personnel psychology internationally. The Erasmus Mundus Program. In R. Griffith (Ed.), *Internationalizing the Curriculum in Organizational Psychology*. New York, NY: Springer Science + Business.

Matefi, G., & Häring, E. (1993). *Inventory of regulations in the field of psychology in European countries*. Bonn, Germany: BDP.

McPherson, F. (1988). Psychologists and the EEC. *The Psychologist, 9*, 353–355.

Milchman, M. S. (2012a). From traumatic memory to traumatized remembering: Beyond the memory wars, Part 1: Agreement. *Psychological Injury and Law, 5*, 37–50.

Milchman, M. S. (2012b). From traumatic memory to traumatized remembering: Beyond the memory wars, Part 2: Disagreement. *Psychological Injury and Law,* 5, 51–62.

Milne, D. L. (2007). An empirical definition of clinical supervision. *British Journal of Clinical psychology, 46*, 437–447.

Misiak, H., & Sexton, V. S. (1966). *History of psychology: An overview*. Oxford, UK: Grune and Stratton.

Moskovitz, M. (1977). Hugo Münsterberg: A study in the history of applied psychology. *American Psychologist, 32*(10), 824–842.

Muzio, D., Hodgson, D., Faulconbridge, J., Beaverstock, J., & Hall, S. (2011). Towards corporate professionalisation: The case of project management, management consultancy and executive search. *Current Sociology, 59*(4), 443–464.

Nadler, J., Thompson, L., & van Boven, L. (2003). Learning negotiation skills: Four models of knowledge creation and transfer. *Management Science, 49*(4), 529–540.

Neave, G. (2003). The Bologna Declaration: Some of the historic dilemmas posed by the reconstruction of the community in Europe's systems of Higher Education. *Educational Policy, 17*, 141–164.

Newstead, S. E. (1994). The psychology curriculum and the training of psychologists in Europe. *News from EFPPA, 8*(4), 11–14.

Newstead, S. E., & Makinen, S. (1997). Psychology teaching in Europe. *European Psychologist, 2*(1), 3–10.

Nixon, M. (1990). Professional training in psychology: Quest for international standards. *American Psychologist, 45*(11), 1257–1262.

O'Donohue, W. T., & Ferguson, K. (2003). Introduction: Ethics, the good, the bad, and the ugly. In W. O'Donohue & K. Ferguson (Eds.), *Handbook of professional ethics for psychologists* (pp. 1–14). Thousand Oaks, CA: Sage.

Organisation for Economic Co-operation and Development (OECD). (2009). *PISA 2006 Technical report*. Paris, France: Author.

O'Neill, O. (2002). *A question of trust. The BBC Reith lectures 2002*. Cambridge, UK: Cambridge University Press.

Ones, D. S., & Dilchert, S. (2012). Environmental sustainability at work: A call to action. *Industrial and Organizational Psychology: Perspectives on Science and Practice, 5*(4), 444–466.

Onstenk J. (Ed.). (2002). *Op zoek naar een krachtige beroepsgerichte leeromgeving* [In search of a powerful profession-oriented learning environment]. Den Bosch, Netherlands: CINOP.

Peiró, J. M. (2014). Roles and responsibilities of international psychology organizations in improving psychology education and training. In R. Silbereisen, P. Ritchie, & J. Pandey (Eds.), *Psychology education and training*. Hove, UK: Psychology Press.

Peiró, J. M., & Carpintero, H. (1978). Los primeros Laboratorios de Psicología y su influencia en la aparición de esta ciencia [The first laboratories of psychology and their influence on the nature of science]. *Análisis y Modificación de Conducta, 4*(5), 129–158.

Peiró, J. M., & Lunt, I. (2002). The context for a European framework for psychologists training. *European Psychologist, 7*(3), 169–179.

Peiró, J. M., Tordera, N., & Potocnik, K. (2012). Retirement practices in different countries. In M. Wang (Ed.), *The Oxford handbook of retirement* (pp. 510–540). New York, NY: Oxford University Press.

Peterson, C., & Park, N. (2005). The enduring value of the Boulder Model: "Upon this rock we will build". *Journal of Clinical Psychology, 61*, 1147–1150.

Podlesek, A., & Zabukovec, V. (2012). *EuroPsy* in Slovenia, The Education program for mentoring supervised practice. *European Psychologist, 17*(4), 337–340.

Poortinga, Y. H., & Lunt, I. (1997). Defining the competence of psychologists with a view to public accountability. *European Psychologist, 2*(4), 293–300.

Poortinga, Y. H., & Lunt, I. (2011). Psychology as a profession and a science: The change from EFPPA to EFPA. *European Psychologist, 16*, 2.

Poortinga, Y. H., & Soudijn, K. A. (2003). Ethical principles of the psychology profession and professional competencies. In W. O'Donohue & K. Ferguson (Eds.), *Handbook of professional ethics for psychologists: Issues, questions, and controversies* (pp. 67–80). Thousand Oaks, CA: Sage.

Prieto, J. M., Fernandez-Ballesteros, R., & Carpintero, H. (1994). Contemporary psychology in Spain. *Annual Review of Psychology, 45*, 51–78.

Pulverich G. (Ed.). (1997). *Inventory of regulations in the field of psychology in European countries*. Bonn, Germany: Deutscher Psychologie Verlag.

Quality Assurance Agency (QAA). (2007). *Subject benchmark statement: Psychology*. Gloucester, UK: Quality Assurance Agency for Higher Education.

Raimy V. (Ed.). (1950). *Training in clinical psychology*. New York, NY: Prentice Hall.

Rasmussen, J. (1986). *Information processing and human-machine interaction*. Amsterdam, North-Holland.

Rauhvargers, A. (2011). Achieving Bologna goals: Where does Europe stand ahead of 2010. *Journal of Studies in International Education, 15*(1), 4–24.

Reichert, S. (2010). The intended and unintended effects of the Bologna reforms. *Higher Education Management and Policy, 22*, 1–20.

Rey, R. (1941). L'examen psychologique dans les cas d'encéphalopathie traumatique [Psychological examination in cases of traumatic encephalopathy]. *Archives de Psychologie, 28*, 286–340.

Richelle, M. Porquoi les psychologues? [Why psychologists?] Brussels, Belgium: Dessart.

Rodriguez, D., Patel, R., Bright, A., Gregory, D., & Gowing, M. K. (2002). Developing competency models to promote integrated human-resources practices. *Human Resource Management, 41*(3), 309–324.

Roe, R. A. (1995). Developments in Eastern Europe and work and organisational psychology. In G. Cooper & I. T. Robertson (Eds.), *International review of industrial and organisational psychology* (pp. 175–349). Chichester, UK: Wiley.

Roe, R. (1996). Work and organisational psychology at the cross-roads: A European view. In J. Georgas, M. Manthouli, E. Besevegis, & A. Kokkevi (Eds.), *Contemporary psychology in Europe: Theory, research and applications*. Cambridge, MA: Hogrefe & Huber.

Roe, R. A. (2002). What makes a competent psychologist? *European Psychologist, 7*(3), 192–202.

Roe, R. A. (2007, May). *The competence model as a device for assessing output for the advanced diploma in W&O psychology*. Paper presented at the XIII European Congress of Work and organisational Psychology, Stockholm.

Roe, R. A. (2011). *The future of EFPA. Vision and strategy document*. Brussels, Belgium: EFPA Head Office.

Roe, R. A. (2014). We have always been indigenous. Thoughts about the past and future of psychology. In S. Cooper & K. Ratele (Eds.), *Psychology serving humanity: Proceedings of the 30th International Congress of Psychology. Volume 2: Western Psychology*. London, UK: Routledge/Taylor & Francis.

Roe, R. A., Coetsier, P., Lévy-Leboyer, C., Peiró, J. M., & Wilpert, B. (1994). The teaching of work and organizational psychology in Europe. Towards the development of a reference Model. *The European Work and Organizational Psychologist, 4*(4), 355–366.

Roe, R., & Freeman, R. (2011). 30 years of EFPA: Past, present and future. *European Psychologist, 16*(2), 83–89.

Roe, R. A., & Spaltro, E. (1988). European methodologies in work and organizational psychology. In M. Antalovits, R. A. Roe, & E. Spaltro (Eds.), *Proceedings of the 7th ENOP symposium on "Methodologies in work and organizational psychology"* (pp. 9–28). Budapest, Hungary: Research Institute of Labour.

Roth, A. (2010). Foreword. In I. Fleming & L. Steen (Eds.), *Supervision and clinical psychology. Theory, practice and perspectives*. London, UK: Routledge.

Roth, A., & Fonagy, P. (2006). *What works for whom? A critical review of psychotherapy research*. New York, NY: The Guildford Press.

Routh, D. K., Del Barrio, V., & Carpintero, H. (1996). European roots of the first psychology clinic in North America. *European Psychologist, 1*(2), 148.

Rosenzweig, M., Holtzman, W., Sabourin, M., & Bélanger, D. (2000). *History of the International Union of Psychological Science (IUPSyS)*. Hove, UK: Psychology Press.

Rueschmeyer, D. (1983). Professional autonomy and the social control of expertise. In R. Dingwall & P. Lewis (Eds.), *The sociology of the professions*. London, UK: Macmillan.

Scaife, J. (2001). *Supervision in the mental health professions*. Hove, UK: Brunner-Routledge.

Schön, D. (1987). *Educating the reflective practitioner*. San Francisco, CA: Jossey-Bass.

Schönpflug, W. (1993). Applied psychology: Newcomer with a long tradition. *Applied Psychology: An International Review, 42*(1), 5–30.

Schönpflug, W. (1994). Professional training in psychology departments: A critical analysis. *News from EFPPA, 8*(4), 15–17.

Schorr, A., & Saari, S. (Eds.). (1995). *Psychology in Europe*. Cambridge, MA: Hogrefe & Huber.

Scott, D., Brown, A., Lunt, I., & Thorpe, L. (2004). *Professional doctorates. Integrating professional and academic knowledge*. Maidenhead, UK: Open University Press.

Sejersted, F. (2011). *The age of social democracy. Norway and Sweden in the twentieth century*. Princeton, NJ: Princeton University Press.

Sexton, V. S., & Hogan, J. D. (Eds.). (1992). *International psychology: Views from around the world*. Lincoln, NE: University of Nebraska Press.

Shadish, W. R., Clark, M. H., & Steiner, P. M. (2008). Can nonrandomized experiments yield accurate answers? A randomized experiment comparing random and nonrandom assignments. *Journal of the American Statistical Association, 103*(484), 1334–1356.

Silbereisen, R., & Ritchie, P. (2014). Introduction to psychology education and training. A global perspective. In R. Silbereisen, P. Ritchie, & J. Pandey (Eds.), *Psychology Education and Training. A global perspective*. London, UK: Routledge.

Silbereisen, R., Ritchie, P., & Pandey, J. (Eds.). (2014). *Psychology education and training. A global perspective*. Hove, UK: Psychology Press.

Simon, H. A. (1969). *The sciences of the artificial*. Cambridge, MA: MIT Press.

Sinha, D. (1997). Indigenizing psychology. In J. W. Berry, Y. H. Poortinga, & J. Pandey (Eds.), *Handbook of cross-cultural psychology, Vol. I, Theory and method* (2nd ed., pp. 129–169). Boston, MA: Allyn & Bacon.

Skrtic, T. M. (1991). *Behind special education: A critical analysis of professional culture and school organisation*. Denver, CO: Love.

Slavin, R. E. (2002). Evidence-based education policies: Transforming educational practice and research. *Educational Researcher, 31*(7), 15–21.

Smail, D. (1984). *Illusion and reality*. London, UK: Dent.

Sonnentag, S., & Kleine, B. (2000). Deliberate practice at work: A study with insurance agents. *Journal of Occupational and Organisational Psychology, 73*(1), 87–102.

Sorbonne Joint Declaration. (1998, May 25). *Joint declaration on harmonisation of the architecture of the European higher education system*. Paris, France: the Sorbonne.

Spengler, P. M., White, M. J., Ægisdóttir, S., Maugherman, A. S., Anderson, L. A., Cook, R. S., . . . Rush, J. D. (2009). The meta-analysis of clinical judgment project: Effects of experience on judgment accuracy. *The Counseling Psychologist, 37*, 350–399.

Spielberger, C. (2004). Foreword. In A. Gale & A. Chapman (Eds.), *Psychology and Social problems. An introduction to applied psychology*. London, UK: John Wiley & Sons.

Steen, L. (2012). Formats of supervision. In I. Fleming & L. Steen (Eds.), *Supervision and clinical psychology. Theory, practice and perspectives* (2nd ed.). Hove, UK: Routledge.

Stern, W. (1900). *Über Psychologie der individuell Differenzen: Ideen zu einer "differentiellen Psychologie"* [Psychology and individual differences: Ideas on a "differential psychology"]. Leipzig, Germany: Johan Ambrosius Barth.

Stern, W. (1903). Angewandte psychologie [Applied psychology]. *Beitrage zür Psychologie der Aussage, 1*, 4–45.

Stern, W. (1911). *Die differentielle Psychologie in ihren Methodischen Grundlagen* [The methological bases of differential psychology] (Vol. 1911). Leipzig, Germany: Johan Ambrosius Barth.

Stevens, M. J. & Wedding, D. (Eds.). (2004). *Handbook of international psychology*. New York, NY: Taylor and Francis.

Universal Declaration of ethical principles for psychologists. (2008). Retrieved from http://www.iupsys.net/about/governance/universal-declaration-of-ethical-principles-for-psychologists.html

Veenhoven, R. (2012). *Correlates of happiness* [World database of happiness]. Retrieved from http://worlddatabaseofhappiness.eur.nl/hap_cor/cor_fp.htm. Rotterdam, The Netherlands: Erasmus University Rotterdam.

Wagenaar, R. (2013). Columbus' Egg? Qualifications frameworks sectoral profiles and degree programme profiles in higher education. *Tuning Journal for Higher Education, 1*, 71–104.

Warner, S., & Spandler, H. (2012). New strategies for practice-based evidence: A focus on self-harm. *Qualitative Research in Psychology, 9*(1), 13–26.

Watson, R. I. (1954). *Psychology as a profession*. Garden City, NY: Doubleday.

Whydett, S., & Hollyforde, S. (1999). *The competencies handbook*. London, UK: Institute of Personnel and Development.

Williams, B. A. (2010). Perils of evidence-based medicine. *Perspectives on Biology and Medicine, 53*(1), 106–120.

Wilpert, B. (1990). How European is work and organizational psychology? In P. J. D. Drenth, J. A. Sergeant, & R. J. Takens (Eds.), *European perspectives in psychology* (Vol. 3, pp. 3–20). Chichester, UK: Wiley.

Wilpert, B. (1999). Barriers to the metamorphosis of European psychology. *European Psychologist, 4*(4), 219–226.

Wilpert, B. (2002). Projecting a European diploma in psychology. *European Psychologist, 7*(3), 221–224.

Wundt, W. (1897). *Outlines of psychology*. Leipzig, Germany: Wilhelm Engelmann.

Wundt, W. (1913). *Die Psychologie im Kampf ums Dasein* [Psychology's struggle for existence]. Leipzig, Germany: Kröner.

Zabukovec, V., & Podlesek, A. (2010). *A model of the supervised practice of psychologist*. Ljubljana, Slovenia: Pontes Academic Book Series.

Glossary of Acronyms

APA	American Psychological Association
BFUG	Bologna Follow-up Group
BPS	British Psychological Society
CoTEP	Committee for Training and Education in Psychology
CTF	Common Training Framework
EAC	European Awarding Committee
EAWOP	European Association of Work and Organisational Psychology
ECTS	European Credit and Accumulation Transfer System
EC	European Community
EEC	European Economic Community
EHEA	European Higher Education Area
EFPA	European Federation of Psychologists Associations
ENOP	European Network of Work and Organisational Psychologists
ENPCA	European Network of Psychological Competent Authorities
ENQA	European Association of Quality Assurance
EQAR	European Quality Assurance Register
EQD	European Qualifications Directive
EQF	European Qualifications Framework
ESG	European Standards and Guidelines
ESRC	Economic and Social Research Coucnil
EU	European Union
IAAP	International Association of Applied Psychology
IACCP	International Association for Cross-Cultural Psychology
IUPsyS	International Union of Psychological Science
NAC	National Awarding Committee
NQF	National Qualifications Framework
QAA	Quality Assurance Agency
QF-EHEA	Qualifications Framework of the European Higher Education Area

Appendices

Appendix 1. Member Countries of EFPA (36)

* **countries** with approved NAC (December 2013) and therefore able to award the *EuroPsy*

Austria*
Belgium
Bulgaria
Croatia
Cyprus*
Czech Republic*
Denmark*
Estonia*
Finland*
France*
Germany*
Greece*
Hungary*
Iceland
Ireland
Italy*
Latvia*
Liechtenstein
Lithuania*
Luxembourg
Malta
Netherlands, The*
Norway*
Poland
Portugal
Romania
Russia*
San Marino
Serbia
Slovakia
Slovenia*
Spain*
Sweden
Switzerland
Turkey*
United Kingdom*

Appendix 2. Members of Leonardo 1 Project (1999–2001)

Dave Bartram (UK)
Jesper Döpping (Denmark)
James Georgas (Greece)
Stefan Jern (Sweden)
Remo Job (Italy)
Roger Lécuyer (France)
Ingrid Lunt (UK) Chair
Steve Newstead (UK)
Pirkko Nieminen (Finland)
Torleiv Odland (Norway)
José María Peiró (Spain)
Ype Poortinga (Netherlands)
Robert A. Roe (Netherlands)
Bernhard Wilpert† (Germany)
Ernst Hermann (Switzerland)

Appendix 3. Members of Leonardo 2 Project (2001–2004)

Dave Bartram (UK)
Eva Bamberg (Germany)
Birgitte Bräuner (Denmark)
James Georgas (Greece)
Arne Holte (Norway)
Stefan Jern (Sweden)
Remo Job (Italy)
Roger Lécuyer (France)
Nigel Lloyd (UK)
Ingrid Lunt (UK) Project Director
Pirkko Nieminen (Finland)
José María Peiró (Spain)
Csaba Pleh (Hungary)
Ype Poortinga (Netherlands)
Robert A. Roe (Netherlands)
Tuomo Tikkanen (EFPA President)

Appendix 4: EFPA Regulations Concerning *EuroPsy*, the European Certificate in Psychology (2013)

Note:

The EuroPsy Regulations are followed by a set of appendices, as follows:

Appendix II Framework and minimal standards for the education and training of psychologists
Appendix III Competences and competence profiling
Appendix IV EuroPsy Certificate and application form
Appendix V Supervised practice
Appendix VI Continuing professional development

These are available on the EFPA website: http://www.europsy-efpa.eu/regulations
The appendices referred to in the Regulations below are these appendices.

The *EuroPsy* European Certificate in Psychology (henceforth *EuroPsy*) is intended to provide a standard of academic education and professional training which informs clients, employers and colleagues that a psychologist can be considered to have gained the necessary competences for the provision of psychological services.

EuroPsy aims to set a common standard of competence in all the countries where it is issued. It envisages the free movement of psychologists across the countries of the EU, and in other countries which have accepted the standard, and aims to support mechanisms to facilitate this.

EuroPsy can be awarded to individual psychologists who meet the conditions specified in these EFPA Regulations on *EuroPsy*.

A person in possession of *EuroPsy* will be referred to as a "Registered *EuroPsy* Psychologist."

Section A. *EuroPsy*, the European Certificate in Psychology

Article 1 *EuroPsy*[19] embodies a set of standards of education and training for professional psychologists as described in Appendix II and III.

Article 2 Individual psychologists are eligible to be listed in the European Register of *EuroPsy* Psychologists (henceforth the Register) and to hold the *EuroPsy* if they:

a. have successfully completed a nationally accredited academic curriculum in psychology at a university or an equivalent institution

[19] European Certificate in Psychology from here on refers to the basic European Certificate in Psychology (*EuroPsy*), as described in the Preamble.

that by law or custom leads to a national title or qualification of psychologist, provided the curriculum has a duration equivalent to at least five years of full-time study (300 ECTS) and fits the framework as described in Appendix II;

b. are able to show evidence of supervised practice as a psychologist-practitioner in training for the duration of not less than one year of full-time work (or its equivalent), and of satisfactory performance of this work as evaluated by their Supervisors (see Appendix I and Appendix V); and

c. have submitted a pledge in writing to their National Awarding Committee that they subscribe to the principles of professional conduct set out in the MetaCode of Professional Ethics of EFPA and will conduct professional activities in accordance with the code of ethics of the national association of psychology in the country of practice.

Article 3 Following positive evaluation of the evidence mentioned in Article 2, an individual may be entered in the Register and awarded the *EuroPsy* Certificate.

Article 4 The *EuroPsy* loses its validity after a period of 7 *years*, unless it is revalidated.

Article 5 For purposes of revalidation, the *EuroPsy* can be re-issued to all psychologists who

a) are able to show evidence of maintenance of professional competence in the form of a specified number of hours of practice as a psychologist and continued education and professional development as indicated in Appendix VI;

b) have submitted a pledge in writing to their National Awarding Committee that they subscribe to the principles of professional conduct set out in the MetaCode of Professional Ethics of EFPA and will conduct professional activities in accordance with the Code of Ethics of the national association of psychology in the country of practice.

Article 6 The *EuroPsy* Certificate will be similar in meaning and appearance to the model presented in this document (Appendix IV).

Article 7 The *EuroPsy* details required in the application form are: information on the university education, the supervised practice, including the professional competences, roles and contexts within which the Registered *EuroPsy* Psychologists worked to qualify, and their work experience.

Article 8 The information to be included in the European Register will be: the name and work or home address of the registrant, the university education, the country of practice, the context of practice and the place and date of authorisation by the National Awarding Committee.

Article 9 The Registered *EuroPsy* Psychologist is considered qualified for independent practice as a psychologist, within the professional context mentioned in the Registration Details, in as far as there are no restrictions from national regulations in the country concerned. This applies in all countries where the national Member Association of EFPA has accepted the *EuroPsy* and these Regulations.

Article 10 The Registered *EuroPsy* Psychologist is considered qualified for supervised and/or dependent practice (see Appendix 1) as a psychologist within any professional context, in all countries in which the national Member Association of EFPA has accepted the *EuroPsy* and these EFPA Regulations on *EuroPsy*.

Article 11 The record of a psychologist will be:

a) removed from the Register in the following cases: (i) upon expiry of the *EuroPsy* (cf Art. 4); (ii) upon the request of the holder; (iii) when a court of law or a national committee has imposed a sentence or measure against the holder that prohibits him/her from exercising the profession of psychologist, such as removal from a national register or withdrawal of a national license;
b) marked in the Register as "suspended" when a court of law or a national committee has imposed a sentence or measure that suspends the holder's right to exercise the profession of psychologist. The mark "suspended" will be removed when the suspension in the respective country ends.

Section B. Awarding Agencies

Article 12 The responsibility for awarding the *EuroPsy* and entering an individual into the Register according to these Regulations rests with the European Awarding Committee. This Committee delegates the authority to award the *EuroPsy* in accordance with these Regulations to National Awarding Committees in countries in which the Member Association of EFPA has accepted the *EuroPsy* and these Regulations.

Article 13 a) The European Awarding Committee consists of a Chairperson and up to twelve other Members. They shall each be from a different country within EFPA and represent the main professional contexts of psychology and provide a balance between those working as practitioners and those working at universities and involved in the education of psychologists.

b) Candidates are nominated by the Member Associations. Members are appointed for a term of up to four years, once renewable, by the Executive Council of EFPA.
c) The terms of appointment are set in such a way that three new members can be appointed every two years.

Article 14 The European Awarding Committee is responsible for oversight of the *EuroPsy* and its Regulations and for ensuring that the Registration and award of the *EuroPsy* occurs in accordance with these Regulations.

Its tasks include the following:
a) to receive and evaluate applications from Member Associations to establish National Awarding Committees;
b) to delegate the authority to award the *EuroPsy* to the National Awarding Committees;
c) to provide guidance for the National Awarding Committees;
d) to ensure that national bodies are interpreting the European standards in a similar way and to co-ordinate the work of the National Awarding Committees;
e) to supervise the proper implementation of these EFPA Regulations on *EuroPsy* by each National Awarding Committee;
f) to take steps towards the suspension of a National Awarding Committee if there is evidence of mismanagement or misuse of these EFPA Regulations on *EuroPsy*;
g) to deal with appeals against decisions of National Awarding Committees;
h) to prepare a report every two years for the Executive Council and the General Assembly of EFPA;
i) to maintain contact and arrange an annual meeting with Presidents of the National Awarding Committees;
j) to work with national associations to remedy the causes of a suspension of the National Awarding Committee;
k) to oversee the maintenance of the European Register;
l) to act as consultation body to the European Commission on issues regarding the recognition of psychologists' qualifications in Europe.

Article 15 a) The awarding of the *EuroPsy* within a country will be carried out by a National Awarding Committee that is appointed by the national Member Association of EFPA. The National Awarding Committee will receive the delegated authority to award the *EuroPsy* from the European Awarding Committee. In countries with another (other) representative psychologists association(s) the Member Association is required to seek the collaboration with this (these) association(s) when establishing the National Awarding Committee.

b) The awarding of a Specialist *EuroPsy* Certificate will be carried out by a Specialist National Awarding Committee that is appointed by the national Member Association of EFPA. The Specialist National Awarding Committee will receive the delegated authority to award the *EuroPsy* from the Specialist European Awarding Committee.

Article 16

a) The National Awarding Committee consists of a Chairperson and between four and eight other Members. The members of the National Awarding Committee will represent the main professional contexts of psychology in that country and will provide a balance between those working as practitioners and those working at universities and involved in the education of psychologists.
b) The National Awarding Committee should be representative of the widest community of psychologists in the country concerned.
c) The members of the National Awarding Committee are appointed by the national Member Association of psychologists (Appendix I) for a term of up to four years, twice renewable.
d) The terms of appointment are set in such a way that 2 new members can be appointed every four years.
e) Changes in the composition of the National Awarding Committee require the written approval of the European Awarding Committee in order to retain the delegated authority (see Art. 15) to issue *EuroPsy* Certificates.

Article 17

The responsibilities of a National Awarding Committee include the following:

a) to submit all its procedures for approval to the European Awarding Committee;
b) to stipulate the manner in which an applicant has to submit evidence of professional competencies;
c) to prepare and publish a list of currently approved curricula for academic education in psychology, including the level of degree;
d) to advise institutions of higher learning of conditions for approval;
e) to issue guidelines for the assessment of competences by Supervisors;
f) to prepare a form on professional ethics to be signed by applicants;
g) to determine the fee for administrative costs to be paid by applicants;
h) to nominate a contact person who will be authorised to access the Register;
i) to take a decision on each individual application for the *EuroPsy*, either informing the applicant of the reasons why the application failed or awarding the *EuroPsy*;
j) to issue the *EuroPsy* Certificate to individual psychologists;
k) to keep a record of psychologists awarded the *EuroPsy*;
l) to keep an archive of all application materials for a period of 15 years;

m) to prepare an annual report of activities for the European Awarding Committee;
n) to provide relevant information and participate in the annual meeting of Presidents of the National Awarding Committees;
o) to act as consultation body to the competent authorities for the recognition of psychologists' professional qualifications in the country.

Article 18 A National Awarding Committee that in the opinion of the European Awarding Committee does not work in accordance with these EFPA Regulations on *EuroPsy* shall have its delegated authority removed by the European Awarding Committee, until the failure to observe the EFPA Regulations on *EuroPsy* has been remedied. No *EuroPsy* Certificate can be issued by a National Awarding Committee when its delegated authority has been removed.

Specialist Awarding Committees

Article 19
a) The Specialist European Awarding Committee consists of a Chairperson and up to eight other Members. They shall each be from a different country within EFPA.
b) The Specialist European Awarding Committee shall be representative of the main range of practice in the domain, and including at least one member who is based in a university.
c) One member of the Specialist Awarding Committee shall serve as liaison with the European Awarding Committee and shall serve on this committee.
d) Candidates are nominated by the Member Associations. Members are appointed for a term of up to four years, once renewable, by the Executive Council of EFPA.
e) The terms of appointment are set in such a way that 2 new members can be appointed every two years.

Article 20 The Specialist European Awarding Committee is responsible for oversight of the Specialist *EuroPsy* in that domain and for ensuring that the Registration and award of the Specialist *EuroPsy* occurs in accordance with the Regulations.

Its tasks include the following:
a) to receive and evaluate applications from Member Associations to establish Specialist National Awarding Committees;
b) to delegate the authority to award the Specialist *EuroPsy* to the Specialist National Awarding Committees;

c) to provide guidance for the Specialist National Awarding Committees and others;
d) to develop regulations for training routes and standards in the domain as appropriate;
e) to deal with appeals against decisions of Specialist National Awarding Committees;
f) to provide an annual report on the operation of the Specialist European Awarding Committee for the Executive Council and the General Assembly of EFPA;
g) to meet once a year with the Chairs of the Specialist National Awarding Committees, and with the European Awarding Committee to moderate procedures and to share good practice.

Article 21 a) The Specialist National Awarding Committee consists of a Chairperson and between four and six other Members.
b) There shall be a structural link between the Specialist National Awarding Committee and the National Awarding Committee in a country such that there is some overlap in membership.
c) The Specialist National Awarding Committee shall be representative of the widest community of psychologists in the country concerned in that domain of practice, and may include psychologists who are not member of the national Member Associations.
d) They are appointed by the national Member Association of psychologists for a term of up to four years, once renewable.
e) Changes in the composition of the Specialist National Awarding Committee require the written approval of the Specialist European Awarding Committee in order retain the delegated authority (see Art. 15) to issue *EuroPsy* Certificates.

Article 22 The responsibilities of a Specialist National Awarding Committee include the following:
a) to submit all its procedures for approval to the Specialist European Awarding Committee;
b) to stipulate the manner in which an applicant has to submit evidence of qualification and professional competencies;
c) to determine the Application Fee for administrative costs to be paid by applicants;
d) to take a decision on each individual application for the Specialist *EuroPsy*, either informing the applicant of the reasons why the application failed or awarding the Specialist *EuroPsy*;
e) to enter information on the specialist expertise of individual psychologists into the Register and issue the Specialist *EuroPsy* Certificate to individual psychologists;
f) to keep a record of psychologists awarded the Specialist *EuroPsy*;
g) to keep an archive of all application materials for a period of 15 years;

h) to prepare an annual report of activities for the Specialist European Awarding Committee;
i) to provide relevant information and participate in the annual meeting of Presidents of the Specialist National Awarding Committees;
j) to nominate a contact person who will be authorised to access the Register;
k) to provide information on the Specialist *EuroPsy* to psychologists and others.

Section C. The Procedure for Obtaining the *EuroPsy* Certificate

Article 23 The validity of a *EuroPsy* registration cannot be extended by applying for the same *EuroPsy* Certificate again, but only by revalidation as described in Article 5.

Article 24 The application must be made on a form that is similar in meaning and form to the model included in this document (Appendix IV). The application must provide information on: the university education, the supervised practice, specifying the professional competences and contexts within which s/he has worked under supervision to qualify for independent practice. The applicant must submit authorised reports by his/her Supervisors. The applicant must sign a pledge that s/he will conduct professional activities in accordance with the code of ethics of the national association of psychology in the country of practice.

Article 25 The National Awarding Committee will establish whether the candidate meets the criteria required by Article 2. It will examine the professional competences and professional contexts in which the applicant has worked under supervision and/or independently and decide in which professional context the candidate is qualified for independent practice.

Article 26 The application will only be processed after the candidate has paid the appropriate fee.

Article 27 The National Awarding Committee shall examine the evidence submitted and decide whether or not more information is needed from the applicant. The applicant will be informed whether or not the National Awarding Committee requires further information within 13 weeks of the original application and the fee having been received.

Article 28 Where additional information is required, the applicant shall be informed of the National Awarding Committee's decision within 13 weeks of such additional information having been received.

Article 29 Where no additional information is required, the applicant shall be informed of the National Awarding Committee's decision on whether to award or not to award the *EuroPsy* within 13 weeks of the original application and fee having been received. When the *EuroPsy* is not awarded the applicant shall receive a detailed account of the grounds that lead to this decision.

Article 30 Per the date on which the applicant has been entered onto the European Register, the *EuroPsy* will be awarded to that individual.

Article 31 In order to revalidate the *EuroPsy* Certificate following the end of the period of validity (Article 4) or the period of transitional arrangements (Article 38), the applicant must submit an application, which provides evidence of current competence, to the National Awarding Committee in the actual or intended country of practice

Article 32 The application for revalidation must provide evidence of maintenance of professional competence in the form of a specified number of hours of practice as a psychologist and continued education and professional development, as specified by the National Awarding Committee in the actual or intended country of practice (see Appendix VI).

Section D. Appeal Procedures

Article 33 An applicant whose application for the *EuroPsy* has been rejected by the National Awarding Committee can lodge an appeal against this decision with the national Member Association within the country concerned, providing the grounds for the appeal.

Article 34 This national Member Association will establish an independent advisory committee, consisting of at least three experts, to examine the appeal. This committee will rule on the appeal and provide a written judgement within 60 days. This judgement will be communicated to the applicant and the National Awarding Committee. The independent advisory committee can seek the advice of the European Awarding Committee.

Article 35 Where an applicant's appeal is rejected, the applicant may appeal to the European Awarding Committee (Article 14f). Such an appeal has to be submitted in the English language and must specify the grounds on which it is being made.

Article 36 The national Member Association in a country where delegated powers of the National Awarding Committee have been withdrawn can appeal against this measure to the Executive Council of EFPA. The EFPA Executive Council will seek the advice of a European advisory committee which is established for the occasion and convened by the EFPA President or a deputy.

Section E. Miscellaneous

Article 37 The EFPA Regulations and the appendices on the *EuroPsy* are established and can be changed by the General Assembly of EFPA, by a vote in support of 2/3 of those present. They will be operative with effect from a date set by the General Assembly of EFPA at the moment when they are established.

Article 38

a) Transitional arrangements for the basic *EuroPsy* Certificate will apply for a period of three years after the date of recognition of a National Awarding Committee in a particular country.
b) Transitional arrangements for any specialist *EuroPsy* Certificate will apply for a period of three years after the date of recognition of a Specialist National Awarding Committee in a particular country.
c) Transitional arrangements for the Basic Certificate will apply for an additional period of two years after the date of recognition of a Specialist National Awarding Committee in a particular country. These arrangements exclusively apply to applicants for the specialist *EuroPsy* Certificate issued by that Specialist National Awarding Committee.
d) All transitional arrangements will end in July 2020.
e) Applicants, who before the date mentioned in Article 38 a) and d) have been licensed to practise independently as a psychologist by a national licensing body recognised by the European Awarding Committee, and/or meet the requirements and conditions of practice as a psychologist in their country of practice can substitute listing of their supervised practice as a psychologist, with a record of their work history after they were qualified for independent practice as a psychologist. In these cases evidence of at least three years or the equivalent, within the past ten years, of independent practice as a psychologist, and evidence of current competence and continuing professional development (see Appendix V and VI) is required for the *EuroPsy* to be awarded. In this case the psychologist applying for the *EuroPsy* under these transitional arrangements may have a further two years beyond the end date of the transitional arrangements in order to fulfill the requirements.

Article 39 These Regulations can be extended with rules on Specialist Certificates in designated areas of psychology, which can only to be obtained by holders of the basic *EuroPsy* Certificate. Such rules will be laid down in Annexes to these Regulations, which must describe:

a) The minimum volume of further study, expressed in study hours or, preferably, units of the European Credit Transfer System (ECTS), and the content to be covered.
b) The minimum volume of supervised practice expressed in years, and the minimum volume of supervision expressed in hours, where

supervised practice and supervision are defined as in Appendix I.

c) The requirements with regard to continuing professional development, as defined in Appendix IV.
d) The competences to be demonstrated by the end of period of supervised practice, preferably described in the same manner as in Appendix III.
e) The system of competence development being used, preferably proactive and comprehensive in order to ensure that psychology graduates acquire all competences (professional and enabling) demanded at the specialised level and comprises all relevant facets of professional practice, including ethics.
f) The way in which evidence of further study, practice, supervision and competences is presented.
g) The way in which the evidence of further study, practice, supervision and competences is evaluated.
h) The transitional arrangements, applicable during the period mentioned in article 38b, of which the content should be analogous to that described in article 38e for the basic *EuroPsy*.

Article 40 The *EuroPsy* Regulations and Appendices will be reviewed at least every five years by the *EuroPsy* Coordination Group (ECG), consisting of the President of EFPA, a member of the Executive Council and the President of the European Awarding Committee.

Upon the advice of the ECG the Executive Council will make necessary changes in the Regulations. After the changes have been brought to the attention of the NACs they will apply provisionally until the next General Assembly. To apply further they need to be confirmed by the General Assembly.

1. Register of *EuroPsy* psychologists

Article 41 The European Register of *EuroPsy* Psychologists is held and maintained by EFPA and comprises the national listings of suitably certificated psychologists as provided by each National Awarding Committee.

Article 42 The European Register holds the names and details of all *EuroPsy* psychologists and also indicates on the Register the holders of Specialist Certificates.

Article 43 The information mentioned in the Registration Details of the *EuroPsy* will be recorded in the European Register, which is a searchable online facility available through the internet (www.europsy-efpa.eu/).

Article 44 The entries of the Register for a country shall be updated upon the initiative of the National Awarding Committee when a *EuroPsy* Certificate is issued, re-issued, withdrawn, or expires. The Register shall be updated when a Specialist Expertise Certificate is issued, on the instruction of the National Awarding Committee. Information in the Register may only be changed by EFPA and if authorised by the National Awarding Committee.

Annex I. Requirements for the Specialist Certificate in Psychotherapy

As spelled out in article 39 of the *EuroPsy* Regulations the *EuroPsy* Specialist Certificate will only be awarded to appropriately experienced psychologists who hold the *EuroPsy* Basic (or who are awarded the *EuroPsy* Basic at the same time). By implication, it is only possible to be awarded a Specialist Certificate in countries where both the NAC and the S-NAC has been recognised.

This Annex describes the requirements for the *EuroPsy* Specialist Certificate in Psychotherapy as required by article 39 of the *EuroPsy* Regulations.

Detailed information is available in: "*Application Form for Psychologists to Apply for the Specialist Certificate in Psychotherapy*" and "*Training Standards for Psychologists Specialising in Psychotherapy*," S-EAC Psychotherapy 2013.

1. **Minimum volume and content of further study**
   a. At least 400 hours of further study (16 ECTS).
   b. The content varies with the institution's curriculum and/or the psychologists' learning trajectory.

2. **Minimum volume of supervised practice and supervision**
   a. At least three years of postgraduate (post eligibility for *EuroPsy* Certificate) practice, of which 500 hours is supervised practice.
   b. At least 150 hours of supervision (on average 50 per year).

3. **Requirements on continuing professional development**
   These requirements are being developed.

4. **Competences to be demonstrated**
   A list of competences is being developed. Reflection is required on six principles, i.e., Psychologists as Psychotherapists; Inquiry and Communication; Psychotherapeutic Practice and Understanding; Personal and Professional Development; and Ethical and Competent Practice; and Further Professional Development.

5. **Competence development**
   No specific system of competence development is applied. Competence development is implied in training in one or more psychotherapeutic models.

6. **Evidence to be presented**
   Applicants need to:
   a. submit an Application Form, which includes a personal statement on the six principles mentioned above; training, learning and experience in psychotherapy; supervision arrangements; and research and publications (optional)
   b. submit a logbook to evidence the specialism.
   c. submit referee forms, completed by two referees, if deemed necessary.
   d. submit a statement by the supervisor.
   e. Submit a structured CV.

7. **Evaluation of evidence**
   a. The evaluation of the further study is carried out by the S-NAC on the basis of the credentials of the training curriculum, the trainers/supervisors, and the training institution (which should preferably collaborate with academic or research institutions).
   b. The evaluation of other aspects is carried out by the S-NAC on the basis of the applicant's statement, the referee forms, and the supervisor's statement.

8. **Transitional arrangements**
   Applicants who wish to obtain the Specialist Certificate in Psychotherapy under article 38 must either show a Letter of Recognition obtained in a pilot project recognised by EFPA or meet the following criteria:
   - be enrolled in a national register that allows them to work as psychologist and psychotherapist
   - hold a Basic *EuroPsy* Certificate (with Health context) or possess the requisites that allow them to apply jointly to the Basic and the Specialist Certificate; they are first assessed for the Basic Certificate and once acknowledged, for the Specialist Certificate,
   - document their work experience and Continuous Professional Development activities by providing evidence of competences gained during a period of at least six years within the last 15 years of independent practice as a psychologist and psychotherapist.

9. **Additional requirements**
   At least 100 hours of personal development (personal therapy).

Annex II: Requirements for the Specialist Certificate in Work & Organisational Psychology

As spelled out in article 39 of the *EuroPsy* Regulations the *EuroPsy* Specialist Certificate will only be awarded to appropriately experienced psychologists who hold the *EuroPsy* Basic (or who are awarded the *EuroPsy* Basic at the same time). By implication, it is only possible to be awarded a Specialist Certificate in countries where both the NAC and the S-NAC have been recognised.

This Annex describes the requirements for the *EuroPsy* Specialist Certificate in Work & Organisational Psychology as required by article 39 of the *EuroPsy* Regulations.

Detailed information is available in: "*Towards The Specialist Certificate: Revised Proposal And Operational Guidelines*," Provisional S-EAC W&O Psychology, 2013.

1. **Minimum volume and content of further study**
   a. At least 90 ECTS of further study (2400 hours), of which 60 (1600 hours) should be devoted to courses and 30 (800 hours) to applied research or assessment or intervention.
   b. The content that must be covered is provided in a specialist curriculum framework, i.e. the ENOP-EAWOP model.
   c. In the case of countries or individuals with early specialisation, specialist expertise acquired during the final two years of their initial 5-6 year qualification may be recognised up to a maximum of 30 ECTS. This means that minimally 60 ECTS remain to be acquired after the study requirements for the basic *EuroPsy* have been met.

2. **Minimum volume of supervised practice and supervision**
   a. At least three years of postgraduate practice, of which 400 hours per year (in total 1200 hours) being supervised practice, labelled as 'coached professional practice'.
   b. At least 150 hours of supervision (on average 50 per year).

3. **Requirements on continuing professional development**
   At least 100 hours (4 ECTS) of personal professional development at the moment of application, included in the 90 ECTs for further study (see 1a).

4. **Competences to be demonstrated**
   Competences to be demonstrated are those defined in *EuroPsy* (*EuroPsy* regulations, Appendix III). They are applied to professional work at the specialised level.

5. **Competence development**
   Coached professional practice is based on an explicit system of competence development. This system takes a pro-active approach to competence development. It ensures that psychology graduates acquire all competences (professional and enabling) demanded at the specialised level and comprises all relevant facets of the profession, including ethics.

6. **Evidence to be presented**
   Applicants need to:
   a. submit an Application Form, which includes further study, supervised practice and continuous personal development activities;

b. submit a structured curriculum vitae;
c. submit a logbook (or portfolio) that provides evidence of competence in the specialism;
d. take part in a Competence Assessment Interview, in order to deepen or clarify some details of the CV, if deemed necessary.

7. **Evaluation of evidence**
   a. The evaluation of study components is carried out by the S-NAC in the same manner as in *EuroPsy*, i.e. based on their content and the accreditation of the institution offering these components (preferably academic institutions).
   b. The evaluation of competences is carried out by the S-NAC on the basis of the portfolio and the Competence Assessment Interview.

8. **Transitional arrangements**
   Applicants who wish to obtain the Specialist Certificate in W&O Psychology under article 38 must meet the following criteria:
   - be enrolled in a national list that allows them to work as psychologist,
   - hold a Basic *EuroPsy* Certificate (with W&O context) or possess the requisites that allow them to apply jointly to the Basic and the Specialist Certificate; they are first assessed for the Basic Certificate and once acknowledged, for the Specialist Certificate,
   - document their work experience and Continuous Professional Development activities by providing evidence of competences gained during a period of at least five full time years within the last 10 years of independent practice as a W&O psychologist; the evidence is to be assessed by means of a structured CV and, if required by the SNAC, by a Competence Assessment Interview.

Appendix 5. EuroPsyT Framework for First Phase

Type of Content/Objectives	Individuals, Groups, Systems/Society
Orientation *Knowledge*	Methods in psychology History of psychology Overview of specialities and fields in psychology
Explanatory theories *Knowledge*	General psychology Neuro-psychology Psychobiology Cognitive psychology Differential psychology Social psychology Developmental psychology Personality psychology Work & organisational psychology Clinical & health psychology Educational psychology Psychopathology
Technological theories *Knowledge*	Data and test theory Questionnaire theory Evaluation theory
Explanatory theories *Skills*	Assessment skills training Interview skills training
Technological theories *Skills*	Test and questionnaire construction training Group intervention training
Methodology *Knowledge*	Introduction to methods, e.g., experimental methods Qualitative and quantitative methods
Methodology *Skills*	Experimental practice, Methodological & statistical practice Data acquisition training, qualitative analysis
Ethics *Knowledge and skills*	Ethical codes and professional ethics
Academic skills *Skills*	Collecting information/library & bibliographic skills Reading/writing papers Research ethics
Non-psychology theories *Knowledge*	Epistemology Philosophy Sociology Anthropology

Appendix 6. EuroPsyT Framework for Second Phase

Type of Content/Objectives	Individual, Group, Society
Orientation *Knowledge*	Orientation on context of practice and possibilities for specialisation
Explanatory theories *Knowledge*	Courses on explanatory theories of general psychology and/or psychobiology and/or developmental psychology, and/or personality psychology, and/or social psychology, e.g. theories of learning, cognitive architecture theory, advanced personality theory.
	Courses on explanatory theories of work & organisational psychology and/or educational psychology and/or clinical psychology and/or psychological subdisciplines, e.g. theories of work performance, theories of situated cognition, theories of leadership, theories of personality disorders.
Technological theories *Knowledge*	Courses on technological theories of general psychology and/or psychobiology and/or developmental psychology, and/or personality psychology, and/or social psychology, e.g. psychometric theory, EEG assessment theory.
	Courses on technological theories of work & organisational psychology and/or educational psychology and/or clinical psychology and/or psychological subdisciplines, e.g. theories of work analysis, analysis of learning needs, theories of counselling and psychotherapy.
Explanatory theories *Skills*	Skills training in applying above mentioned explanatory theories in assessment within research/laboratory settings, e.g. training in EMG measurement, training in personality assessment.
	Skills training in applying above mentioned explanatory theories in assessment within applied/field settings, e.g. training in error analysis, assessment of learning disorders.
Technological theories *Skills*	Skills training in applying above mentioned technological theories in interventions within research/laboratory settings, e.g. training in test construction, design of a learning experiment.
	Skills training in applying above mentioned technological theories in interventions within applied/field settings, e.g. training in the design of performance rating systems, the design of a training system, the development of a therapeutic plan, psychotherapy.

(continued on next page)

Appendix 6. (continued)

Type of Content/Objectives	Individual, Group, Society
Methodology *Knowledge*	Advanced Research Design. Basic and advanced multivariate statistics, including ANOVA. Multiple regression analysis, Factor analysis. Qualitative Research Design, including advanced interviewing and use of questionnaire, qualitative data analysis.
Methodology *Skills*	Skills training in above mentioned methods and techniques.
Ethics *Knowledge and skills*	Knowledge of ethical principles and their application. Skills training in the application of ethical principles and ethical codes to professional practice.
Academic and generalprofessional skills *Skills*	Skills training in report and article writing. Skills training in professional interviewing etc.
Non-psychology theories *Knowledge*	Theoretical and practical courses on topics from other disciplines, relevant for professional activity, e.g. medicine, law, business economics
Basic research competence	Research project (thesis)

Appendix 7. Minimum Requirements (in ECTS) for Education for Independent Professional Practice in Psychology

Phase	Component	Individual, Group, Society	Total
1st Phase: (Bachelor or equivalent)	Orientation	The curriculum should include orientation to psychology, its sub-disciplines and areas of professional activity	Min 125
	Theoretical courses and practical exercises	Min 60 Min 20 Min 20	
	Academic skills	Academic skills training should be included	
	Methodology	Min 30	Min 45
	Non-psychology theory	Min 15	
			Total 180
2nd Phase: (Masters or equivalent)	Theoretical courses, seminars, assignments etc.		Min 60
	Internship/stage/Placement	Min 15–30	Min 30
	Research project/thesis	Min 15–30	
			Total 120
3rd Phase	Supervised Practice	Min 60	**Total 60**
			Total 360

Index